T0330279

GLOBALIZATION UNDER AND
AFTER SOCIALISM

EMERGING FRONTIERS IN THE GLOBAL ECONOMY

EDITOR
J.P. Singh

SERIES BOARD
Arjun Appadurai
Manuel Castells
Tyler Cowen
Christina Davis
Judith Goldstein
Deirdre McCloskey

GLOBALIZATION UNDER AND AFTER SOCIALISM

AFTER SOCIALISM

The Evolution of Transnational Capital in
Central and Eastern Europe

BESNIK PULA

STANFORD UNIVERSITY PRESS
STANFORD, CALIFORNIA

Stanford University Press
Stanford, California

Printed in the United States of America on acid-free, archival-quality paper

Library of Congress Cataloging-in-Publication Data

Names: Pula, Besnik, 1975– author.
Title: Globalization under and after socialism : the evolution of transnational capital in Central and Eastern Europe / Besnik Pula.
Other titles: Emerging frontiers in the global economy.
Description: Stanford, California : Stanford University Press, 2018. | Series: Emerging frontiers in the global economy | Includes bibliographical references and index.
Identifiers: LCCN 2017055038| ISBN 9781503605138 (cloth : alk. paper) | ISBN 9781503605985 (epub)
Subjects: LCSH: Globalization—Economic aspects—Europe, Eastern—History. | Europe, Eastern—Economic conditions—1945– | Europe, Eastern—Economic policy—1945-1989. | Europe, Eastern—Economic policy—1989– | Europe, Eastern—Foreign economic relations.
Classification: LCC HC244 .P97 2018 | DDC 332/.04240943—dc23
    LC record available at https://lccn.loc.gov/2017055038

Typeset by Newgen in 10/14 Minion Pro

To my parents, Bardh and Lule, for their love and support.

Contents

GLOBALIZATION UNDER AND
AFTER SOCIALISM

Introduction

The reigning image of state socialist economies as they existed during the second half of the twentieth century is that of fully closed, autarchic systems. Today, by a number of measures, including dependence on foreign direct investment (FDI), export specialization, and the dominance of transnational corporations (TNCs) in the local economy, the ex-socialist economies of Central and Eastern Europe are among the most globalized in the world. Was the socialist past merely an obstacle these countries needed to overcome to join the global economy? Or, did socialism instead lay the groundwork for the region's present-day globalization? *Globalization Under and After Socialism* tackles this puzzle through an analysis of institutional reform and globalization in the East European ex-socialist economies from the 1970s through the first decades of the twenty-first century. Specifically, I focus on what are today known as the Central and East European states. The geographical designation of Central and Eastern Europe has varied usages. In this book I include Bulgaria, the Czech Republic, Hungary, Poland, Romania, Slovenia, and Slovakia. The historical sections also discuss Yugoslavia, Albania, the German Democratic Republic (GDR), and the Soviet Union, but these cases receive uneven and partial attention. The term "East Europe" is used more broadly as a designation for the ex-socialist states of Europe.

The ex-socialist economies would seem to represent some of the world's most unlikely places for the emergence of transnationally integrated economies. Indeed, by most accounts, the legacy of socialist industrialization was a

1

burden that needed to be overcome rather than a basis to advance the region's political and economic transformation. Could institutional developments in the area of trade, technology, and international economic cooperation during the socialist era have in fact laid the basis for the region's globalization? This book aims to argue precisely that, showing how trade and reform policies during the socialist period created the organizational and institutional basis for the region's economic globalization in the 1990s and 2000s, and that history has much to do with where these states stand today in the global economy.

What has East Europe's globalization looked like, and why does it matter? The fall of Communist Party rule in East Europe after 1989 unleashed one of the greatest experiments in economic reform in modern history. In a moment of exuberance, analysts declared the victory of capitalism and liberal democracy, even that the world had reached "the end of history" (Fukuyama 1992). Economic reforms, many designed with the aid of Western advisors, aimed at implementing markets in ways that would radically reshape the formerly centrally planned systems. A burgeoning academic literature grew around the problem of transition, a powerful organizing concept that was soon embodied in international financial institutions such as the European Bank for Reconstruction and Development (EBRD), established for the specific purpose of financing and monitoring East Europe's transformation. For the EBRD and others, one of the main organizational tasks in relation to the newly anointed transition economies became the benchmarking of "transition," with the region's past quickly fading into the background and standardized quantitative indicators of an idealized market economy model used to measure the region's progress. In academic debates, as well, for a considerable period, the legacies of socialism dropped from view. When spoken of they were described largely in negative terms—obstacles that had to be overcome if democracy and markets were to be implemented successfully. This left the impression that the trajectory of postsocialist states and economies had much to do with what their politicians did, but very little to do with where their institutions and economies came from.

In making these remarks, my aim is not to take the opposite view—that is, to glorify the socialist past or ascribe it undue merit for a future its bearers neither envisioned nor intended. Instead, my goal is to present an empirically nuanced and theoretically attentive argument on what about socialism did matter in the making of postsocialist economies. The focus on globalization is not arbitrary. Indeed, I show that the origins of East European globalization are to be found in the socialist experience. That is, the prevailing feature of present-day Central and East European economies, their reliance on FDI and the depth of the transnational integration of their key industries, was a process whose development was laid out during institutional reforms these states undertook in the 1970s and 1980s, as they attempted to gain access to, and better integrate with, Western trade, finance, and production. The experience of that period laid the groundwork for the region's future transformation and the patterns of postsocialist development that emerged in the early twenty-first century.

Suggesting that the structural conditions for Central and East Europe's glo-balization were laid out during the socialist period is not an effort to remove contingency and politics from the picture or to present a linear and evolu-tionary narrative of change. Indeed, the making of globalized economies was infused thoroughly by the political choices made by successive (socialist and postsocialist) political elites; moreover, different paths of integration with the global economy have had divergent outcomes for domestic institutional devel-opment. From this general perspective, then, I take a historical-institutionalist view on the transformation of socialism. The familiar themes of institutional stickiness, path dependence, cumulative causality, and unintended conse-quences pervade the analysis. Rather than the "transition" view of equal starting points where all ex-Communist states and societies enjoy equal opportunity in benefiting from globalization, the historical view taken here shows that starting points to globalization were not the same and that, in that game, some already had a head start. More regionally and historically informed analysts acknowl-edge this. What this book does is take a comparative and historical approach to identify what exactly about the experience of socialist industrialization made countries different in organizational and institutional terms, and how that mat-tered causally. Ultimately, in Central and Eastern Europe the question is not *if* states globalize their economies, but *under what terms* do they do so and in what role are their industrial capabilities cast in the twenty-first century inter-national political economy? This new international role ultimately shaped their domestic institutional development. The path of getting there marked the polit-ical crossroads these countries found themselves at during the early 1990s and forms some of the dilemmas of future development these countries face today.

The Argument in Brief

I explore two sets of outcomes in this book. The first are the region's differenti-ated capacities for rapid transitions from socialism to transnational capitalism through an FDI-driven investment and export policy. I argue that the origins of these capacities lay in the structure of ties that these economies began creating with TNCs beginning in the 1970s. It was 1970s reform socialism, I argue, that first laid the groundwork for the transnational capitalism of the 1990s and 2000s. The exhaustion of Stalinist industrialization, world economic opportunities in the 1970s, and the politics of reform within the socialist countries intersected in ways that led socialist states toward variants of import-led growth models that depended heavily on Western finance and export markets. While these growth models faltered in the 1980s, they created crucial ideational and organizational legacies that proved critical after 1989.

The political revolutions of 1989–1992 and the final collapse of the Soviet-led international socialist economic bloc turned East Europe decisively in the direction of market reform. The experience of import-led growth led the economies of Central and Eastern Europe toward developing industrial enclaves that were relatively competent world-market actors. These created the basis for the region's turn toward FDI and the making of what some have called its "manufacturing miracle" (Bohle and Greskovits 2012) of the 2000s and 2010s. These unevenly distributed capacities launched the region's first postcommunist divergence as it began its uneven and differentiated integration into the globalized economy of the twenty-first century.

The nature of domestic economic regimes and the emerging international market roles constitute the second outcome examined in the book. While often described as a homogeneous political-economic region, the analysis in Chapter 5 shows important distinguishing features of political economies in Central and Eastern Europe as they integrated into global production chains via flows of foreign capital, industrial restructuring and institutional reform, and accession into the European common market. Here, it shows that the degree to which political economies were export- or domestic-market oriented, the degree to which market reform became politically tempered, and the mode of the economy's incorporation into transnational production chains determined whether the economy assumed an assembly platform or intermediate producer role. These roles are consequential for the role transnational capital has within national economies, but more importantly for the articulation between transnational capital and domestic production regimes. Put differently, I show that transnational capital plays a very different role in each type of economy's postsocialist "dependent development" (Evans 1979): In assembly platforms, transnational production remains largely isolated from the broader economy, whereas in intermediate producers, domestic firms appear as formidable partners and competitors to TNCs thereby enhancing the spillover effects of transnationalization to the broader economy. While radical openness toward transnational capital became Central and Eastern Europe's mantra in the 2000s and 2010s, it is in politically negotiating the terms of transnational capital's entry and the role of state policy toward domestic producer groups that comes to define differences between states like Slovenia, Hungary, and the Czech Republic.

Organization of *Globalization Under and After Socialism*

This book makes its case in the following way. Chapter 1 discusses approaches to East European socialism, globalization, and postsocialist transformation. In considering world-systems, institutionalist, and transitological approaches to East European globalization, I propose my own comparative and historical institutionalist framework that sees the region's world economic integration and institutional transformation in terms of a series of cumulative but nonlinear "punctuated evolutions." Chapter 2 traces the historical origins of East Europe's industrial development as it became excluded from US-led postwar international economic arrangements. It discusses the intensification of trade within the international socialist bloc through the establishment of the Council for Mutual Economic Assistance (Comecon) and the changing economic relations between the Central and East European states and the Soviet Union. The chapter assesses the importance of intrasocialist trade for East European industrialization, highlighting varying patterns of industrialization and national political responses to Soviet domination. This historical background informs the comparative analysis in Chapter 3, which examines causes for the exhaustion of Stalinist industrialization, changing opportunity structures in the world economy, and efforts to reform domestic institutions. In particular, the chapter explores the rise in the 1970s of import-led growth models of industrial upgrade, showing variation across socialist bloc states' engagements with the capitalist world to reflect a variety of domestic and international political priorities. The chapter documents how import-led growth led to the protoglobalization of East European industry as it began to participate, however marginally, in chains of transnational production that cut across the East-West political divide.

Chapter 4 documents the continuities between East European industrial protoglobalization in the 1970s with foreign investment inflows in the early

1990s. It does so by shifting attention from the state to the level of industrial sector and enterprise, to examine patterns of industrial cooperation and specialization that emerged during the era of import-led growth. What emerges as a key asset for East European economies after 1989 are organizational capacities to implement arrangements for the transnational production of goods and to access Western markets. The origins of this capacity lie in the reforms of the 1970s, when East European economies implemented a new model of interfirm cooperation that involved horizontal integration with Western TNCs in the form of product licensing, joint production, and joint research and development (R&D), and vertical integration of East European industry into supply chains with Western industry. These interfirm ties proved central for industrial restructuring after 1989 because they generated an organizational learning experience among both Western firms and East European enterprise that laid the foundation for TNC-driven globalization in the 1990s and 2000s.

Chapter 5 assesses the significance of industrial transnationalization through the 1990s for the international economic roles that the region's countries occupy in the twenty-first-century global economy. While legacies of transnational production provided a structural advantage for countries adjusting to globalization, political choices made during the reform period of the 1990s were also important in the manner in which legacies were mobilized toward postsocialist developmental goals. Rather than follow patterns of structural determination that drew from past decades, the period presented a number of critical junctures that pushed postsocialist economies along divergent paths of transnational integration and institutional adjustment to globalization. In the process, the states of Central and Eastern Europe assumed one among three possible roles in international market integration: assembly platform, intermediate producer, or combined. The chapter presents a counterintuitive finding, that those countries that pursued globalization the hardest became the largest relative losers, becoming increasingly dependent on the capital and technological capabilities of TNCs while seeing the relative decline of domestic skill and technological capacity. Among other countries, large domestic markets kept globalization at bay, thus differentiating economies on their levels of global integration. The analysis in this chapter thus challenges homogenizing depictions of Central and East European economies to show that the economic and institutional outcomes of their globalization have been neither unidirectional nor homogenizing, but determined by both industrial legacies and domestic political contingencies.

Chapter 6 examines comparatively the contingencies of the postsocialist period and the choice of reform orientation during two critical junctures, in 1989 and the late 1990s. The political analysis of this chapter demonstrates how choices of reform orientation in the making of Central and East European political economies were cumulative and path dependent. In the 2000s, FDI-driven development became the norm in most countries. However, the degree to which countries had worked to cultivate domestic capital during the early reform period proved crucial. In cases where postsocialist industrial restructuring relied most heavily on FDI, states eventually lost the advantages of skill formation and endogenous technological development that they had built during the socialist era. By contrast, in cases where postsocialist governments made efforts to cultivate domestic capital and industrial competitiveness, the economy developed greater capacities for sustained global competition and generated political economies supportive of innovation and skill formation through educational policies and pro-worker employment laws. This transpired even in cases where governments initially pursued policies of supporting domestic industry but began in the 2000s to turn increasingly toward FDI, highlighting the importance of institutional residues of past policy choices in the making of postsocialist political economies and the impact on local institutional change of the timing and mode of entry of TNCs. In the Conclusion I remark on the region's developmental challenges after the 2008 global financial crisis and the euro crisis.

Globalization Under and After Socialism

A Comparative and Historical Perspective

What is globalization? Given the ambiguity of the term and the abundance of existing definitions, this question is a good place to start. Definitions of globalization have often varied based on the social or institutional domain that has interested the analyst. A more narrow and widely applicable definition of globalization is offered by Anthony Giddens's (1990) concept of "time-space distantiation," the reduction of space by time with the advancement of communication and transportation technologies alongside the rise of more complex social interdependencies. Giddens sees the disembeddedness of social relations from particular local contexts as the defining feature of modernity, and others have used this insight to argue that globalization amplifies this process by expanding the spatial scope while narrowing the temporal frame of social action (Robertson 1992; Appadurai 1996; Bauman 1998; Sassen 1998; Beck 2000). Even though globalization has been theorized and the concept scrutinized across multiple frames and dimensions, the primary focus in academic debates has rested on the *economic* side of globalization (Stiglitz 2002; Weinstein 2005; Held and McGrew 2007; Rodrik 2011). Following historians of the *longue durée*, world-systems theorists have long held that economic globalization is neither new nor recent. Trade, transnational economic links, and transborder transactions between disparate parts of the world have been a defining feature of modern capitalism since its emergence in the sixteenth century (Wallerstein 1995, 2004). Other theorists have historically situated the more recent iteration of globalization within the context of economic paradigms and developmental policies of the postwar era. Rather than a faceless structural process, globalization entails a set of ideas and a vision about the global management of national economies, involving the internationalization of political authority in multilateral institutions and the adoption of standard rules and policies across national institutions (McMichael 1996; Holton 2005; Robinson 2004, 2014). Globalization thus operates as an ideological and institutional ordering principle whose bearers include a host of global and transnational elites, from state managers to financial and corporate elites to those of international financial institutions like the International Monetary Fund (IMF) and the World Bank.

The question of globalization's origins is inextricably linked with the outcome one believes globalization to be producing. This debate has often pitted institutionalists against critical globalization scholars—and here I ignore diversity within these perspectives to use these two designations loosely. Institutionalists see globalization as a process that flows through and is embedded in the existing institutions of national states and economies. These institutions change very slowly, and hence whatever restructuring takes place under globalization does not ultimately eliminate differences across regions, nation-states, and larger geohistorical conglomerates in terms of local institutions, interests, and cultural identities. In general terms, adherents of the institutionalist perspective argue that while recent decades have involved important transformations in economic institutions and policies given the rise and proliferation of transnational economic practices—including trade, financial flows, and transnational production—these have neither diminished nor displaced the primacy of state institutions (Weiss 1998; Gilpin 2002; Swank 2002; Mosley 2003; Campbell 2004; Streeck 2014). Consequently, major political and economic processes are contained within and their outcomes mediated by domestic institutions.

Critical globalization scholars, on the other hand, see economic globalization as largely driven by the expanding spatial scope of capitalist accumulation (Harvey 2001; Robinson 2004, 2014; Kotz and McDonough 2010). From this view, the capitalist crises of the 1970s in the advanced economies exposed the structural limits of national welfare capitalism. The response of capital was to incorporate new markets and shift the scale of accumulation to the global level, aided in part by the ideological ascendance of neoliberalism. This process resulted in the disintegration of national capitalist classes and the coalescence of a transnational capitalist class (Sklair 2001). The dominance of transnational capital also reoriented the state away from traditional goals of national welfare and developmentalism and the accommodation of transnational production in the growing competition for capital flows (Cerny 1997; Soederberg, Menz, and Cerny 2005).

The theoretical poles of institutionalism and critical globalization have informed the debates around the transition to capitalism in East Europe. Admittedly, in postcommunist studies the focus on democratic and market transitions from the theoretical perspective of "transitology" has limited the scope of alternative critical globalization analyses of East European transformations.[1] In the transitological literature, globalization (though the term is rarely invoked) may have had something to do with the spread of the ideas of liberal democracy and markets in East Europe, but subsequent developments in democratic consolidation and market transition rested largely on the choices of domestic political actors (O'Donnell and Schmitter 1986; Karl and Schmitter 1991; Przeworski 1991; Huntington 1993; Linz and Stepan 1996). Hence, the behavior of political elites, and not global forces, would be determinant of the character of regimes and economic systems in the postsocialist era (Ekiert 1991; Sachs 1993; Boycko, Shleifer, and Vishny 1995; Fish 1998; Bunce 1999a). As Grzegorz Ekiert notes, in the transitological paradigm, "political elites and their strategic choices in various phases of the political and economic transformations acquired paramount importance" (2015, 326). If there was any globalization in East Europe to speak of, whether in economic or political terms, this was largely an externally imposed process. In other words, globalization, like democracy and markets, was a novelty introduced to East Europe with the collapse of the proverbial iron curtain.

As a consequence, past efforts to integrate with the world economy through trade and international borrowing and by joining networks of transnational production seemed to no longer matter in the face of the promising new world of postcommunism.[2] The history of globalization mattered little, as did other legacies of socialism, and was categorically rejected especially in transitological thinking. To quote Ekiert again: "Initial structural conditions and specific historical legacies [were] relegated to the background as causal factors relative to transitional outcomes" (2015, 329). In this epistemic worldview, postcommunism was considered more a beginning than an end; a world born, to borrow an expression from Pierre Bourdieu, in "a world of already realized ends—procedures to follow, paths to take—and of objects endowed with a 'permanent teleological character'" (1990, 53). With democracy and markets—these objects endowed with a "permanent teleological character"—as the objective, the future of East Europe was laden with uncertainty but held little mystery over end goals. The choices needed to attain these goals were readily available, lying in the implementation of now standardized policy scripts of macroeconomic adjustment, deregulation, and privatization. It is not that the past was forgotten, of course, but it became something exogenous to the models of economic and political change that came to prevail. In other words, the past represented a set of initial conditions or cost structures that needed to be taken into account but were not in themselves enabling or determinate of future outcomes. This frame of thought came to inhabit not only the world of scholars and technocrats, but became constitutive of a broader transition culture of postcommunism, in which "transition" became the key regulative idea of the present's relationship to the past. As Michael Kennedy observes,

> Transition culture emphasizes the fundamental opposition of socialism and capitalism, and the exhaustion of the former and normative superiority of the latter. It values broad generalizing expertise around the workings of market economies and democratic polities. Culture and history are not especially difficult to understand in transition culture, and transition culture certainly does not privilege those who are expert in reading complicated and contested histories and cultures. Instead, culture is treated like a hunk of clay that can be reshaped, and history as a path that should inform postcommunist institutional design. Most certainly, culture and history are not recognized to be things that envelop the work of transition itself. (2002, 9)

In itself, "transition" is "a term very well suited . . . to those whose expertise is oriented toward the future, such as those in economic modeling or business plans" (6) and epistemologically "elevate[s] broad, generalizing, and comparative expertise about market economies while diminishing the value assigned to those who know how socialist institutions work and how local networks operate" (10). Within postsocialist countries, anticommunist "memory entrepreneurs" in academia, civil society, and politics also worked to flatten out the complexities and ambiguities of the Communist period into an unequivocal dark age of repression and national shame, with market liberalism, circulating in both academic-technical and popular "folk" varieties, offered as a path toward national redemption and renewal (Mark 2010; Appel and Orenstein 2013; Ban 2016).

This broader epistemic paradigm in postsocialist studies spread beyond the narrow field of scholarship on democratization and economic reform. It may have contributed to the partial stunting of critical globalization scholarship on

East European transformations, as the belief that the post-1989 period represented the original encounter between East Europe and globalization came to inform understandings even among those who rejected the specific assumptions and frameworks of transitology. Two perspectives emerged out of research written from a critical vein. The first appropriated the Marxist and "materialist" assumptions of the critical globalization perspective. This perspective has been confined to a small number of studies, and its emphasis is largely on postsocialist economic reforms and transnational capital creating the conditions for the "transnationalization of the state." This view sees globalization largely imposed, if not entirely from the outside, then certainly by the convergence of interests and collusion between powerful external and domestic forces as these economies opened in the course of the 1990s (Holman 2001; Shields 2004; Bohle 2006; Drahokoupil 2009).

An alternative critical perspective typically associates globalization with particular ideational forces, and in particular the rise of neoliberal ideology. From this perspective, in East Europe the forces of globalization have primarily manifested themselves in the form of ideas, not material (class) interests. Neoliberalism's introduction into East Europe as a particularly zealous form of "market fundamentalism" (Stiglitz) led to a determined effort towards radical liberal market reform in the region (Gowan 1995; Wedel 1998; Appel 2000). In that sense, neoliberal ideology helped legitimize the policies and processes of domestic institutional adjustment required for globalization—what might be called the domestic "institutional assimilation" of globalization through a "rolling-out" neoliberalism (Appel 2000, 2004; Peck and Tickell 2002; Orenstein 2008; Birch and Mykhnenko 2009). Neoliberal ideology also served to legitimize the social structural outcomes that the transition to a globalized capitalism created. The globalization of East European economies, in this view, was embodied first and foremost by the ideas held by market reformers and their international supporters, who proceeded to "institute" globalization domestically. Broadly, from this view, globalization and the creation of postsocialist markets went hand in hand: "Postsocialist transformations and intensification of globalization happened simultaneously" (Bandelj 2008, 57).

Soviet Socialism and World Capitalism: What Relation?

Conventional Cold War scholarship treated East Europe as "other" and described Western liberal capitalism and Soviet socialism as two opposed, competing, and irreconcilable ideologies and sociopolitical systems (Deudney and Ikenberry 1991). From this perspective, the iron curtain represented more than a geopolitical divide. It was also a fundamental rift that hid deeper cultural and historical differences between the two parts of the continent (Wolff 1994). Before 1989 it was world-systems scholars who developed an interest in interpreting the role of socialism and the international socialist bloc in the context of what they theorized as a *capitalist* world-system.[3] In his original formulation, Immanuel Wallerstein (1974, 1979) argued that Cold War divisions into rival ideological and sociopolitical blocs, rather than embodying deep political, cultural, and historical differences between East and West, instead represented a division of the capitalist world-system into a core and a global periphery competing against the political and economic pressures emanating from the core. In this interpretation, state socialism as a sociopolitical system was both genetically and structurally derivative of, rather than a systemic alternative to, the capitalist world-system. For Wallerstein, the socialist bloc exhibited behaviors typical of developing semiperipheral states—that is, policies aimed to (temporarily) withdraw the state from the capitalist world economy in order to improve its status within it. The Soviet model of socialism, later transplanted onto Central and Eastern Europe, was but one variation in the theme of developmental intervention by political elites through which marginalized states sought to match the military, economic, and technological standards set by the core states of the capitalist world economy. Christopher Chase-Dunn (1980) further developed Wallerstein's initial formulation with an effort to demonstrate the subordinate but dependent position of socialist bloc economies in the capitalist world-system.

Chase-Dunn's discussion of socialism in the world-system created significant debate among historical social scientists, but for the most part, the debates concentrated on theoretical criticisms of the world-systems approach and political and ideological concerns over the prospects and possibilities of other socialisms. While controversial, the world-systems perspective inspired alternative critical approaches to the historical role of Soviet and Third World variants of socialism and its relationship with the capitalist world. Jadwiga Staniszkis (1989) built on the insights of world-systems theory to argue that the collectivization and privatization of property rights was a strategy for the bloc's erection of an "ontological barrier" against Western capital. Under these terms, the relationship between the Soviet bloc and the capitalist world economy could not be described by the "normal" terms of (capitalist) dependency relations (Dos Santos 1970; Clark and Bahry 1983; Luke 1985). While the USSR could use its military power and vast natural resources to cordon itself off from the core of the world economy, the smaller states of Central and Eastern Europe faced dual subjection in the form of economic dominance from the Western core and military dominance from the Soviet empire. Staniszkis described this condition as a situation of "dual dependency"—that is, the region's simultaneous political domination from the imperial center (the Soviet Union) and economic dependence on the capitalist world economy (dominated by the core economies of advanced capitalist states). Dual dependency was not merely the expression of a political subordination or a historical contingency, but constituted a necessary functional relationship that mediated the existence of socialism as a sociopolitical apparatus within the capitalist world economy (Staniszkis 1989). A backward and forward slide from adversarial, competitive, and cooperative relations with the core of the world-system was the resulting pattern in Soviet and East European relations with the West. Under dual dependency, Central and East European socialist states in particular faced a conundrum of standing subordinate to the Soviet empire's political and military dominance, yet finding their economies dependent on capital from the West. In the late 1980s, Staniszkis (1989, 1990) saw this developmental tension resolved increasingly in favor of the core's dominance, as East European reformers began instituting an "ontological opening" to Western capital with the restoration of private property.

Among Western social scientists, world-systems scholars were some of the few to attempt to seriously parse the relationship between socialism and world capitalism. The relevance of these past debates is that they present a theoretical opening in light of the earlier questions raised about globalization—was the Soviet Union and its socialist bloc allies subject to globalization pressures emanating from the capitalist world? Of course, world-systems theory is an awkward position from which to ask that question, given Wallerstein's well-known rejection of the idea of globalization (Robinson 2011). At the same time, unlike the Manichaean view embedded in Cold War scholarship, world-systems theory at the very least raised the possibility that relations between world capitalism and Soviet socialism were characterized by certain systemic features. Considering that the era of late twentieth and early twenty-first century globalization is marked by certain qualitative features that make it distinct from prior episodes of global economic integration, imperialism, and dependency, world-systemic interpretations of socialism can serve as a useful base from which to begin to explore the question. To do so, the world-systems view of Soviet socialism must itself be subject to critical reassessment.

Examining systemic relations between the socialist bloc and the capitalist world economy using a world-systems perspective presents both theoretical and empirical difficulties. The long criticized theoretical problem of world-systems analysis is its privileging of systemic analysis in which the nature of constituent parts is determined by the whole, with political and economic relations largely cast in functional terms (Skocpol 1977; Gorin 1985; Sewell 1996). World-systems scholars applied this framework in interpreting the historical role of Soviet socialism. Chase-Dunn described socialist states as mere "functional parts of the capitalist system" (1980, 522). As a result, we end up with the familiar problems of functionalism: the favoring of structural relations over agency and the flattening of world ontologies by the treatment of all existing institutions and ideologies as derivative phenomena whose character and content is determined by the nature of the larger ecology (system).[4] As a critic noted, the framework ultimately denied the causal autonomy of socialist states, elites, and social relations, as these seemed to exercise no meaningful agency of their own. It tended to repress the fact that "the structure and logic of the socialist systems [were] radically different from those of the capitalist societies; that this logic [was] the dominant factor in the dialectic of internal and external forces" (Gorin 1985, 364).

While lying within a world-systems framework, Stanszikis's dual dependency perspective attempted to restore the autonomy of socialist states and societies and proceeded to complicate the structural relations between socialist states and world-systemic forces. A number of critical scholars building on the insights of world-systems theory began to integrate the developments of the 1970s and explore their structural effects on socialist systems, going beyond the functional relations between unit and system posited by Wallerstein and Chase-Dunn. Rather than seeing structural relations between socialism and the capitalist world economy as fixed, they developed a more dynamic mode of structural analysis that incorporated the effects of structural change in the world economy beginning in the 1970s.

Staniszkis's work served as an inspiration to József Böröcz (1992), who reinterpreted the developmental path of socialist states by distinguishing between two periods. In the first period, lasting from the postwar establishment of state socialist regimes in Europe and through the 1960s, the logic of dual dependency favored the coercive logic of Soviet imperial dominance over the "negative dependency" on the Western core of the world economy. Starting in the 1970s, this logic began to change. During this second period, the socialist bloc experienced a rapid expansion of trade with the West. Financial flows intensified while its foreign debt skyrocketed. As a result, dependency relations experienced a qualitative transformation. It was no longer about negative dependency via the rejection of the basic institutions of capitalism but about the reemergence of "linkages of direct financial and technological dependency" (89) between East European and Western capitalist economies. The (re)integration of the socialist bloc into the capitalist world economy took place primarily through the channels of global finance, which began its expansion in the 1970s. These deepening linkages transformed the character of dual dependency, establishing a new "pragmatic equilibrium" between its imperial and world-economy components, until its unraveling in 1989. The final stage of restoration of property rights marked not only the end of socialism as a counterhegemonic project but also created "the opportunity for [capital] to valorize [Central and East] European labor without having to take the circuitous route through private lending to the socialist state" (97).

Like the theory that served as its inspiration, the dual dependency framework left little room for the agency of local actors in setting the terms or determining the outcomes of transformative processes. The problem of agency appears particularly muted in the case of East European transformations after 1989, since the goals of change appeared contradictory from a world-systems perspective: a revolutionary change in terms of politics (democratization), but with a reactionary purpose among its goals (the restoration of capitalism). Staniszkis (1990) saw this contradictory project as lying with the conservational efforts of East European political elites, confronted by systemic contradictions at the top and popular pressures for reform from below. For this reason, she predicted that the region would transition toward "political capitalism," an economic system in which the institution of property rights would proceed to consolidate the domination of existing elites alongside new capitalist sociopolitical arrangements. This assessment was not entirely wrong. "Nomenklatura capitalism" did emerge in postcommunist Russia and across a number of other ex-Soviet states. It was less pronounced in Central and Eastern Europe (Eyal, Szelényi, and Townsley 1998; Hanley 2000; King and Szelényi 2005). The Central and East European pattern leads to further complications in interpreting systemic change as being driven primarily by the interests of dominant elites; indeed, as Gil Eyal and his colleagues (1998) found in their research in Central and Eastern Europe, the collapse of socialist regimes did not prove to be favorable to the political survival or economic enrichment of high party elites.

Still, the acknowledgment by the dual dependency view that East Europe's socialist economies were already participating in the structures of world capitalism *prior to 1989* suggests an interesting starting point for an *institutional* analysis of the globalization of state socialist and postsocialist economies. A critic of the world-systems approach to socialism observed that, when examining economic relations, world-systemic perspectives ignored the fact that, although "economic exchanges among the socialist societies and between them and the capitalist world are affected by the dynamics of capitalism in important ways, these relationships [were] radically different from those among capitalist countries, since they are filtered through the structures and mechanisms of these countries" (Gorin 1985, 364). When Zeev Gorin speaks of exchanges "filtered through the structures and mechanisms of these countries," he is calling for institutional analysis. More importantly, an institutional approach establishes an empirical basis for examining the nature of dependency relations and organizational and institutional change. It also recognizes the importance of the goals of agents and the historical context of their ideas about change. Such historical contextualization helps gauge the significance of the presumed deepening "incorporation" of socialist states into world capitalism while avoiding exaggerated claims or sweeping explanations.[5] This alternative perspective assumes that state socialist actors did not only passively react to developments in the world economy but were influenced by and helped shape the ideas and opportunities world economic change represented.

The broader significance of this in relation to literatures on East European transitions is that globalization, rather than a Western project *imposed* on East Europe from the outside, can be better understood as a constructive, rhizomatic, and relatively open-ended process whose features were shaped by the *active agency* of East European actors. By this, of course, I do not mean to imply that these actors had an equal and symmetrical role in the making of globalization alongside powerful financiers, transnational corporate elites, and neoliberal reformers of the core capitalist states. However, by navigating at the margins and helping shape the articulations of globalization in both pre- and post-1989 East Europe, local elites and other actors played their role in molding globalization in forms amenable to local conditions and harnessing its forces in the service of domestic goals. Going beyond a world-systems framework means accepting that there are actors, ideas, and institutional forms in East

Europe that reflect endogenous causal processes carrying local histories and are not merely reactionary to, and derivative of, the institutions, ideas, and agency of hegemonic actors. This restoration of agency in historical change brings us back to the role of institutions in the globalization of East European economies.

Globalization and the Socialist States: A Historical-Institutionalist Perspective

It may seem anachronous to apply the term "globalization" to the era before 1990, since the term itself was not popularized until that time (Beck 2000). But as students of the global economy have noted, many of the features we presently associate with globalization had their origins in some of the structural changes taking place in the world economy beginning in the 1970s. The term "globalization," then, is here used not to refer to a "thing," a state of being, or a set of ideas, but to structurally transformative processes of the post–Bretton Woods era that laid the groundwork for the global economy of the late twentieth and early twenty-first centuries. Engaging with the history of globalization in East Europe from an institutionalist standpoint involves several tasks. First, it requires *defining* what we understand by globalization during the socialist era. Second, it involves *theorizing* the relationship between global economic change and locally embedded ideas, organizational practices, and institutions in the socialist world. Finally, it requires asking the question of relevance—that is, did the early globalization experience matter for *postsocialist* trajectories? In other words, what causal relationship is there, if any, between structural change under pre-1989 globalization and *institutional outcomes* observed in these states in the era of post-1989 globalization? And what exactly do these institutional outcomes consist of as they emerge in the early twenty-first century? That is, do different forms of engagement with globalization lead to different *kinds* of transnational economic integration, enabling globalization to either support, or be detrimental to, the long-term developmental goals of these polities and societies? In the end, that analysis casts a normative judgment on globalization itself, thereby contributing to debates about the relative benefits and perils that globalization has offered to countries aspiring to join the exclusive club of wealthy nations (Evans 1995; Amsden 2001; Kohli 2004; Gereffi 2009; Rodrik 2011).

Even those who largely identify globalization with the rise of ideas embodied by neoliberalism and the Washington Consensus note that structural changes in the organization of the world economy beginning in the 1970s pre-figure the key features of the globalized economy of the late twentieth and early twenty-first century. These transformations precede the formal global ascendance of neoliberal ideology in the 1980s and its challenge after the 2008 global financial crisis (McMichael 1996; Harvey 2005; Crouch 2011; Duménil and Lévy 2011). These changes include the quantitative growth and qualitative transformation of trade, financial flows, and production (Sassen 1998; Simmons 1999; Gilpin 2001; Frieden 2006). The architecture of the postwar Bretton Woods system facilitated the growth of trade among advanced Western economies, but in the 1960s and 1970s opportunities multiplied for developing states to gain a steadily growing share of advanced country markets. By 1973 the role of trade in the economy had more than doubled in Western Europe and quadrupled in Japan (Frieden 2006, 346). Globally, the period between 1970 and 1980 saw the largest increase in the size of trade in world gross domestic product (GDP) in the postwar period, driven largely by developing countries. In 1981 the share of trade as a percentage of world GDP reached 35 percent, a level that would not be attained again until the late 1990s. In some ways, then, the decade of the 1970s marks the era when postwar trade patterns were becoming disrupted by the rise of new trading powers in the periphery, and advanced economies reacted with shifts in policy to deal with the decline in their relative competitiveness in the world economy (Arrighi and Drangel 1986).

In addition to the expansion of energy and commodity trade by developing nations, the rise of East Asian exporters was deeply disruptive to the competitive structures of the North Atlantic nations (Amsden 2001). The share of East Asian exports to member nations of the Organization for Economic Cooperation and Development (OECD) nearly doubled between 1970 and 1980. Competitive pressures from East Asian manufacturing exporters, led by Japanese firms' competition in traditional industrial areas like steel production and the manufacture of automobiles and high-technology goods, generated a backlash in the advanced countries in the form of demands for protectionist policies. In the course of the 1980s, Western states saw a partial return to protectionism to deal with the rise in competitive pressures from East Asia (Gilpin 2001). While protectionist measures, mainly in the form of nontariff barriers and "voluntary restraints," reduced global trade volumes during the 1980s—aided in part by falls in commodity prices and the debt crises of Latin America—the structural changes of the 1970s led to a number of policy shifts, particularly in the developing and socialist states. These policy shifts, alongside the example set by the East Asian export-driven model, increasingly challenged traditional import-substitution policies, and these states began seeing trade as critical to development (Frieden 2006, 351–357). In particular, policy orientations in both developing and socialist economies came more and more to value exports to the advanced economies as a means for making developmental gains. These policies, of course, unfolded within the context of the fiscal, monetary, and economic policy autonomy that for developing countries had been enshrined in the international monetary and financial arrangements of the Bretton Woods system. From their end, socialist states believed that they could gain and maintain access to capitalist markets and technology even as most stood outside of the formal institutions of postwar international capitalism.

More important than trade in the 1970s was the rise of global finance. Indeed, according to most accounts, it was the forces of global finance, rather than trade, that drove the paradigmatic shift from Bretton Woods to neoliberalism and globalization (Harvey 2005; Glyn 2006; Duménil and Lévy 2011). Growth in international financial flows between the early 1970s and the early 1980s outpaced growth in trade. During that period, foreign investment by transnational corporations grew from $15 billion to $100 billion a year. International lending grew from $25 billion to $300 billion a year, while international financial markets grew from $160 billion in 1973 to $3 trillion in 1985 (Frieden 2006, 397). Structural problems in the advanced countries were behind the growth of global finance in part. As balance of payments problems, inflationary pressures, and the need to finance deficits grew, policymakers sought new sources of raising capital while avoiding policies that would worsen recessions or impose higher taxes on their citizens (Helleiner 1996; Krippner 2011; Streeck 2014). At the same time, the Organization of the Petroleum Exporting Countries (OPEC) raised oil prices in 1973, creating a dollar glut in offshore eurodollar markets, as OPEC states reinvested their oil dollars in Western financial institutions (Allen 2009). With excess dollars on their hands and few opportunities for profitable investment in the advanced countries, Western commercial banks and investors began a lending spree to developing and socialist governments, whose debt levels soared during the decade of the 1970s.

The third aspect of structural change during the 1970s was the rise and global expansion of TNCs, particularly in the area of manufacturing. In the 1960s, apart from the United States, only a small number of European nations had manufacturing firms operating subsidiaries outside of their home economy. During this time, US-based manufacturing companies were dominant in the size and extent of their subsidiary networks worldwide, controlling 83 percent of all TNC subsidiaries in 1962 (Kentor 2005, 272). But the composition of global TNCs began to transform dramatically, and by 1998, 81 percent of subsidiaries were controlled by firms based in states other than the United States. The momentum for change began in the 1970s. Indeed, as Jeffrey Kentor documents, the dominance of US firms in global TNC networks peaked at 1971, with the subsequent years exhibiting the largest wave of growth among non-US (particularly European and Japanese) TNC networks. The expansion of TNC networks coincided with growing flows of FDI, the principal means by which TNCs established manufacturing operations in offshore locations. In the early 1970s, 90 percent of US-based TNC subsidiaries were located in European economies and Japan. The emergence of new TNC networks controlled by European and Japanese-based companies diversified the regional spread of TNC networks. By the 1990s, US, major European, and Japanese manufacturing TNCs maintained only a minority of their subsidiaries in other rich economies, having spread their networks increasingly toward developing nations.

The dramatic shift in the organization of worldwide production networks prompted some of the first analyses of globalization in the area of production. John Dunning (1988) observes that in the decades between 1960 and 1985, what transformed was not only the size and composition of TNC networks but also their character. Increasingly, TNC investments were driven not by the goal of controlling access to natural resources or producing goods for sale in the host (recipient) economy, but to base production in those economies within networked and integrated frameworks of TNC production. Dunning points out that this period saw "a shift away from traditional import-substituting and resource-based FDI to that designed to promote an integrated structure of production by [TNCs] and their affiliates" (1988, 83). In addition to the reorganization of production along networked (transborder) operations, TNCs also began moving away from increasingly competitive low-cost and standardized technology sectors and turned toward complex goods. Early researchers noted the high correlation between high innovation and the propensity to engage in FDI in the 1970s and 1980s (Dunning 1988, 94). Hence, TNCs sought to maintain their competitive edge not only by their ability to produce cheaply but also through their control of proprietary processes and technologies. Control of proprietary technologies gave TNCs an increasing advantage over nationally based competitors, a process that concentrated manufacturing power through "technological accumulation" (Pavitt 1987; Cantwell 1989). Increasingly, the control of dominant capital and technological goods was transferred from firms operating within the bounds of nation-states to transborder, networked TNCs (Herrigel and Zeitlin 2010). The development literature grappled deeply with the questions of the rise of TNC dominance and its consequences for developing economies, producing influential analyses such as Fernando Henrique Cardoso and Enzo Faletto's (1979) critical revision of the theory of economic dependency and Peter Evans's (1979) novel concept of "dependent development." In these revised views, insofar as TNCs enabled developing countries access to capital and new technologies and products, they could serve as potential allies in the process of development. This new engagement with TNCs began undermining the view that foreign capital is inherently detrimental and exploitative for developing economies, a mainstay of traditional dependency scholarship (Frank 1966). Views in socialist countries also began to change, as Chapter 3 documents.

During the crisis years of the 1970s, the actions of Western TNCs reflected not only their efforts to maintain technological dominance in an increasingly crowded world market for goods but also to confront the recessions, macroeconomic instability, and labor demands in the advanced economies. A common term used to describe TNC restructuring during this period was "rationalization"—that is, the shifting of operations away from the advanced toward developing countries. Folker Fröbel, Jürgen Heinrichs, and Otto Kreye (1980) note that the 1970s marked a period when foreign investment from advanced economies, particularly toward developing countries, grew, even while domestic investment was on the decline. This, for the authors, was a deliberate process. They note that "stagnating output, short-time working and mass redundancies in numerous countries do not . . . necessarily reflect the fate of individual companies. On the contrary, many companies, both large and small, from the industrialized countries are expanding their investments, production capacities and employment abroad, especially in developing countries, whilst their investments, production capacities, and employment at home are stagnating or even declining" (3). This new TNC-led reorganization of worldwide production resulted not only in the growth of foreign investments, but profound structural changes in skill, employment, and quality of work, creating what the authors saw as an emerging "new international division of labor." This new international division of labor increasingly shifted low-end, labor-intensive work away from the advanced countries to take advantage of the cost benefits of developing countries. In the process, these shifts were leading to the erosion of national production regimes and remaking the nature of labor markets across both advanced and developing economies. Recognition of the growing role of TNCs was not limited to scholars in the West. A doctoral dissertation written at the Jawaharlal Nehru University concluded worryingly that

> the skill, the speed and ease with which [TNCs] move enormous liquid funds from one country to another act as an unsettling effect on the international monetary system. . . . [T]he theories of international trade have lost relevance because of the significant increase in intracompany transfers, growing practice of transfer-pricing and jumping trade and tariff barriers by locating production plants in various national jurisdictions but obeying the central command of corporate headquarters. Possession of and control over sophisticated technology have invested the corporation with superior bargaining power enabling them to extract unconscionable prices for the licensing or sale of such technology. (Shanker 1979, 301–302)

Raymond Vernon (1971), writing in the early 1970s, could already discern the threats to national sovereignty that the rise of TNCs represented to both advanced and developing states, as the control of technology and the shifting of production diminished the capacities of states to tax, carry out monetary policy, and implement traditional developmental goals. And by the mid-1980s, Susan Strange (1986) could already raise the alarm over the rise of global finance and the dangers of "casino capitalism." These patterns highlight the fact that the structural changes we have come to identify with globalization were already underway in the 1970s.

I recall these common patterns and themes in the globalization literature to remind the reader of the kinds of structural changes in the capitalist world economy that confronted the socialist world during the 1970s and 1980s. To be sure, during this period Soviet and Third World socialist states engaged in their own variant of globalization through deepening ties of trade, technical and military aid, and cultural exchanges. This politically driven "socialist internationalism" of the periphery, however, differed significantly in its aims and practices from core globalization and during its existence functioned as a "possible might have been—as an alternative model for conducting international relations" (Imlay 2009, 541). But, as we will see, many socialist reformers in East Europe took a keen interest in the rise of trade, global finance, and transnational production in the capitalist world and saw in them a unique set of opportunities for upgrading the path of socialist economic development. The

East Asian export model affected the thinking of socialist reformers, and many advocated reforms that would ease restrictions and institutional obstacles to interacting with the capitalist world. The globalizing world of the 1970s seemed rife with opportunities for convergence—namely, the standing official belief among socialist planners that socialist countries can, and will, catch up developmentally and technologically with the advanced capitalist countries. Early globalization affected the socialist world at the level of ideas about the role of socialist states in the world economy, and the opportunities opened up by early globalization were the trigger for processes of organizational change within these economies as they adjusted to the rise in global interactions beyond the socialist bloc. Change at the level of ideas and organization became cause for institutional adjustments within the governance of socialist economies as they shifted away from traditional Stalinist planning toward decentralized systems of economic governance that assigned an increasingly important role to trade and cooperation with the capitalist world.

It is not that the dynamics of the world economy and their impact on the socialist bloc went unnoticed by Western academic observers of East European economies prior to 1989 (e.g., Perlmutter 1969; Wilczynski 1976; Tyson and Kenen 1980; Brada 1985b; Holzman 1987; Lavigne 1991). But, with few exceptions (e.g., Ban 2012), after 1989 many of these observations appeared irrelevant in the face of the new epoch of democracy and markets that the (now former) socialist states had entered. The dual dependency view portrayed these interactions in systemic and encompassing terms, leaving out the internal dynamics within socialist states that led to particular policy choices and structuring increasingly varied forms of integration with the emerging global economy.

Socialist Globalization and Postsocialist Development

In this book I seek to restore not only the historical but also the *causal* significance of these past transformations in accounting for the present. One need not only challenge the notion that socialist economies were unperturbed by developments of the post–Bretton Woods world economy but also trace causal links between past reforms and later trajectories. While not dismissing the radical political and institutional discontinuities of postsocialism at the macro level, the argument frames the analysis of the organization of production under socialism and postsocialism as one following a "punctuated evolution." Punctuated evolution is characterized by "evolutionary periods of social learning during which self-reflexive actors gradually adjust their institutions in ways that are constrained by already-given institutional practices, rules, routines, and cognitive schema." But these evolutionary adjustments "are punctuated . . . by crises that involve open struggles over the very core of the institutional status quo and that eventually result in truly fundamental institutional transformations" (Campbell 2004, 34). The metaphor of punctuated evolution softens the standard assumptions of a radical and incommensurate break between past and present that stands as the fundamental assumption of transitology (Campbell and Pedersen 1996). It also forces us to examine the dialectical relationships between gradual and rapid change, and processes of contestation over institutions whose origins may lie much farther in the past than the present epistemic field of vision allows.

If concern over the socialist past ultimately lies with explaining the present, what are the *outcomes* of interest, and why do they matter? That is, if East Europe's engagement with globalization began much earlier than commonly presumed, does that mean that the region's globalized economies of the early twenty-first century represent the unfolding of the logic of the ever expanding geographic scope and organizational scale of capitalist accumulation as described by critical globalization scholars? While mature globalization has expanded transborder networks of capital accumulation, particularly with the rise of global finance, the distinct feature of Central and Eastern Europe's globalization is that its dominant form is not primarily in the area of finance, but in production. The *realm of production*, and, particularly, *manufacturing industries*, has been the premier site of the region's global integration. Since global manufacturing is structured by hierarchically organized chains of value-added activity, the location in which industries find themselves in these networks is crucial to ascertaining the potential developmental effects of global production for the local economy (United Nations Conference on Trade and Development [UNCTAD] 2007; Gereffi 2009). Transborder participation also differs between typical TNC-based subsidiary production and independent participation in global supply chains through subcontracting ties (Gereffi, Humphrey, and Sturgeon 2005). These multiple dimensions suggest numerous possibilities for transnational production, varied economic and political impacts of transnational production on domestic institutions, and in combination provide a means for classifying distinct roles that states and their industrial sectors occupy within global production regimes.

Put in other terms, different modes of transnational integration assign states and their economic sectors distinct *roles* in the twenty-first century global economy. In this book I identify three such roles in the postsocialist economies of Central and Eastern Europe: assembly platform, intermediate producer, and combined. As Chapter 6 shows, the origins of socialist globalization in combination with the politics of postsocialist reform explain why some countries appear to have done better in using globalization to upgrade their industrial status, and why for others, integration in global production has combined absolute gains (in productivity and market share) with relative losses (in industrial status). As that chapter shows, this outcome depended on the orientation of postsocialist reform policies, and particularly on the choice to gain export market share by integrating directly with transnational manufacturing or to "go it alone" and attempt to engage domestic producers to compete in the world market directly. What this means is that the postsocialist era represented its own set of contingent choices for economic and industrial policy, but that in relation to the process of globalization, these choices were contingent because *where countries already stood and how they got there mattered for their possible futures.*

Methodology of *Globalization Under and After Socialism*

To develop my claims in this book, I employ a multimethod research approach, relying variously on case discussion, structural comparisons, and statistical analysis drawn from historical documents, secondary sources, historical and recent economic data, and over fifty interviews with a broad base of institutional actors across five countries. This research is incorporated within the realm of a case-based, comparative historical analysis (Tilly 1984; Griffin 1992; Steinmetz 1998; Arrighi 1999; Mahoney, Kimball, and Koivu 2009). I use quantitative analyses to test, support, and extend the findings of qualitative case-based research and examine ancillary hypotheses and expectations generated by the qualitative findings, for example, by examining the extent to which observed policy goals and outcomes match. Application of these combined methods in a macrolevel, comparative historical frame means three things. First, within-case analysis of historical cases is performed using what Tulia Falleti and James Mahoney (2015) call "inductive process tracing" (see also Mahoney 2012; Beach and Pedersen 2013; Collier 2014). Inductive process tracing involves "[deriving] propositions and [formulating] sequences from empirical observation" (Falleti and Mahoney 2015, 229). This method is most productive in theory building and is a strategy best employed for unconventional cases for which theoretical expectations are not readily available. "Inductive process tracing plays a large role in the construction of any complex, conjunctural, and multilayered historical narrative. . . . [T]he analyst cannot anticipate in advance many of the key events that comprise sequences and processes of central analytical importance" (229). Given the complex and layered histories of East European globalization prior to 1989, and the not readily obvious connections of those histories to political and economic transformations after 1989, the method serves to "[pull] out and [assemble] events into coherent and connected sequences" (230). Second, causal processes are reconstructed using a comparative sequential method (Rueschemeyer and Stephens 1997; Falleti and Mahoney 2015). The goal in the analysis is to comparatively examine if and when temporal sequences empirically traced out across cases combine into coherent *causal sequences* that are tied together by shared mechanisms leading to shared outcomes (Tilly 2001; Mayntz 2004; Gorski 2009; Grzymala-Busse 2011). A sequential analysis can also accommodate conjunctural events—that is, the combination of two or more independent causal sequences (Paige 1999; Mahoney 2000). For example, both the pressures of globalization and the particular politics of post-1989 transitions can be analytically treated as causally distinct processes that jointly determine the transformation of economic institutions in East Europe. World-systems and dual dependency perspectives treat these processes as intricately intertwined, and as a result local change merely reflects causes that are endogenous to the functional demands of the larger system (e.g., the systemic demands of capitalist accumulation lead to the removal within states of institutional barriers against private capital accumulation). By contrast, transitological approaches begin their analysis by treating a given historical situation as an initial condition for outcomes that the theory considers relevant, such as democratic consolidation and economic reform, which subsequently produce varied outcomes. Both perspectives obscure the possibility that the combination of domestic organizational changes induced by globalization and postcommunist reform politics, while temporally concurrent, may in fact represent a *contingent conjunction* between what are causally independent processes (Steinmetz 1998; Paige 1999). This view makes it possible to analytically separate causal processes and thus avoid collapsing the processes of globalization as inherent in the logic of postcommunist democratization and marketization. If two or more conjuncturally combined sequences reflect independent causal processes, then there exists the potential for one process to either block or amplify the other, or to combine in ways that launch a new transformational process. This suggests a different logic of postsocialist transformation from that typically employed in the transitions literature, since it assumes that economic outcomes in postsocialist East Europe are not that of postcommunism establishing a historical tabula rasa that postcommunist reformers inscribe at will, but a critical juncture in which antecedent conditions generate the (nonetheless limited) range of possibilities for agents to negotiate and enact transformational change.

This historical perspective on postsocialist transformations falls in line with recent efforts by scholars of postcommunism to more directly engage with the importance of legacies of socialism in determining postsocialist trajectories of democratization and economic reform (Ekiert and Hanson 2003a; Tismaneanu et al. 2006; Beissinger and Kotkin 2014; Pop-Eleches and Tucker 2017). Much, though not all, of this scholarship takes its inspiration from the work of Kenneth Jowitt (1992), who emphasizes the distinct character of Communism (or, as Jowitt terms it, Leninism) as a world-historical force and associated historical experience. Jowitt's concept of Leninism represents an effort to use a Weberian comparative historical frame to steer clear of the pitfalls of both the essentialism of Cold War scholarship (with its emphasis on the presumably immutable features of Soviet totalitarianism) and the universalism of various modernization perspectives on Soviet socialism as an alternative (and potentially convergent) model of bureaucratic (or capitalist) modernity. In contrast, Jowitt describes and theorizes the experience of Leninism by emphasizing its "genetic" and "developmental" features that led it to constitute a distinct "historical individual" containing its own set of organizational imperatives, ideological tensions, and institutional contradictions (Bunce 1999b; Sil 2006). Jowitt argues that the "Leninist extinction" in 1989–1992 left in its wake societies characterized by political cultures of mistrust in public institutions, divided elites, weak governance, and fragmented body politics. Jowitt believes these features would continue to define the postcommunist world. Yet divergent patterns of political and institutional development in the region since 1989, and particularly successful efforts to consolidate democratic regimes and build market institutions in Central and Eastern Europe, have denied reality to some of Jowitt's more pessimistic predictions.[6] The benefit of a longer historical view of the region's institutional transformation and development after Communism has not resolved the question among historically minded social scientists of what, if any, of socialism's—

or even precommunist—legacies still remain or have mattered in the course of transformation. For scholars arguing for the importance of legacies, there is little consensus on which particular legacies matter more, even when there is consensus on the normative object or outcome in question (Kotkin and Beissinger 2014). As Rudra Sil points out, part of the problem in examining the impact of Communist legacies from a comparative historical perspective stems from the failure of many scholars of postcommunism to "articulate a coherent theoretical framework that could focus attention on the dimensions along which transformation processes could be systematically compared and contrasted across postcommunist and other settings" (2006, 234). There is also, as Grzegorz Ekiert and Stephen Hanson (2003b) point out, the methodological issue of how legacies are defined and theorized to exert causal influence. For some, legacies have been conceptualized as underlying "deep structures" of slow-changing behavioral habits involving processes of "cultural transmission" from the past that continue to exert causal power in the present (Janos 1993; Putnam 1993; Kubik 2003). For others, legacies operate more pragmatically as "structural enablers" that exert causal power during significant turning points of transformative change that have long-term consequences for institutional development (Ekiert 2003). The methodological strategy followed here is of identifying legacies as the product of antecedent processes whose causal powers become important during periods of dramatic institutional change and whose patterns of change across similar cases cannot be fully accounted for by differences in proxy variables (Kitschelt 2003; Wittenberg 2015). Rather than reflecting the logic of deeply inculcated cultural patterns, this definition of legacies follows that originally developed by Ruth Berins Collier and David Collier (1991) as structures that become causally active during "critical junctures" of structural and institutional change. In this view, legacies are not persistent cultural patterns transmitted from the distant past, but elements or structures that recur over time and become causally relevant in the determination of the mode, direction, and speed of change during a given temporal juncture. In this sense, legacies are not hapless inheritances from history but specific institutions (or agentic capacities) that are produced at particular moments in history and exert causal power because their institutionalization provides them with mechanisms of reproduction (cf. Stinchcombe 1968; Sewell 1996; Pierson 2004). A legacy thus has a beginning, a duration, and an end—it constitutes, in other words, "the outcome to be explained, not the antecedent or the mechanism linking antecedent and outcome" (Wittenberg 2015, 369). Put in other terms, contra Jowitt's expectation that legacies will *always* matter, I posit that legacies matter, but not always and not forever. More crucially, one of the key lessons of macrohistorical analysis is that what appear as marginal elements of a social formation often prove much more determinant of its future forms than what are considered to be its defining features. Postcommunist transformations have been no different. Hence, *which* legacy will come to matter at a particular juncture of structural change is determined by the contingent set of problems actors are presented with, and by the solutions they conjure out of materials inherited from the past, rather than the mindless enactment of some immutable body of beliefs and social practices carried from the past into the present.

The particular legacy I consider in this book is that of socialist industrial development. In this vein, the work of Béla Greskovits and collaborators (Greskovits 2004, 2014; Bruszt and Greskovits 2009; Bohle and Greskovits 2012) has been crucial in developing frameworks to think about the impact of socialist industrial legacies on patterns of postsocialist development and global economic integration. Their work challenges the narrow confines of postcommunist studies and its standard set of questions and conceptual frameworks organized around issues of democratic and market transitions and brings the analysis of postsocialist economic transformation into dialogue with research in globalization and dependency (Cardoso and Faletto 1979; Evans 1979, 1995; Amsden 2001; Gereffi, Humphrey, and Sturgeon 2005) and international and comparative political economy (Katzenstein 1985; Hollingsworth and Boyer 1997; Kitschelt et al. 1999; Hall and Soskice 2001; Streeck 2009; Beramendi et al. 2015). In a foundational theoretical statement, Greskovits (2004) argues the folly of measuring and explaining patterns of economic "transition" in East Europe by gauging progress through each postsocialist country's abstract enactment of markets; instead, Greskovits aims to demonstrate how postsocialist developmental paths were largely determined by the structure and composition of leading industrial sectors that states inherited from the socialist era. Greskovits suggests that developmental trajectories leading toward rapid global integration were found in states in which leading economic sectors combined flexible mixes of capital, products, and skill, and could muster effective developmental alliances involving the state and national and/or transnational capital. Working out of these divergent industrial bases, the developmental potentials of postsocialism were largely exhausted by the late 1990s: "New reforms in the second half of the 1990s appear to be less effective levers of economic restructuring than the measures implemented earlier in the decade. . . . As a consequence, in many countries, reformers' capabilities to enforce, by policy packages, significant shifts from less satisfactory to more promising developmental trajectories, seem to have come close to their limits" (Greskovits 2004, 201). Both the insights that socialist industrial legacies proved vital in determining possible developmental paths during the critical juncture of early reform, but that by the 2000s had largely exhausted their transformative force, are crucial for the analysis carried out here. However, unlike Greskovits's treatment of the region's global integration as one beginning in earnest in the 1990s, in this book I push the process further into the past and examine patterns of socialist economic policies and strategies of global integration that proved essential in *generating* the flexible product and skill mixes and local capabilities for technological assimilation that Greskovits identifies as crucial for rapid industrial transnationalization after 1989. I also assess the impact of policies and strategies of industrial transnationalization in Central and Eastern Europe by showing that articulations with the politics of reform were important in determining the full developmental impact of socialist industrial legacies. The analysis also corrects the export bias of recent work by considering the role of domestic markets in either tempering or exaggerating the dependency impact of transnational forces in Central and Eastern Europe's economic transformation in the 2000s and beyond. To this effect, Chapter 5 identifies and describes three distinct international market roles assumed by Central and East European economies in the course of the 2000s and 2010s: assembly platform, intermediate producer, and combined. Each role signifies a particular mix between transnational versus domestic capital and technology, on the one hand, and export specialization versus domestic market orientation of producers, on the other. While the first part of the book is focused on the role of socialist industrial legacies in variously enabling patterns of postsocialist global integration, the second part explains divergent patterns of global integration and the ultimate transcendence of socialist legacies and their succession by new competitive dynamics unleashed by the deepening of Central and Eastern Europe's transnational integration in the twenty-first century.

The Limits of Autarchy in the Periphery 2

Trade, Planning, and East European Industrialization, 1946–1969

As to the future, it appears to me that further progress in the Socialist countries will lead to the formation of a single Socialist economic system. The barriers which separated our economies under capitalism will gradually disappear . . . making national frontiers pointless.

—Nikita S. Khruschev, *Pravda*, Moscow, 1959[1]

The 1970s may have represented the unleashing of the first wave of globalization, but the problems and conundrums faced by East European elites during that decade originated in the larger set of developmental challenges they faced in the postwar period. Soviet dominance in Central and Eastern Europe, patterns of postwar industrialization, and the separation of European economies into rival blocs all played an important role in the kinds of policy choices Central and Eastern European political elites faced in subsequent decades. Moreover, many of the reform attempts of the 1970s originated in the limits of industrial development that these economies appeared to have reached in the 1960s.

In particular, after Joseph Stalin's death, Soviet leadership began taking a fresh view on the importance of trade and its role in internal and intrabloc development. Despite Stalin's efforts to organize a distinct socialist trade bloc, the limits of endogenous industrial development led socialist leaders ultimately toward the discovery of the unity of the world market. In the 1950s and 1960s, Soviet trade policies opened the door for greater economic interaction across the European economies both within and, partly, outside the Soviet bloc. By the 1960s, socialist economists, planners, and reformers began seeing in the West not an adversary to be defeated, but a partner whose knowledge and technology could serve the domestic aims of economic development. These policy changes are examined primarily through the evolution of Comecon and its role in organizing patterns of socialist intrabloc trade.

Intrabloc relations were important for the rapid industrialization of socialist economies. This chapter discusses the international political context in which Central and Eastern European industrialization policies emerged and resulting patterns of industrial specialization. In that context, this chapter considers aspects of the centrally planned economy as they interacted with trade policy, patterns of industrialization, and the building of capital and technology bases.[2] To be sure, many institutional features of central planning made trade and industrial specialization more difficult. I examine these problems through a discussion of some of the classic theories in the international political economy of socialism and the insights they provide on the systemic relationships between trade, technology, and industrialization. The limitations that domestic institutions placed on trade provided the impetus that partly motivated the wave of economic reform in the USSR and, subsequently, in the rest of East Europe.

This chapter is intended as a historical overview of Central and Eastern Europe's integration into the Soviet economic sphere and its effects on patterns of industrialization and trade. It is organized into five parts. First, I discuss the international context of the early Cold War, economic reconstruction and trade policies, and the formation of Comecon. Second, I discuss early Cold War tensions and the impact of geopolitics on the character of Central and Eastern European industrialization. Third, I turn to the post-Stalin period, when Soviet leaders begin increasingly to see Comecon as a tool of deeper regional economic integration. Fourth, I examine the benefits of intrabloc trade by comparing the region with other socialist and developing states to demonstrate how membership in Comecon aided in facilitating rapid industrialization. Finally, I discuss the challenges Soviet and Central and Eastern European leaders saw in expanding trade with the West. In the 1960s in particular, Soviet leadership made efforts to expand cooperation ties with Western (and particularly West European) states, in ways it believed benefited its own economy. These reforms would lay the basis for important institutional changes and restructuring in East Europe during the subsequent decades.

The Politics of Soviet Economic Dominance in Central and Eastern Europe and the Rise of Comecon

With the exception of what was to become East Germany and parts of Czechoslovakia, the Central and Eastern European nations after World War II were primarily underdeveloped agrarian economies (Lampe and Jackson 1982;

Chirot 1989; Berend 1998). Some nations achieved small successes in spurring industrial development during the interwar era, but these were limited both by dependency on capital and technology from the West as well as by the continued power of conservative agrarian elites. In Hungary and Romania, politics and the economy were dominated by landowners and nobilities tied to monarchical courts, while in countries like Yugoslavia, Poland, and Bulgaria, consisting of large populations of peasant smallholders, governments were unable to muster the resources necessary for rapid economic growth. The postwar period presented Central and Eastern European nations with a fresh opportunity to restart the process of industrial development. Conservative elites were largely defeated in the war or marginalized soon thereafter, peasantries came under the spell of an international revolutionary movement, and the West, including the United States, appeared in a generous disposition. This situation would change rather quickly after 1948, when rising tensions between the United States and the USSR led to the erection of what would become lasting political and economic barriers between the European nations east of the Elbe.

The dramatic geopolitical changes did not forfeit, however, Central and Eastern Europe's opportunity for industrial development. In fact, they may have had the very opposite effect, in that industrial growth became not only a stated policy goal but also the very means by which the Soviet-supported regimes in the region would legitimize their rule (Jowitt 1992; Bunce 1999b). Soviet socialism, it was promised, would beat capitalism at its own game. To accomplish this aim, Stalin created Comecon, the socialist bloc's first multilateral organization. While initially a weak organization with few real functions, Comecon grew in importance as the Soviet Union sought increased trade and industrial specialization in its sphere. Comecon also served as an important framework for Central and Eastern European industrialization, which was in large part determined by shared technologies, technical training and assistance, and provision of basic supplies. While not as extensive as what would emerge in the West under the European common market, the interdependency that developed among the USSR and its Central and Eastern European allies played a crucial role in the origins, development, and ultimate downfall of socialist industry.

The establishment of Comecon came partly in response to increasing divisions between the United States and the Soviet Union over influence in Europe. The creation of Comecon in 1949 under Moscow's initiative was in large part a Soviet response to the Marshall Plan and the formation in the same year of the Organization for European Economic Cooperation (OEEC) as the body charged with managing US aid distributions in Europe. Moscow's creation of Comecon served the goal of offering an alternative to the Marshall Plan, especially in the context of still unconsolidated Communist control in Central and Eastern Europe. Formally, the United States included the USSR among those invited to join the Marshall Plan, and senior Soviet representatives participated at the OEEC meeting in Paris where the disbursement of aid was discussed. However, the Soviets ultimately rejected the terms of the Marshall Plan and withdrew, forcing other applicants from Central and Eastern Europe, like Czechoslovakia, to withdraw as well. Following the formation of Comecon, the USSR and its Central and Eastern European allies temporarily suspended participation in the United Nations Economic Commission for Europe (UNECE), a body for European economic cooperation set up under the aegis of the United Nations (Kock 1969, 35–61).

In the early years, Comecon was a loose body without any real organizational structure. Its existence was based on a founding statement issued in January 1949 after a meeting of founding member states (USSR, Czechoslovakia, Poland, Hungary, Bulgaria, and Romania), but no charter was drafted nor any permanent organizational body set up. The founding statement emphasized the need to strengthen trade among the socialist countries and charged the United States, United Kingdom, and other Western countries with deliberately undermining the economic recovery of Central and Eastern Europe. The statement also rejected the Marshall Plan as a "dictatorship" that violated the national sovereignty and the economic interests of Europe's small states. This came just as the US Congress reauthorized the Export Control Act, which targeted exports to the USSR and its allies, and the US government increased pressure on West European governments to restrict their trade with the emerging Soviet bloc.[3]

Comecon's thin organizational structure reflected Moscow's preference for bilateral arrangements for the conduct of aid, trade, and other relations with its new allied regimes in Europe. During the early years, Moscow also subjected individual states to different treatment. Moscow demanded war reparations from Hungary, Romania, and Bulgaria given their wartime alliance with the Axis powers and pursued a deindustrialization policy in Czechoslovakia. East Germany was not admitted into Comecon until 1950 and was forced to pay war reparations to the USSR until 1954. Until Stalin's death, Moscow employed more indirect means of control in these countries. As P.J.D. Wiles (1969) points out, both domestic and international politics dictated to Stalin to support the

creation of Comecon, but there was little interest in making it a viable organization for economic coordination. Coordination was limited and carried
out primarily through the operation of an "informal empire" consisting of an
"uncoordinated and irregular system of oppressive devices . . . 'advisers' at all
levels, mixed companies, overweening ambassadors, Party channels, occupying
troops, reparation agreements, etc." (314).

While the establishment of Comecon was driven by political motives, the
gradual transformation of the Soviet sphere into a trade bloc cannot be understood without recognizing the intricate relationship between Soviet aid, trade,
and Central and Eastern European industrialization. This linkage was crucial
particularly as the USSR's economic role in the region evolved in the course of
the 1950s. Soviet policy of forced reparations and deindustrialization had to be
balanced against the interest of securing the rule of Moscow loyalists across
Central and Eastern Europe. The latter became particularly urgent after 1948,
when tensions between the United States and the Soviet Union were at their
height. At the same time, the legitimacy of Communist rule across the region
depended heavily on the success of Communist governments in economic reconstruction and industrialization. Catching up with Western industry had
been the ideological promise of Soviet Communism, which offered what was
often portrayed as a shortcut to an industrial society. Managing relations with
the new socialist regimes also proved challenging. In 1953, Moscow had to bow
down to popular pressures when a series of rebellions led the USSR to end its
demand for burdensome reparation payments from East Germany. The events
in Hungary in 1956 threatened the unity of the socialist bloc after the already
embarrassing defection of Yugoslavia in 1948, not to mention increasing tensions with the new Communist government in China and the growing intransigence of Albania's Communist leadership (Stone 1996, 30).

While the USSR had been providing basic food aid to its allies in Central
and Eastern Europe immediately after the war, the policy shifted toward more
direct support for industrialization efforts via the provision of technical aid,
machinery, and infrastructural development. This came in line with the adoption by all Central and Eastern European states of Soviet-style central planning. Ideologically, the Communist Party of the Soviet Union (CPSU) claimed
that "the laws of development of the Socialist revolution and of the building
of Socialism in the USSR are not of local, specifically national, significance:
they are of international importance" (quoted in Kaser 1967, 17–18). This suggested that the techniques and policies of industrialization that had been

developed in the USSR were of universal applicability. Politically, it led the now entirely Communist-run party-states of Central and Eastern Europe to abandon alternative developmental models and mimic Soviet institutional design in economic planning. Soviet economic aid followed the shift to central planning. East Germany, initially used by Moscow as a source of economic advantages, became the largest recipient of Soviet economic aid in Central and Eastern Europe after 1954.[4]

With the extension of the Soviet industrialization model in Central and Eastern Europe came a set of patterns of development that stemmed directly from the institutional mechanisms and economic goals of Central and Eastern European planning officials. The key premise of these was an overwhelming focus on heavy industry (metallurgy, heavy metals, and energy production) in the context of national developmental plans aimed, at least nominally, at achieving maximum autarchy. In this context, economic integration, coordination, and specialization at the bloc level were still far-fetched goals. Planning officials across the bloc focused on achieving national output goals and pursuing the development of domestic industries. As a result, by the 1950s, there was much excess capacity in heavy industry, yet other sectors, such as light industry and agriculture, lagged behind. While enabling rapid industrialization in what were at the time largely underdeveloped, agrarian economies, the pattern of development determined by the structure of domestic institutions, distinct national economic goals and priorities, and weak coordination mechanisms would become an important liability in the bloc's economic evolution—and a key problem that leaders attempted to address via reforms in the 1960s and 1970s.

The first wave of reforms were introduced soon after Stalin's death. This followed reforms that were undertaken in the USSR's own system of planning and economic management. From the first five-year plan in 1929 and until 1949, planning in the USSR was led by the state planning agency Gosplan. In 1949 Nikolai Voznesenski, the powerful head of Gosplan, fell out of favor with Stalin and was arrested and executed. The planning system was subsequently reorganized to weaken Gosplan's autonomy in favor of direct ministerial control of economic production plans (Nove 1966, 66–67). After Stalin's death, a number of other reforms reorganized the planning system, and in 1957, under Nikita Khrushchev's leadership, reforms decentralized planning authority to regional economic councils (*sovnarkhozy*) established throughout the USSR. The *sovnarkhozy* were assigned direct control over larger industrial enterprises within their regions.

It was also under Khrushchev that Soviet leadership sought a new role for Comecon. Soviet leaders were particularly interested in expanding capabilities for economic coordination and specialization among members, especially as trade integration was deepening in the capitalist countries of Europe. For most of the 1950s, Comecon largely remained an organizational empty shell. Most trade among members was conducted bilaterally. While all Central and Eastern European states traded with the USSR, not all members had established active trade links or even formal trade agreements with each other. This partly reflected Stalin's policy of maintaining individual Central and Eastern European states under Soviet economic dependence as well as preventing the rise of regional industrial powerhouses in East Germany and Czechoslovakia that could threaten Soviet economic primacy (Smith 1983, 27). Recognizing that this strategy had created inefficiencies within the bloc, Soviet leadership sought to bolster Comecon as a central institutional feature of what it dubbed the emerging "world socialist system" and "international socialist division of labor" to rival trade integration in the capitalist world. At the same time, the USSR was undergoing domestic economic reforms as well as rapidly expanding its trade with both Comecon and the West (Hanson 2003, 80–87).

As a result of Soviet efforts, in 1959 Comecon gained a formal charter. Soviet leadership made further efforts to promote specialization within the Soviet economic bloc via the joint issuance in 1962 of the "Principles of the International Socialist Division of Labor" (reprinted in Butler 1978, 14–32). In the meantime, Comecon was given its own organizational legs with an executive committee and permanent standing committees on scientific and technical cooperation. The impetus for Comecon's consolidation during Khrushchev's leadership was both economic and political. Economically, Soviet leadership believed that better integration and coordination would benefit industrial development across the entire bloc. It was becoming evident that the autarchic developmental model followed by the USSR in the 1930s and immediately after the war was impossible to follow in the small, resource-poor economies of Central and Eastern Europe. Individual countries pursued similar industrialization goals, leading to limited diversification in economic activity. What were perceived as comparative advantages of individual economies based on natural resource endowments or the availability of existing stocks of capital and labor were not being put to full use. Politically, the Soviets with their Central and Eastern European allies saw in Comecon a response to the establishment of the European Economic Community (EEC) and the European Free Trade

Association (EFTA). In addition to consolidating political and economic dominance over the Soviet bloc, Soviet leadership's consolidation of Comecon as a
full-fledged trading bloc served intrabloc geopolitics as well. First, it allowed
Moscow to isolate China, which was kept at arm's length by being admitted into
the organization only as an observer. Chinese discontent with such arrangements in the context of growing political and ideological disagreements lasted
until the Sino-Soviet split in 1960, when China abandoned all goals of economic integration with the Soviet bloc. Yugoslavia was also granted observer
status after partial reconciliation with Yugoslav leadership, while Albania was
expelled after the Albanian Communist Party increasingly sided with China
in Sino-Soviet clashes. The prospects for non-European socialist countries to
become full members brought Mongolia, North Vietnam, North Korea, and
Cuba into the organization.[5]

Socialist unity on the economic front clearly depended on political developments in the relations between the USSR and other socialist states. But di-
verging economic interests among Comecon members also led to fissures. As
noted, Comecon member states varied widely in resources, levels of industrialization, and specialization. In particular, Romanian leadership became increasingly unhappy with some of the long-term plans that were being drawn
up under Moscow's direction. It was opposed to maintaining Romania's role
in the bloc as a producer and exporter of basic commodities and wished the
country to pursue a policy of extensive industrialization. Romania's economic
goals and how they related to trade and specialization within Comecon would
become a vexing issue for decades to come. Polish leadership, however, saw
value in greater coordination and specialization; it went as far as proposing
that economic planning shift to the level of Comecon as a whole. The leaders
in Moscow entertained this idea with some seriousness, and ultimately party
elites proposed joint planning within Comecon. In 1962 Soviet leadership also
offered to reduce or even abandon the production of particular goods if it was
determined that such goods could be produced more efficiently in other socialist countries (Kaser 1967, 107). While the idea of joint planning was never discussed within Comecon, Romanian leadership expressed strong opposition to
any such proposal, stating in an official declaration in 1964 that, "transmitting
such levers [of economic planning] to the competence of super-state or extra-
state bodies would turn sovereignty into a notion without any content." It suggested that the decision to relinquish national planning authority to Comecon
or some other jointly constituted body ought to be a question left to individual

countries to pursue but not imposed on Comecon as a whole. "The idea of a single planning body for [Comecon] has the most serious economic and political implications . . . undoubtedly, if some socialist countries deem it fit to adopt in the direct relations between them forms of cooperation different from those unanimously agreed upon within [Comecon], that is a question which exclusively concerns those countries" (quoted in Kaser 1967, 108). In Comecon's July 1963 conference, the idea of joint planning was abandoned, and in its stead the members decided to establish a bureau of the Executive Committee, with the role of facilitating consultations among members in the coordination of economic plans. While in the 1950s regional economic integration was precluded by Stalin's goal to maximize his political leverage over Central and Eastern European party-states by making individual economies as dependent as possible on the USSR, in the 1960s Soviet interest in greater integration and specialization was hampered by Central and Eastern European concerns that giving up economic policy authority would amount to the ceding of national sovereignty.

Political resistance in the 1960s spurned sectoral specialization at the bloc level, as each member continued to pursue goals of comprehensive and semiautarchic industrial development. A degree of specialization was no doubt dictated by factor endowments, but ironically, in the end these primarily affected the USSR, which assumed the role of a basic commodity supplier to the Central and Eastern European nations. The latter increasingly built their domestic manufacturing base through reliance on Soviet commodities and the Soviet economy as a target for their exports. A degree of intrasectoral specialization was ultimately achieved through bilateral agreements or cooperation through Comecon committees, especially when spearheaded by Soviet policy (Brada 1988). But, while failing to attain Khrushchev's grand goal of the deep economic integration of the socialist bloc, Comecon accomplished several things. First, it facilitated intrabloc trade by establishing a common pricing system, currency exchange policy, and a clearinghouse system of payments based on the convertible ruble. Comecon also served as a venue facilitating the creation of bilateral bodies for technical cooperation, which helped organize sectoral industrial links, especially in coal, steel, electricity generation, oil, and later in more advanced fields like the computer hardware industry. These institutional mechanisms greatly facilitated efficiency in planning domestic trade policy and led to the long-term embeddedness of the socialist industrial economies in the Comecon bloc.

Industrialization in Central and Eastern Europe after 1948

While the Central and Eastern European economies were greatly underdeveloped compared to those of Western Europe in 1945, they differed tremendously in comparative levels of development and industrialization among themselves. As pointed out, Czechoslovakia was the most advanced industrial nation in the group. During the war, German-occupied regions had seen significant investment in heavy industry employed in support of Nazi Germany's war economy. Hungary inherited a number of light industries that dated from the Habsburg era, while Poland had developed extensive trade ties with Great Britain in the course of the 1930s, connected to agriculture and extractive and light industries. After the war, however, both Hungary and Poland were still mainly agrarian economies. After 1945, a good number of industries in Soviet-occupied territories of what was to become the GDR were placed under Soviet control; others were dismantled and their machineries shipped to the USSR. Romania and Bulgaria were the most underdeveloped of all, with nearly two-thirds of their active populations employed in agriculture.

Agrarian systems in the region also differed as a result of patterns of land ownership and prewar political regimes and social structures. Hungary, Poland, and Czechoslovakia had the most land concentrated in large plots (over one hundred hectares) and owned by a small minority. The agrarian economy played a smaller role in Czechoslovakia, but the country was divided between the more industrialized regions of Bohemia and Silesia and the agricultural Slovak lands. In the latter, most land had been under the control of the Hungarian nobility, a situation that changed only after the enactment of the Beneš decrees in 1946, resulting in the disenfranchisement and forced removal of the Hungarian minority on charges of collaboration with the Nazis (the German minority in the Czech lands experienced the same fate). In Poland nobility-controlled land existed parallel to a large population of smallholders, while in Romania most agricultural production was based on sharecropping. In Bulgaria the peasant population consisted almost entirely of smallholders. These reflected in the patterns of interwar politics. In Hungary the landowning nobility had played a prominent role in interwar politics, while in Poland and Czechoslovakia its role was counterbalanced by bourgeois and working classes in the latter, and large numbers of politically organized smallholding peasants in the former (Stokes 1989).

During the interwar years, nationalist goals of economic self-sufficiency led governments to rely on a combination of protectionist policies, state-led development, and nationalization of foreign-owned assets to spur economic growth. These succeeded in generating a degree of industrial development in parts of Central and Eastern Europe in the 1930s. However, most industrial development depended highly on West European technology, know-how, and markets, and especially the German industrial behemoth. The Great Depression significantly derailed state-led policies of industrial development and the introduction of protectionist policies in Europe led to the loss of markets for manufactures. Small domestic markets limited the potential for growth, and protectionist measures led most industries to rely on high domestic prices, making them less competitive on world markets (Smith 1983, 21–23; Berend 1998, 234–239).

The desires of Central and Eastern European political elites for rapid industrialization received a renewed impetus after the war. Postwar National Front governments, which were dominated by Communists but included within them a variety of Socialist, Peasant, and Nationalist parties and old regime elements, approached postwar economic policy with significant differences in goals and means. With the decimation of the nobility and the historical weakness of bourgeois interests, as well as past reliance on the state for industrialization, there was general consensus across all parties on the need for state-led development. However, during 1945–1947, the degree of state control in the economy was hotly debated between the parties, and different approaches prevailed in different countries. While the Communist parties typically favored the adoption of Soviet-style planning, other parties still saw private-sector activity playing an important role. In Hungary, Social Democrats proposed that only industries that were "monopolistic in character" be placed under state control, such as mining, banking, transportation, and some manufacturing sectors. In Czechoslovakia, Communist leadership under Klement Gottwald nationalized large industries but still envisioned a role for the private sector. In Poland, initial plans envisioned up to 40 percent of the labor force being employed in the private sector after nationalization.

However, disagreements quickly developed between Communists and other parties, especially Socialists and Social Democrats, on the degree of state control of the economy and sectoral priority. In Hungary, Social Democrats favored the development of labor-intensive consumer industries as opposed to the Communist predilection for heavy industry. Hungarian Social Democrats also wished to see a more rapid return to prewar levels of consumption, as opposed to the path of forced savings and high investment demanded by Communists. Similar disagreements over sectoral priorities emerged between Communists and Socialists in Poland. A major point of contention between the Communist and Socialist and Social Democratic proposals was that the latter strategy not only prioritized consumption but also relied heavily on the importation of manufactures from Western Europe. This approach was unacceptable not only to Soviet-oriented Communists but also to various nationalist elements of the postwar regimes who wished to see a decisive break from prewar economic dependency on the larger economies of Western Europe, especially Germany (Spulber 1957; Smith 1983, 27; Fowkes 2000, 33–40).

The disagreements between Communists and their allies would be resolved swiftly and conclusively after 1948, when Soviet pressure led to the start of purges and elimination of non-Communists from governments across Central and Eastern Europe. Soon after, parties rivaling the Communists were banned as single-party People's Republics were established across Central and Eastern Europe and the remaining vestiges of parliamentary democracy dismantled (Fowkes 2000, 37–40). The consolidation of Communist control of Central and Eastern European states, and of Soviet control over Communist parties across Central and Eastern Europe, rapidly eliminated alternatives to Soviet central planning. However, the implementation of the Soviet model in individual Central and Eastern European countries would turn out to be a protracted process, and in some cases a rather incomplete one. In the Stalin years, the direction of economic planning was also heavily influenced by instructions on priorities issued by Moscow and dependence on Soviet assistance, both financial and technical.

The nationalization of industry and the establishment of planning administrations modeled on Gosplan were done rather quickly. By 1949, as a result of governmental decrees, 85 percent or more of industrial workers were employed in state-controlled enterprises in Hungary, Poland, Czechoslovakia, and Romania (Smith 1983, 30). In Czechoslovakia the assertion of central control over industry led to the abolition of worker councils, which had independently organized to take over factories in 1945, showing that Communist leadership, while claiming to represent the working class, had little genuine interest in industrial democracy (Fowkes 2000, 35). In Romania as well as in Bulgaria, the nationalization of industry was partly aided by the establishment of joint ventures with Soviet enterprises. Such arrangements lasted until 1954, when

Khrushchev relinquished Soviet control over joint enterprises. Soviet-style firm management, including preference for large industrial enterprises, also took root during the early years.

Much less progress was achieved in the second component of the Soviet developmental model, the collectivization of agriculture. Soviet industrialization was based on the Preobrazhensky model of increased investments in industry arrived at through forced savings in agriculture—once called by Leon Trotsky the "socialist mode of primitive accumulation."[6] This model proved difficult to implement in most countries, as prewar land ownership patterns and political resistance held back Communist goals of collectivization. While collectivization was performed relatively quickly in Czechoslovakia (and a less daunting process given the smaller size of the farming sector), by 1952 collectivization had slowed in all countries. In Poland collectivization was attempted halfheartedly and ultimately abandoned as a policy. In the other countries, collectivization was not completed until 1966 (Smith 1983, 30).

The difficulties of collectivization limited the ability of planners to increase investments by mobilizing forced savings in agriculture, leading to greater reliance on Soviet assistance. Stalin's geopolitics and the breakout of the Korean war played a decisive role in the direction of Central and Eastern European industrialization. In 1950 Stalin instructed the Communist parties of Central and Eastern Europe to revise planned output by increasing production levels in heavy industry in support of Soviet war efforts in the Korean peninsula and in preparation for possible war in Europe. This led to a major push in Central and Eastern Europe for the development of heavy industries producing goods for military use. Iron and steel production received the largest share of investments, even in countries like Hungary and Romania, which lacked major raw mineral deposits. Manufacturing was oriented toward the production of armaments and military transportation equipment. Even Czechoslovakia, which had better developed engineering and consumer goods industries, was pushed toward the manufacture of military goods. The disproportionately large investment in heavy industry and military-use machinery would dramatically affect the course of Central and Eastern European industrialization for decades (Smith 1983, 31–33; Fowkes 2000, 43; Zubok 2007, 78–85). Khrushchev's economic reforms were partly motivated by the goal of correcting the Stalin era's biases. While Khrushchev persuaded many Central and Eastern European leaders to follow his lead in reemphasizing agriculture and consumer goods, his criticisms against the goals of national self-sufficiency were less successful, as his failed efforts to introduce Comecon-level planning demonstrated.

Comecon: Dependency, Exploitation, or Integration?

Scholars still debate the question of whether the Soviet Union benefited economically from its dominance of Central and Eastern Europe or whether supporting the region was a drain on Soviet resources (Stone 1996; Spechler and Spechler 2009). The origins of the debate lie in the 1970s and 1980s, when three prominent theories emerged among Western observers to explain the political economy of Soviet trade relations: the totalitarian model, the subsidy model, and the customs union model. Each of these are discussed in turn.

The totalitarian model saw Soviet trade mainly as a political instrument of Soviet foreign policy (Brzezinski 1967). The Soviet Union used trade with its Central and Eastern European allies to consolidate its hold over the region, given its geopolitical interests in securing political and military control. In this reading, the economics of Soviet trade with its allies were largely tied to a political function given Soviet geopolitical interests in securing its sphere of influence against Western threats. At base, political motives stood at the formation of Comecon, and political motives sustained Comecon throughout the era of its existence.

Subsequent work increasingly challenged this purely instrumentalist view of Soviet economic influence in Central and Eastern Europe. The subsidy model was first elaborated by Horst Mendershausen (1959, 1960). In its original incarnation, the thesis claimed that relations between the Soviet Union and Central and Eastern Europe were exploitative and beneficial to the Soviets. Mendershausen aimed to demonstrate this through Soviet trade data that suggested that the USSR was importing underpriced (in world market terms) goods from its Central and Eastern European allies. In the 1980s Michael Marrese and Jan Vanous (1983) took a fresh look at Central and Eastern European trade data in the period 1960–1980 and reversed the thesis by showing that, in fact, the USSR was subsidizing Central and Eastern European economies by providing the region with underpriced commodities while paying high prices for Central and Eastern European goods. These negative terms of trade for the USSR were further exacerbated by the oil price shock of 1973. Soviet supplies of oil to Central and Eastern Europe continued to increase steadily throughout the 1970s even as the price charged for oil remained significantly below the world market price. In Marrese and Vanous's interpretation, the Soviets provided this subsidy in exchange for "unconventional gains from trade"—that is, obtaining acquiescence for Soviet foreign policy and political loyalty to Moscow. In some ways the subsidy model helped bolster while at the same time refine the totalitarian model, in that politics were still the primary driver of Central and Eastern European trade relations. For instance, Marrese and Vanous calculated subsidy differentials for the various Central and Eastern European states, aiming to show that subsidies were greatest for the most loyal regimes. They found that throughout the period under question, the largest Soviet subsidies went to East Germany and Czechoslovakia, the two most loyal and strategically important Soviet allies, while the lowest to Bulgaria and Romania. Indeed, for most of the 1960s, Bulgaria and Romania received a negative subsidy. In the Romanian case, this was to be interpreted as punishment for Romania's defiance of Soviet foreign policy in the Eastern Bloc, especially its refusal to support Soviet intervention in Czechoslovakia in 1968.

The trade economist Franklyn Holzman (1976) developed an alternative framework to understand the political economy of Soviet trade. Holzman applied the Heckscher–Ohlin theorem of international trade to Comecon to argue that patterns of trade within the bloc reflected relative factor endowments. He combined this view with Jacob Viner's (1950) insight of the trade-diverting effects of customs unions as protective tariffs raised the costs of trade with nonmembers while intensifying trade between members. Comecon was thus an "autarchic customs union" whose prices reflected *internal* relative factor endowments while trade closure distorted those prices from those prevailing on the world market.

These effects were observed both in the structure of trade and in the relative prices found within Soviet-bloc trade. In this model Soviet abundance in natural resources, not only relative to Comecon members but the world, made it inevitable that the USSR would specialize in the export of basic commodities, while the growing capital richness of Central and Eastern Europe led this group to specialize in manufactures, with the USSR as their primary "captive market." What Marrese and Vanous saw as differential subsidies to particular states could instead be interpreted as reflections of relative factor endowments (Holzman 1986). As Josef Brada argues, following Holzman's interpretation,

> [the] divergence between intraunion and world-market prices affects the distribution of the gains from trade among the integrating countries . . . [because]

integration will increase the proportion of gains obtained by those integrating countries that have abundant endowments (relative to other integrating countries) of the input that is scarce (relative to the rest of the world) within the union. Conversely, those integrating countries that are abundantly endowed (relative to other integrating countries) with the factor that is abundant (relative to the rest of the world) in the union will receive a smaller share of total gains than they would receive under free trade. (1985a, 88)

Thus, what Marrese and Vanous observed in their data were not subsidies, but "the amount of gains from trade that are redistributed among integrating countries [since] they do trade at terms of trade that differ from those prevailing on the world market" (Brada 1985a, 88).

There are, of course, several difficulties in adjudicating between the subsidy and customs union model, given the intricacies of trade within a centrally planned economy. First, while it is one thing to observe differentials between intra-Comecon and prevailing world market prices, it is difficult to gauge the rationale behind differences in intra-Comecon relative prices, given the largely "artificial" (i.e., administratively established) prices of Comecon-produced goods (Kornai 1991). Since prices reflect administrative fiat rather than costs, it is difficult to determine the extent to which prices reflect efficiency as understood in neoclassical economic terms. This becomes especially crucial in determining the value of Central and Eastern European manufactures. While, in theory at least, the USSR could have more easily diverted its commodity exports toward other (i.e., non-Comecon) nations willing to pay a world market price, such flexibility was presumably less possible for Central and Eastern European manufactures given product specificity and generally poorer quality in comparison to Western-made goods. Moreover, a great deal of these manufactures were producer goods for whom demand could be found only within Comecon, given similar industrial structures, technologies, and production techniques—that is, given "exclusive complementarities" (Clark and Bahry 1983, 280) that made these goods of little use to other economies. The same problem that applied to prices applied to currencies as well. With nonconvertibility and formal exchange rates established via administrative means, the value of such currencies was also arbitrary from the perspective of market valuations. In world market terms, however, based on sheer quantities and world market demand for goods, it may appear that the USSR did have an upper hand. Theoretically, at least, if political obstacles and other incentives with Central and Eastern European trade were removed, the USSR could have potentially expanded its exports more easily given the more readily available demand for basic commodities in the world market, despite their apparently lower value-added nature. This is especially true for high-demand commodities that the USSR produced in abundance, such as oil, gas, grain, and cotton.[7]

Holzman's model combines the role of both internal institutional structures and bilateral trade links to explain what he calls the "trade averse" nature of the centrally planned economies. First, the requirement within Comecon to maintain balances of trade between members forces states to export high-priced goods for which there is a shortage in the domestic economy and others to accept goods that they produce abundantly themselves. This proviso creates inefficiencies and waste throughout the system. Second, since prices and currency values are administratively governed, comparative efficiency and product quality assume secondary roles to sheer quantities of goods traded. Moreover, as Holzman (1976) points out, while growth in the output of the national economy was a central goal, trade behavior under central planning was patently nonmercantilist (Lavigne 1991). Given that quantity considerations outweighed all other concerns for planning authorities and industrial managers, exports of goods were seen as an economically wasteful activity. Since planners needed to account for the production needs of the entire industrial system, planning for exports could be extremely cumbersome and, indeed, costly and unnecessary, especially when resources could be put to better use for the needs of the domestic economy. In addition, given that export earnings almost always accrued to the state, managers had little direct incentive to pursue sales in foreign markets. At the same time, planners were governed by an incentive to avoid reliance on foreign suppliers of raw materials or other goods, given unreliability and unpredictability of supplies that lay beyond their direct control. These issues induced planners and industrial managers to avoid imports and rely as much as possible on domestically sourced goods. As a result, the systemic incentives of a centrally planned system resulted in a trade-averse economic system in which both planners and managers had more reasons to avoid foreign trade rather than to embrace it as policy and operational strategy.

In theory, as Holzman notes, a centrally planned system ought to have been more responsive to signals of efficiency and competitiveness at the sectoral level when engaging with international markets. That is, a centrally planned system should have been more effective in balancing resources by importing large quantities of domestically scarce goods from countries that can supply them

Although poorer, the USSR caught up with this part of the world by 1950, and by 1969 a significant distance emerges between it and Latin America. The latter period is also one when the USSR was making important advances in space exploration, rocket propulsion technology, and nuclear energy, displaying not only greater material wealth but also important technological advancement.

The case of Central and Eastern Europe (without the USSR) is just as impressive, if not more so. Initially lagging far behind the Latin America-8 group, it not only caught up with the region, but by the mid-1960s surpassed the Latin American industrializers in per capita terms. And these are countries that are mainly resource-poor and began the postwar period with a small capital base. Central and Eastern Europe and the USSR do just as impressively when compared with the larger group of Latin American countries (Latin America-15 in the table), which includes poorer and politically more unstable countries such as Bolivia, Guatemala, Panama, Haiti, and Honduras. While the levels of development of these countries were on average lower than that of the USSR and Central and Eastern Europe, bear in mind that in 1946 countries like Bulgaria and Romania were very much underdeveloped agrarian nations, as were many parts of the USSR and Yugoslavia.

This illustration is not meant as a vindication of central planning or to "prove" the superiority of socialist as opposed to capitalist approaches to industrialization. It is merely to illustrate the intense resource mobilization undertaken by the Central and Eastern European states and the relative effectiveness of the Comecon framework in creating the basis for rapid industrialization in Central and Eastern Europe. Soviet dominance in Central and Eastern Europe, as Cal Clark and Donna Bahry (1983) have observed, resulted in a distinct socialist variant of "dependent development." While the region's economic incorporation in the Soviet sphere was achieved largely by coercion, and was initially characterized by distinct elements of exploitation, in the subsequent period it translated into local gains due to the combination of ideological goals, political interest in industrialization, and institutional homologies enabling the circulation and diffusion of technical and organizational skills and techniques. In later decades, the structure of industrial development in the region led to the creation of exclusive complementarities between the USSR and Central and Eastern Europe. That is, emergent structures of economic interdependence "became increasingly costly in terms of potential domestic economic disruption for the East European states to break" (280). Put succinctly, "unlike dependent development on the capitalist periphery, the large-scale [Soviet] industrialization programs brought material benefits and a rising standard of living to a large proportion of the East European populations, and the external exploitation associated with capitalist dependence [in the later period] was largely absent as well. Still, the very structure of this political economy portended future problems" (283–284).

More importantly for our historical consideration here, however, is that for domestic party elites, rates of industrialization and growth seemed dissatisfying. The limits of growth under central planning were recognized as soon as the early 1960s, and efforts at reform were begun as early as 1953 by Stalin's successors. Clearly, while comparing Latin America and the socialist bloc as two semiperipheral developing regions is sensible in theoretical terms, Soviet and Central and Eastern European leaders certainly did not judge their economic performance by the standards of the Chilean or Argentinian economies. Their point of reference was always the industrial West, and in that comparison the Soviet bloc, it was increasingly recognized, was falling further behind.

Trade and Intrabloc Industrialization: Bulgaria and Albania

The centrality of the region's economic integration to local industrialization is best illustrated by the underperformance of Communist-ruled countries in East Europe that were left outside of the Soviet trading system. In 1948 Western aid saved the economic policies of Tito's Yugoslavia after its break with Stalin, allowing it to pursue a third course in the building of non-Stalinist socialism. In 1955 Khrushchev initiated a rapprochement with Yugoslavia. Though thereafter Yugoslavia maintained less intimate relations with the USSR, the thaw allowed Yugoslavia to begin reestablishing trade relations with the USSR and the remainder of Comecon. Romanian leadership grumbled about Soviet policy and the slow pace of industrialization but was nonetheless kept inside the bloc. One of the most troubling economic fates befell Albania, which in 1955 was expelled from Comecon and whose leadership subsequently maintained a hostile attitude toward the USSR throughout the period of Communist rule.

Albanian leadership became increasingly dissatisfied with Soviet policy, especially after Stalin's death. In 1948, when Yugoslavia broke with the USSR, the Albanian Party, which had during the war been closely allied with and supported by the Yugoslav Communists, broke its ties to Belgrade and sided with Moscow. The growing animosities between the Soviet and Chinese parties provided the opportunity for the Albanian Party to express its grievances over Soviet policy and side with China in ideological disputes. The Albanian Party also became increasingly vocal against Khrushchev's leadership, especially after the "secret speech" in which he denounced Stalin's policies (Biberaj 1990). In 1955, fed up with Albanian intransigence, Khrushchev cut diplomatic relations with Albania and placed the country under an economic embargo. This would prove disastrous for Albania as its economy and industrialization goals relied heavily on Soviet and other Comecon assistance (Mëhilli 2017, 130–150). Attempts at mediation by other Comecon members ultimately proved futile, and in 1960 Albania entered into a close alliance with China.

Several theories attempt to explain Albania's break with the USSR. Ideological differences between Khrushchev and Albania's party leadership under Enver Hoxha is one commonly cited reason. Hoxha critiqued Khrushchev's reforms and charged that his willingness to cooperate with the capitalist West were increasingly deviating from the postulates of Marxism-Leninism. Mao Zedong's criticism of revisionism in Soviet policy followed along these lines. While ideological disagreements were significant, what likely led to the Soviet-Albanian break were Albanian perceptions of marginalization in the Soviet sphere. After World War II, Stalin saw little use for Albania, and at one point suggested that it be incorporated into Yugoslavia (Djilas 1963). The infamous "percentages agreement" of October 1944 between Stalin and Winston Churchill, where the two agreed on the division of spheres of influence in Europe, did not even list Albania as an area of interest for either party. Fortuitously, the Albanian Communists were victorious in the war and consolidated power in the country after 1945. After Stalin's break with Yugoslavia, Albania came to receive greater amounts of Soviet aid and support. However, this lagged behind and was at lower levels than that of other Communist-ruled countries; as a result, progress in Albania's economic reconstruction was slow. Geographical isolation may partly account for this sluggishness, given that after 1948, Albania was surrounded by two hostile states. To its north stood "revisionist" Yugoslavia, while to its south was Greece, whose Communist movement suffered defeat in 1949. As a result, Albania lost direct territorial links to the Soviet empire. Dissatisfaction with Soviet policy intensified after Khrushchev's succession to the Soviet party leadership, and there is evidence that Khrushchev saw Albania as little more than a convenient port to station the Soviet navy (Vickers 1999). Relying on archival materials, Elidor Mëhilli (2017, 191–203) shows that disappointment with Soviet aid and economic support was among the chief causes of the

Albanian Party's decision to break with the USSR. In the end, whether siding with China in Sino-Soviet disputes was sincere or a failed opportunistic ploy to pressure Moscow is a moot point. At the same time, the extreme ideological position that the Albanian Party maintained domestically and staked during the Sino-Soviet conflict precluded the option to engage the West as Yugoslavia had done in 1948. Albania's limited policy options were compounded by the praetorian nature of Albanian party politics. The break with the USSR provided an opportunity for Hoxha to engage in another round of violent purges within the party, thus solidifying his control and shutting out voices of dissent within the ranks.

In the context of this chapter's illustrations of regional patterns of industrialization, the Albanian case demonstrates the significance of membership in Comecon in the process of Central and Eastern European industrialization. By comparing Albania's growth with that of Bulgaria, we can gauge the impact of isolation from Comecon on industrial development within each country.

Postwar Albania inherited a largely agrarian economic structure and was the poorest and least developed country in the entire Soviet bloc. However, Bulgaria was not too dissimilar from Albania in economic terms. According to Maddison Project (2013) data, in 1950 Albania's per capita GDP was $1,001 compared to Bulgaria's level of $1,651. By 1962 Bulgaria's per capita GDP had almost doubled, whereas Albania's had managed to grow to only $1,511. This difference holds even when considering that the rate of population growth in the two countries during this period did not differ significantly.

A better indicator of Bulgaria's postwar industrialization is the structure of its exports. As noted, in the immediate postwar period, Bulgaria's exports consisted mainly of primary goods, especially agricultural products. This pattern began to change rapidly in the 1950s, as Bulgaria started to increase its exports of manufactured goods, reflecting changes in its domestic economic structure. Albania's export structure changed very slowly, and by 1964, 95 percent of its exports were still primary goods—chiefly foodstuffs. During the 1960s, Albanian exports expanded to include metals and mineral raw materials. However, manufactures never became prominent in Albanian exports, up through the demise of the Communist regime in 1991.

The economic fate of Albania stands out even more when contrasted with the general trend of industrial growth in Central and Eastern Europe. Alan Smith (1983, 203–204) cites data from the Polish economist Stanisław Gomułka showing that within Comecon, the expansion of industrial output during the early period of central planning was greatest in the least developed countries of Bulgaria and Romania, and lowest in the industrialized economies of Czecho-slovakia and the GDR. Gomułka's point in the analysis was to demonstrate the trade-offs between extensive development, productivity, and growth. In-dustrialization produced high and rapid gains in underdeveloped economies, as capital was added and a large, underemployed "reserve labor army" in the countryside was put to work in mines and on factory floors. Gomułka's eco-nomic analysis is complemented by Soviet aid data cited by Giovanni Graziani (1981, 69), showing that through 1972, Soviet direct assistance in the construc-tion of industrial plants was highest among the less industrialized countries.[9] The key point here is that the capital needed for extensive growth required—in the capital-poor economies—access to financing, technology, and technical training. Albania's exclusion from Comecon and, more specifically, the discon-tinuation of economic relations with the USSR, effectively crippled Albanian industrialization.

With its domestic industrial base and its postwar control of East German and Czechoslovak industries, the USSR provided other Comecon members ac-cess to both the technologies and the technical training and support required for industrial development. The diffusion of technology and expertise—in ad-dition to offering a large market to absorb the very manufactures that the Cen-tral and Eastern European nations were now producing—was a central part of successful industrialization in Comecon. Yugoslavia managed to get around its banishment from Comecon by opening to the West. After 1960 Albania, how-ever, sought aid and support from China, itself a highly underdeveloped coun-try. This course proved disastrous even in terms of the Stalinist approach to industrialization that the Albanian Party followed. But the contrasting fates of Albania and Bulgaria sufficiently illustrate why economic ties to the USSR and the Comecon framework remained central to Central and Eastern European industrialization and why Central and Eastern European party-states would continue to value those ties.

Trade with the West until 1965

Geopolitical developments in the context of the Cold War led political and strategic interests to override Soviet economic interests in expanding trade and economic cooperation with the West. However, pursuing increased trade, espe-cially with Western Europe, was not a goal that was ever completely abandoned by the USSR, and less so by the smaller economies of Central and Eastern Europe. After all, prior to World War II, the smaller Central and Eastern European nations had, as a matter of course, conducted most of their trade with the West European capitalist nations.

During the Cold War, "economic warfare" was the term used to describe relations between the two competing blocs. It is clear, however, that in this war, capabilities were asymmetrical. In the immediate postwar period, the USSR's war-ravaged economy was in no position to represent an economic threat to the United States. With the growing polarization and division of Europe after 1948, the rise of the Soviet economic bloc came mainly as a response to measures for greater bilateral and multilateral trade and economic cooperation in the West. A series of US-led initiatives were knitting Western economies into tighter economic relationships, turning the region away from the autarchy and protectionism of the 1930s. These measures included, in addition to the Marshall Plan, the establishment of the Bretton Woods institutions and the signing of the General Agreement on Tariffs and Trade (GATT) in 1947, all of which were constituted exclusively or almost exclusively by the United States and its West European allies. Within Europe, the growing number of regional organizations like the OEEC (later OECD), the European Coal and Steel Community, EEC, and EFTA intensified West European trade and financial ties. During the Stalin years, the USSR either turned a cold shoulder to such initiatives or was deliberately excluded, in a mutually reinforcing pattern of animosity and distrust.

Soviet leadership did not, at least rhetorically, reject greater European economic integration, but preferred to develop trade and economic ties mainly under the auspices of UN-mandated structures like UNECE. Stalin saw the alternative, non-UN-based multilateral organizations and initiatives as tools of US foreign policy. The Marshall Plan in particular was seen as threatening Soviet influence in Central and Eastern Europe. As discussed earlier, the hasty push to establish Comecon was partly a response by the USSR to what it saw as increasing US encroachments on European, and potentially Central and Eastern European, economies. These encroachments would, as Soviet leadership under Stalin reasoned, have inevitable political consequences that would undermine the stability and loyalty of the new Communist-led regimes of Central and Eastern Europe and threaten Soviet control of the region and ultimately, perhaps, isolate the USSR from any significant role in Europe (Zubok 2007).

In effect, however, the USSR's foreign economic policy after 1948 was mainly defensive in nature. A great deal of the USSR's industrial capacities had been destroyed during the war. In 1945 the level of production of basic staples like bread, meat, and butter was less than half that before the war (Zubok 2007, 52). In 1948 the USSR's per capita GDP was estimated at no more than a quarter of that of the United States (Hanson 2003, 244). Europe's economies were recovering and being rebuilt with American aid, while the continued control of colonial territories in Africa and Asia by imperial powers like Great Britain, France, and the Netherlands meant that abundant overseas resources were still held under their control—a fact by no means lost on Soviet leadership (Sanchez-Sibony 2014). Holzman points out that "the USSR was in the position not of primarily trying to 'hurt' the United States and its allies—since this was hardly feasible—but rather making itself as invulnerable as possible to Western economic warfare" (1976, 125). Soviet archives reveal that vulnerability to Western, and especially American, economic power was precisely the fear leading Moscow to reject membership in the Bretton Woods institutions (Zubok 2007, 51–52). On the US end, undermining Soviet economic recovery and industrialization was driven mainly by political and military concerns over the growing Soviet military threat, especially after the USSR's development of the atomic bomb in 1949. The policy of applying widespread trade embargoes against the USSR and its Central and Eastern European allies after 1948, and the discriminatory treatment of the USSR and Central and Eastern European states by the erection of protectionist barriers through mechanisms such as the EEC and EFTA, further contributed to the division of the continent's economies and the reinforcement of divergences in industrial structures and patterns of growth. Ironically, Western policy of keeping Central and Eastern European economies at arm's length were critical in aiding and reinforcing the Soviet project of making these economies as dependent as possible on that of the USSR.

While these policies contributed to a slowdown of East-West trade, they did not result in its total disappearance. Sectors of the Soviet bureaucracy were aware that, despite important technological breakthroughs in certain areas, Soviet industrial development would be impossible without access to Western technology. After Stalin's death, the initiation of economic reforms in the USSR and the steady exertions of national economic sovereignty in Central and Eastern Europe created opportunities for a gradual rise in East-West trade.

Soviet interest in expanding trade with the West grew in the early 1950s. In 1952 Soviet leadership organized a conference in which Western business leaders were enticed to pursue trade and investment opportunities in the USSR. While Western commercial actors were more pragmatic in their dealings with the USSR, Western trade restrictions made it unlikely that Western business interest in the USSR would translate into meaningful cooperation. Khrushchev's economic reforms also favored expanding commercial ties with the West. As a result, efforts to expand trade intensified in the 1960s, when Soviet leadership under Khrushchev began seeing trade with the West as potentially economically beneficial for the USSR (in addition to using bilateral arrangements to improve relations with individual West European nations, thus sidestepping the United States).[10]

Holzman (1976, 132–148) cites several reasons for the period's gradual policy change. First, by the mid-1950s, the Central and Eastern European economies were successfully wed to that of the USSR. Communist Party rule was also relatively secure in the region and, despite the display of popular dissatisfaction with the regimes in East Germany in 1953 and Hungary in 1956, all serious opposition had by that time been exiled, imprisoned, or killed. Second, policies of industrialization were beginning to bear fruit in both the USSR and Central and Eastern Europe. The USSR and Central and Eastern Europe experienced an economic miracle of sorts in the 1950s, registering annual rates of growth of 8 to 10 percent. Soviet and Central and Eastern European leaderships gained confidence in their ability to take on the West in economic terms. Third, on the Western side, the United States' hand in enforcing restrictions on West European trade with the Soviet bloc was weakening. Blocking access to Marshall Plan funds was a key threat that the United States used to ensure that its European allies implemented trade restrictions under the informally run, Paris-based Consultative Group and Coordinating Committee (CoCom) set up in 1950. Through 1954, the list of goods banned from trade with the USSR and its allies covered as much as half of all internationally traded goods (Mastanduno 1992). The end of the Marshall Plan removed some US leverage, while West European governments began pushing against what they saw as CoCom's excessive trade restrictions. West European nations were also driven to expand trade with the USSR and Central and Eastern European countries as they registered improvements in their own trade balances, and such concerns could no longer serve to limit imports. Restrictions against extending credit facilities to socialist countries, which the United States had also demanded, were also eased, enabling Western loans to finance external trade with the socialist economies. Finally, in Central and Eastern Europe, the seeking out of expanded trade ties with the West may also have been driven by national interest—that is, the goal of decreasing economic dependence on the USSR. Yugoslavia had followed this path in the 1950s, and it appeared as an increasingly appealing option for leaders in other Central and Eastern European party-states, particularly Hungary and Romania.

Soviet leadership also began to recognize that the EEC was gradually remaking the economic map of Europe. The major capitalist crisis predicted by Stalin never came. Instead, EEC economies were growing at impressive rates as was trade between them. Already in the early 1960s, Khrushchev noted the "internationalization of production in the aggressive bloc of Common Market nations" (quoted in Pisar 1970, 17). What lay on the horizon was greater industrial integration and specialization across states, rather than national autarchy. Khrushchev made important efforts during this time to increase coordination mechanisms within Comecon. Soviet leadership had, by 1960, led a successful effort to synchronize the five-year planning periods of the USSR and most Central and Eastern European nations, a definitive step toward better coordination. Another significant change in this period was the introduction of world market prices as the referential basis for intrabloc trade, which would have important ramifications, as subsequent sections discuss. In addition to its practical aspects, the turn to world market prices helped bury Stalin's contention in his *Economic Problems of Socialism in the USSR* (1952) that socialist economic integration would produce an alternative global trade system that would directly rival the capitalist world. Somewhat ironically, Soviet leadership's rediscovery of the unity of the world market vindicated Stalin's prewar opponents Leon Trotsky and Raya Dunayevskaya, who argued that no amount of state control over the economy would allow the USSR to escape the "law of value" so long as capitalist accumulation continued to exist at the worldwide scale.[11]

In the 1960s technology became another important factor that drove the USSR and Central and Eastern European leaderships to seek greater economic ties with the West. Growth was beginning to falter, and the limitations of the socialist model of extensive industrialization were becoming more apparent. Light industries producing consumer goods lagged behind, and the existing heavy industry was operating with what was increasingly becoming outdated technology and producing, by Western standards, poor-quality goods. Trade with the West came to be increasingly accepted as a means toward introducing better technology and improving production techniques. In addition to the direct import of technology, great emphasis was put on contracting builders of turnkey plants. In the 1960s much of the expansion of the USSR's chemical industry, particularly in the production of mineral fertilizers, was accomplished in this manner (Hanson 1981, 161–185).

Partly as a result of these developments, there grew a flourishing Cold War academic industry on the study of the extent, intensity, value, and economic, political, and military repercussions of East-West technology transfers. In the course of the 1960s and 1970s, Western observers pointed out that the USSR was increasingly falling behind in technological sophistication (Brada 1985b). Awareness of this technological lag was beginning to be voiced in the USSR as well. As a group of prominent Soviet scientists pointed out in an open letter to their government,

> the gulf between the US and us is all the greater in the newest and most revolutionary sectors of the economy. We are ahead of America in coal extraction, but behind in oil, gas and electric energy; we are ten years behind in chemicals and infinitely behind in computer technology. . . . We simply live in another era.
> (quoted in Pisar 1970, 27)

Technology transfer remained a lingering concern for US policymakers, and it was seen as just as dire a threat in the 1970s as in 1948. The problem, according to a congressional report published in 1979, was that "trade with a potential adversary will inevitably, to some extent, strengthen the economy and military capability of the trading partner" (US Congress 1979, 3). Given this opinion, three decades into the Cold War, US policy sought to question in earnest "the value and wisdom of selling US goods and technology to the Communist world" (3). Despite the ease of official trade restrictions in the course of the 1960s and the brief period of détente beginning in 1969, limiting Soviet access to what were deemed "sensitive" and "dual-use" technologies listed high on the agenda of US foreign policy.

The importation of Western technology, especially in sectors in which Soviet leadership deemed the USSR to have fallen behind, continued to remain a priority for Soviet economic policy in the 1970s and 1980s. It was an item of similar high concern for the other Central and Eastern European party-states. But these policies had to work around a number of legal, political, and institutional constraints. As an OECD report pointed out in 1985, Soviet adoption of Western technology was limited by Western export controls, but also by the capacity of the Soviet economy to assimilate and diffuse new technologies. These problems stemmed from the institutional constraints, incentives, and bottlenecks of the planning system. The ability to finance new technology purchases was also a challenge (Bornstein 1985). The latter represented an enduring structural problem for the USSR and the other Central and Eastern European party-states, given the nonconvertibility of their currencies. Indeed, a number of Western estimates showed that in the course of the 1960s and 1970s, the USSR had to draw on its gold reserves in order to finance Western imports. During the Khrushchev years, gold reserves were estimated to have fallen by as much as $1 billion on account of the USSR's trade deficit with the West (Hanson 2003, 83–87). Clearly, without access to hard currency—which could be obtained either through exports to hard currency markets or by borrowing—expanding trade with the West was unsustainable in the long run. Recent archival research reveals that Soviet foreign trade officials grappled with this problem for a long time (Sanchez-Sibony 2014, 106–113). Fortuitously, structural changes in the world economy beginning in the 1970s would provide the socialist states with opportunities that could seemingly address all their problems in one swoop, but with consequences that none could foresee in that decade. Chapter 3 discusses these.

Conclusion

The rise in Cold War tensions led to the division of the European economies along bloc lines, a pattern reinforced by both adversaries through trade embargoes (by the United States) and efforts at preventing US economic power from penetrating what the USSR saw as its sphere of influence in Europe. With the consolidation of party-states after 1948, Central and Eastern Europe embarked on a path of industrialization by central planning, collectivization and integration into the Soviet-led trade bloc under the Comecon framework. After Stalin's death, Comecon became increasingly important for facilitating industrial development and economic integration among the East European economies, with the USSR solidifying its role as a source of capital, commodities, and a captive market for Central and Eastern European products in the context of growing intrabloc interdependence. The rapid industrialization of capital-poor economies like Bulgaria and Romania indicates the key role played by the Soviet-led trading system in creating the conditions for the region's growth (seen especially in contrasts with Albania's go-it-alone Stalinism), albeit in forms that generated growing sets of exclusive complementarities that revealed the dependence of the region's industrial development on the Soviet economy and its technical and technological standards.

At the same time, in the course of the 1960s, Soviet and Central and Eastern European party elites were becoming aware of the limits of bloc autarchy. In response, the USSR under Khrushchev began exploring ways to expand trade and commercial ties with the West. It also made efforts to reform Comecon in ways that increased integration and specialization within the bloc. In the process, Comecon facilitated the region's gradual reintegration into the world economy. It began by such seemingly innocent policies such as using world market prices as the basis for intrabloc trade. It included efforts, begun under Khrushchev, to engage in cooperative agreements with Western firms as well as the admission of the need to gain access to Western technology.

These efforts transformed the nature of Comecon but also revealed the institutional constraints limiting the kind of growth sought by economic planners and reformers in Central and Eastern Europe. In the 1960s it became increasingly clear to East European elites that stronger and deeper engagement with the West would be necessary to move beyond the limits of extensive growth. Chapter 3 discusses how structural changes in the world economy and domestic pressures in the late 1960s and 1970s combined in ways that dramatically remade trade, financial, and technology relations between Central and Eastern Europe and the West.

Upgrading Socialism   3

Technology, Debt, and East European Reform, 1968–1985

We are aware that an epoch-making rearrangement in the international division of labor is taking place. We must find our place in this new international economic order.

> —Director of Intercooperation, Hungary's agency concerned with relations between socialist and capitalist enterprises[1]

While our main foreign trade is with the socialist world, we shall enhance our foreign trade structure and balance with the capitalist world, increase the share in exports of the manufacturing industry and enlarge output of goods in demand in foreign markets. We also have in mind new forms of foreign economic ties under which we are granted credits, equipment and licenses to build new enterprises, belonging to our state, in cooperation with foreign firms, and we pay for this with part of the output of these or other enterprises.

> —Leonid Brezhnev, *Report of the CPSU Central Committee and the Immediate Tasks of the Party in Home and Foreign Policy*, 1976[2]

This chapter presents a structural account of East Europe's industrial transformation during the era of reform socialism. I use "reform socialism" here to refer to the period of economic reform in socialist states introduced beginning around 1968, when economic problems like technological backwardness, low productivity, and poor product quality became apparent to Communist leaderships across the region. While reforms were carried out unevenly, they are significant in that they coincide with a number of important developments in the world economy. The rising costs of energy are the first among these developments. The climbing world market price of oil and other energy products gave an unwelcome jolt to Soviet economic planners, leading to important political strain within the bloc and the ultimate change in Comecon price formulas to account for world market price fluctuations. The second structural change involved the steadily expanding role of global finance in the 1970s, enabling the massive increase of foreign borrowing by socialist countries. Finally, the end of the "golden age" of postwar economic growth and the spread of major recessions in the Western economies gave an impetus to policymakers, especially in Europe, to attempt to revive economies by boosting trade. This provided an important push for West European policymakers and large business groups to seek to expand market access to the socialist bloc, just as leaders in the latter came to increasingly value the access of their economies to Western markets.

This chapter traces international trade and credit patterns alongside domestic policies of administrative reform and industrial upgrade in the era of reform socialism. I argue that the 1970s were a crucially transformative decade for socialist economies. In particular, reforms that increasingly decentralized trade authority away from central ministries to enterprises and FTOs gave these actors direct exposure to the competitive pressures—and thus the dominant actors—of the world market. This exposure proved important in two ways: first, by creating linkages with Western industries and markets, and second, by imbuing socialist enterprises to seek to build the technical and organizational capacities necessary to effectively participate, if not outright compete, in capitalist markets.

The chapter is organized into five sections. The first discusses the rise of the reform socialist movement out of the domestic political upheavals and intra-elite conflicts in East Europe in the course of the 1950s and 1960s. It outlines the basics of reform and approaches taken toward reform across the region. The second discusses the importance of economic crisis in the West beginning in 1973, the new set of opportunities it created for Central and Eastern European states, and how those intersected with domestic reform. The third section identifies three models of Central and Eastern European engagement with the capitalist world in the 1970s and 1980s: import-led growth, Stalinist globalization, and Comecon integrationism, followed variously by the region's states. The fourth section evaluates empirically the effects of Western technology imports on the socialist economies' integration with Western markets, finding that heightened technology imports ultimately did not displace the role of domestic institutions on determining growth. The chapter concludes by outlining changes in industrial structure and organization that grew out of the experience of the 1970s and 1980s and set the stage for the onset of economic liberalization reforms in the early 1990s.

Reforming Central Planning

The inefficiencies and, more critically, the structural limits of Stalinist central planning became apparent early in the era of postwar industrialization. Chapter 2 highlights Khrushchev's reforms in the USSR, which aimed to correct gross underdevelopment in Soviet light industries and to initiate the administrative decentralization of the planning process and coordination between organizational units of production. Under Khrushchev, more investments were made in agriculture and light industry, and trade with the West resumed. However, reforms faced tough political resistance and ultimately failed to transform Soviet planning in fundamental ways (Nove 1992).

In Central and Eastern Europe, party leaders and economists were also preoccupied with reform. Khrushchev's openness for reform offered what seemed an opportunity for important revisions to the excessively bureaucratized, command model of Stalinist central planning. At the same time, unlike the USSR, in the Central and Eastern European countries central planning was a more recent institutional implant. As a consequence, bureaucratic interests were not as entrenched within the political and economic structure, nor was ideological commitment equally strong as in the USSR. As a result, the economic system seemed more pliable to modification or—possibly, as some reformers hoped—even transformation into something radically different.

Reform proposals emerged as early as 1955 but were derailed by both political resistance and domestic upheavals. In the early 1960s, the most radical of reform proposals emerged in Czechoslovakia. A great deal of the reforms were based on what was known as the Brus Program, from the ideas of the Polish economist Włodzimierz Brus. Brus proposed a radical overhaul of central planning that incorporated elements of the market in the operation of the economic system, but where the state continued to play a role in controlling the social costs and externalities that would accrue in a purely capitalist economy (Brus 1979). "Market socialism" was one of the names used to describe the ideas of Brus and likeminded economists such as Oskar Lange and Ota Šik. Building on a neoclassical economic model, market socialism promised to provide the means of balancing between "private" (producer and consumer) preferences for things such as greater income, more leisure time, and high-quality goods, and "social" (planner) preferences for collective goals such as high investment ratios, maximizing aggregate output, efficient use of resources, and full employment (Bockman 2011). Institutionally, these would be achieved through the devolution of enterprise control to workers, the freeing of trade unions from party control, and the relinquishing of physical output plans for indirect control over enterprises through macroeconomic tools such as the determination of wage levels, investment ratios, and interest rates. To allow the aggregation of social preferences, the reformed system would also require fundamental political democratization, giving workers and consumers greater say in policy making.

It is a sign of the relatively fluid and open nature of the political environment in East Europe in the immediate post-Stalin years that ideas as radical as those of the Brus Program ended up in the Czechoslovak reform proposals of 1968. Indeed, these reforms "proposed to give a far greater role to market demands [in decision making] . . . than that envisaged by Brus' model" (Smith 1983, 68). The proposals aimed to create an economic system that was described as "market-type state capitalism, guided by econometric forecasting, tools of indicative planning, opened up to foreign competitive imports, possibly with elements of employee participation in management, and surely with trade unions returned to their role as autonomous interest organizations of labor" (Holesovsky 1977, 714). In addition to making central planning indicative and limiting its scope to long-term targets, enterprises would be encouraged to maximize gross income, with excess income (profits) placed in funds for bonuses, reinvestment and technical improvements, and social activities. The state would use fiscal policy instead of direct command to ensure that excess income was not captured by managers and workers in the form of excess wages and personal bonuses. Limited price controls would remain in force during an intermediate period, but in the long run these would be dropped as retail prices would be determined by the market. The financial sector would also operate on a market basis, with centrally determined interest rates the main mechanism used by the state to influence financial policy.

The market socialist option was certainly not the only proposal on the table, though most of its ideas made it onto the desks of fellow economists more than on the agendas of central committee meetings. At least two other reform movements among this group are important to note. Centralized reformers wished to improve the planning process by devolving part of the decision-making process to the enterprise level, but not radically change the planning system itself. The changes they advocated involved mainly administrative decentralization within the planning system. Among important movements along these lines were the Liberman proposals in the USSR, which pushed for giving wider decision-making authority in investments and output to the enterprise, while using profitability measures to assess enterprise performance. The 1963 reforms in the GDR followed the model proposed in the USSR by Evsei Liberman, and one of its key features was the strengthening of the *Vereinigungen Volkseigener Betriebe* (Associations of Publicly Owned Operations—VVB). The VVB were national associations that subsumed a number of enterprises and took over aspects of planning authority from the central planning board.

Differing more in emphasis than in substance, "computopians" were mainly statisticians and mathematical economists, many of whom were housed in the newly established Central Economics and Mathematics Institute in Moscow. This group believed that planning could be made more efficient via improvements in the planning process itself as better information, more sophisticated mathematical models, and greater computing power was put to use in all stages of the planning process. In political terms, centralized reformers and computopians offered a safer bet to conservative party elites than market socialists, since they tinkered at the edges with the administrative structure of the planning system and did not demand—like the market socialists—radical political reforms that would undermine the party's political monopoly. The centralized and computopian reforms would entail transferring greater control over economic policy to technocrats in the planning administration and the enterprise sector but would not have planners lose oversight of enterprises. Yugoslavia's seemingly successful experiment in enterprise self-management and decentralization also encouraged market socialists.

Technocratic imperatives remained consistent in the reforms adopted during most of the 1960s, but by 1968 reforms were either blocked (especially as a result of the events of the Prague Spring) or backtracked as a result of a conservative backlash and bureaucratic obstinacy. Promises of improvements in economic performance also proved ephemeral. The Kosygin reforms of 1965 in the USSR, based on Liberman's proposals, made significant changes, such as introducing profit measures for enterprise performance, but measures to devolve authority to enterprises to make independent investment decisions were soon retracted. Although overall output grew between 1966 and 1970, these remained below planned levels. In particular, while wages grew dramatically, productivity did not improve. Many blamed this development on the new incentives for enterprises to accumulate bonus funds based on higher profits. Profits also accumulated unevenly across sectors, as light industries accumulated more than the traditional heavy industry sector, creating imbalances in the economy (Adam 1989, 53). The introduction of profits could also not help make enterprises more efficient since wholesale prices—the prices used by enterprises for their sales—continued to be centrally administered. By 1970, under Brezhnev, most of Alexei Kosygin's reforms were retracted or new measures introduced that practically annulled any attempts to devolve substantial control from the center.

Greater openness toward experimentation existed in Central and Eastern Europe in the 1960s. In addition to the reasons previously outlined, Khrushchev and his immediate successors saw Central and Eastern Europe as a laboratory in which reform policies could be developed and tested in practice before being considered for adoption in the USSR. This partly explains the relative tolerance Moscow displayed toward the more radical proposals for market socialism throughout the 1950s and early 1960s put forth by Czechoslovak, Hungarian, and Polish economists. These experiments came to an abrupt end in 1968, however, after Soviet tanks rolled into the streets of Prague in response to the mass protests led by students and intellectuals. The fallout from the Soviet intervention in Czechoslovakia resulted in the downfall of reformers in the Czechoslovak Party. Reformists were blamed for stirring unrest, and under newly installed General Secretary Gustáv Husák, the Czechoslovak economic reform program was swiftly shelved. Many of the reforms that were implemented after 1966 involved devolution of authority to the enterprise level. Changes such as the introduction of gross income as a measure of enterprise performance, autonomous control over wages, independent bank financing of investments, and greater worker self-management in enterprises were systematically retracted as central control was reinstituted.

Surprisingly, while the 1968 events in Czechoslovakia led to the collapse of economic reforms there, they continued unabated in Hungary, where the reforms begun under János Kádár in 1956 intensified with a new economic reform program introduced in 1968. Hungary's reform program was also inspired by the market socialist movement. One of the reform architects, Rezső Nyers, described Hungary's reform as one that would "integrate central planning and the market mechanism," but its goals were not as radical as those envisioned by Brus (Adam 1989, 72).

The Hungarian reforms, which came to be known as the New Economic Mechanism (NEM), did away with compulsory plan targets and created flexibility that allowed readjustment to planned output based on changing economic factors. Enterprises were also assigned the task of developing their own production plans, which would be better reflective, the reformers thought, of enterprise preferences. Enterprise plans would not require approval from the center. This was thought to be more in line with the actual workings of central planning, in which plans were often subject to revision and actual enterprise performance often deviated from those foreseen by the initial plan. The center reserved the right to approve large investment projects. This change, it was hoped, would enable the center to balance and prioritize investments at the macroeconomic level, while at the same time giving sufficient autonomy to enterprises to respond to market or quasi-market price signals. Reform of the price system was aimed at making the latter more reflective of conditions of supply and demand. In the place of an entirely administered price system, the reforms were inspired by the Yugoslav system of tiered prices. The price system was to contain both administratively set and free prices. The former would be further subdivided into fixed prices, prices limited by a ceiling, and prices allowed to fluctuate within a set range. Free prices were applied most sweepingly for producer goods as well as a range of consumer goods such as clothing, household items, and luxury goods.[3] Export and import prices would be determined by world market prices, translated into a domestic price via a standard currency conversion formula. In the long run, price controls would be entirely removed, reformers hoped.

Alongside devolution of production authority to enterprises, the performance of the latter was also made accountable by profit measures. A variety of regulations stipulated the distribution of profits into enterprise wage and investment funds, which were also heavily taxed. In principle, enterprises were expected to generate sufficient revenue and earn enough profits to pay their own wages and finance their investments. In practice, few enterprises were able to accomplish this, and many had to rely on subsidies to cover the wage bill and on state banks to provide investment funds.

While the Hungarian economy registered growth during the early reform years, in 1973 the reforms came to a standstill. Enterprise control was decentralized, but structural dependence on the center for investment funds, subsidies, tax breaks, and wage support precluded any meaningful separation of enterprises from their branch ministries: "The quest of enterprises for subsidies and tax reliefs brought about a situation in which bargaining about output targets, which was characteristic of the centralized system, was replaced by bargaining about application of regulators, subsidies, tax reliefs and prices" (Adam 1989, 88). More importantly, the perennial macroeconomic problem of the centrally planned economy, in which the growth of the wage bill consistently outstripped the growth of productivity, was not overcome by the NEM's innovations. But the decentralization of foreign trade authority brought on by the NEM would have an important impact in enabling increased interaction with Western firms and markets. This would have a lasting impact on the future transformation of the Hungarian economy, as the following section shows.

In his assessment of the reforms of the 1970s, Brus (1979), now writing from exile in the United Kingdom, argues that the process of devolution ended up strengthening the intermediate organizations—that is, the industrial associations that bridged the center with the enterprise as the unit of production. Devolution, he argues, resulted in greater concentration of authority in these intermediate organizations. They followed the original example set by the GDR's creation of the VVBs. Imitating this model, the "Large Economic Organization" emerged as the central institutional form for organizing planning and production (*Wielka Organizacja Gospodarcza* [WOG] in Poland, *Výrobni Hospodářská Jednotka* [VHJ] in Czechoslovakia, *Centralele* in Romania, and the *Durzhavno Stopanstvo Obedinenie* [DSO] in Bulgaria). "In all cases of genuine increase of autonomy of industry vis-a-vis governmental economic apparatus," Brus argues, "it was the association (or similar body) which became the main beneficiary and not the unitary enterprise of the traditional type" (260). The reform in effect implemented what was a structural necessity. As Paul Wiedenmann (1981) argues, this structural problem consisted of the administrative challenge of planning for an ever larger economy with ever increasing units of production and ever growing numbers of intermediate and final goods to produce. The growing scale of the industrial economy made reliance on traditional planning impractical and increasingly daunting. To deal with the increasingly herculean task of managing the economy, authority was first devolved from the center to the intermediate organizations. When decentralization proved problematic, as the resulting intermediate (industrial) associations created new problems of coordination, authority was concentrated again by reducing the number of intermediate organizations (and, in some cases, reasserting the center's control over output plans). The backtracking across the socialist economies did not restore the old Stalinist system of direct top-down control over enterprises; it was rather a reassertion of central authority within the already restructured system that now increasingly relied on intersectoral bargaining and negotiated agreements on supplies and output levels between planner and producer (Kornai 1991, 118–127).

A combination of domestic political pressures and/or economic weaknesses, of a degree that could potentially threaten regime legitimacy, spurred party leaderships to contemplate reform in Hungary, Poland, and Czechoslovakia. As a result, in the late 1950s and 1960s, these countries were at the forefront of reform efforts. These factors were not present in Romania or Bulgaria, which faced neither domestic upheavals nor significant shortfalls in economic output. Indeed, for most of the 1960s, the Romanian and Bulgarian economies were the highest growing in Comecon, and perhaps in all of Europe. The reforms in these countries seemed to result from the local parties' efforts to jump on the bandwagon of an existing trend and the need to improve efficiency of administrative methods of planning given the growing size of industry. But this context also illustrates why the motivation for reform in these two countries was not as strong as in Hungary and Poland (and Czechoslovakia until the internal party coup reversed the reforms), and why the reform templates used there were less radical.

In retrospect, the most critical aspect of the post-1968 reforms was a growing awareness of the region's integration into the world economy. In 1967 the Romanian Party organized a major conference on foreign trade, the chief message of which was centrality of foreign trade in Romania's future development (Spigler 1973, 18). In 1969 a party report went even further when it called on Hungarian policymakers to abandon the approach in which economic policy is developed within an exclusively national framework. The thinking no doubt seeped beyond the borders of Hungary. Structurally, taking into account world economic conditions was becoming a greater necessity given the long decade of steadily expanding trade. Throughout the 1960s, levels of trade in Central and Eastern Europe had grown at a rate higher than economic growth. Trade with the USSR expanded most rapidly, but trade with the West came to assume a more prominent role in the 1970s. In the 1960s trade with Third World nations was also assuming an increasingly important role and offered new export opportunities and sources of raw materials. The policies of the reform socialism era were in some ways both a response to growing domestic needs as well as the result of a growing realization that those needs cannot be met by reliance on domestic resources alone. By the mid-1970s, the process of Central and Eastern Europe's integration into the world economy was very much in high gear, facilitated in no small way by the tumultuous economic events taking place in the West.

"Epoch-Making Rearrangements": World Economic Restructuring and the New Era in East–West Economic Cooperation

A series of momentous events took place across the two political-economic blocs in the course of the late 1960s and early 1970s that marked an important turning point in the world economy. Politically and diplomatically, changing world political conditions, including the rise of Japan and the Federal Republic of Germany (FRG) as economic powerhouses, China's opening to the West, and the achievement of nuclear parity with the USSR, steered the Nixon administration toward a balance-of-power approach in its relations with Moscow. Brezhnev, who had assumed power in 1964, continued his predecessors' policies of negotiating nuclear controls with the United States and saw the easing of tensions in Europe as beneficial to the USSR for both strategic and economic reasons. The spearhead of détente, however, was Chancellor Willy Brandt's *Östpolitik*—the FRG's establishment of diplomatic relations with Moscow and the eventual mutual recognition of the FRG and the GDR, reducing the hostility between the two Germanys that had been one the key pillars of Cold War policy in Europe. The prospects for stable peace in Europe seemed to grow especially after the Helsinki Final Act in 1975, signed by the United States, the USSR, and their respective allies in Europe, established the Council for Security and Cooperation in Europe (CSCE). The intensified diplomatic links opened the door for greater trade, especially as the FRG began expanding its commercial interests in East Europe.

A second impetus for Western interest in Central and Eastern European trade came after 1973, when recession-hit European businesses sought to gain a foothold in Central and Eastern European trade. The extension of export credits greatly facilitated these inroads. The FRG and other European nations were at the forefront of this move. The United States, though acting to strengthen commercial ties with the socialist bloc—including taking measures such as establishing the Bureau of East-West Trade at the Department of Commerce—was, however, prevented from granting most favored nation (MFN) status to the USSR and other Central and Eastern European states due to restrictions stemming from the Jackson-Vanik Amendment passed by Congress in 1974.[4] Nonetheless, one important development in US policy that, if not promoting, at least did not work to hinder growing East-West trade *in Europe* was the easing of CoCom restrictions on the reexport of US-engineered technologies by West European allies. The restrictions put into place in the 1950s threatened to deny exports of US technology to any state that reexports such technology to a Communist country. These drastic restrictions were scaled back in the 1970s by the Nixon and Carter administrations, despite strong domestic pressures against such changes. The restrictions were also less effective in practice since the United States had lost the technological leading edge it had held in the 1950s. Additionally, in the United States, the locus of advanced technological development had shifted from the military to the private sector, creating additional difficulties for the enforcement of export restrictions (Mastanduno 1992, 143–219).

The most crucial factor that enabled the explosion of East-West trade in the 1970s lay outside of direct control of the policy of either set of governments. This was the dramatic expansion of lightly regulated dollar-denominated money markets in Europe. Commonly known as eurodollar markets, these offshore dollar and other hard-currency markets emerged as a combination of a number of processes. The first involved British interest in preserving London's status as a world financial center in the Bretton Woods era. Lax regulation, a long tradition in currency trade, tight monetary policy by the Bank of England, and bankers finding creative ways of getting around US restrictions on interest payable on short-term dollar deposits helped turn London into the center of the international dollar trade already in the 1950s (Schenk 1998; Helleiner 1996). By the 1960s, growing export earnings added to the accumulation of dollar surpluses across Western Europe. European banks found innovative ways of using these dollar reserves to devise and sell dollar-denominated bonds and other securities. But the real boon for eurodollar markets came after the oil crisis of 1973. After OPEC's takeover of crude oil pricing, the sudden rise of oil prices flooded the oil-exporting nations with excess dollar earnings. A great deal of these petrodollars were deposited with banks in London and elsewhere in Europe, producing an international dollar glut. Roy Allen estimates that, from a $59 billion of turnover for the entire year in 1970, eurodollar markets grew to an average turnover of $300 billion *per day* in 1980. "By the late 1980s," Allen writes, "global financial markets were generating a net international flow of funds of more than $3 trillion each month . . . [of this], $2 trillion was so-called stateless money, which is virtually exempt from the control of any government or official institution, but available for use by all countries" (2009, 3). Unlike national banks, eurodollar markets often lack reserve requirements, making them a source for an almost limitless supply of quasi money. Milton Friedman, writing in 1970, pointed out that lack of reserve requirements and

other regulations gave eurodollar markets the capacity to produce hard currency merely by putting "the bookkeeper's pen at work" (1970, 8). Most importantly, lax lending restrictions made this excess supply of hard currency an easy
sort of credit for developing countries, including those of the socialist bloc, and
banks were very eager to lend (Kindleberger 1978; Darity and Horn 1988). As
Darrell Delamaide writes, during the 1970s the eurodollar market functioned
"a bit like Oz":

> For companies and countries with extra cash, the Euromarket was an investors'
> paradise. Assets were liquid, anonymity reasonably sure, and returns high. For
> a borrower, it was a cash machine. The market mobilized millions of dollars
> overnight, with only a few telexes and no red tape. (1984, 40)

In the 1970s eurodollar markets became the chief source of hard-currency
borrowing for Central and Eastern European countries (Zloch-Christy 1987).
Typically, a set of banks would jointly provide a pool of credit to a client in the
form of syndicated loans. It made no difference if the borrower was a firm or a
government. The introduction of syndicated loans permitted eurodollar institutions to extend credit over several years. However, in order to minimize risk,
banks rolled over loans every six months, and in the process revised the interest rate charged based on current market rates (Delamaide 1984, 41–43). Under
these terms, the costs determined by change in credit market conditions were
swiftly passed on to the borrower.

While the 1973 OPEC crisis flooded eurodollar markets with hard-currency
deposits, it also inaugurated a period of recession, high inflation, and interest
rate instability in the United States. From its postwar high of about 8 percent in
1969, the Federal Reserve's annual average federal funds rate fell to a little over
4 percent in 1972. By 1974 it approached 11 percent. A period of rate reductions
followed, leading most Central and Eastern European governments to continue
planning domestic growth based on continued international borrowing. However, the second oil crisis in 1979 and the stagflation crisis that afflicted the US
economy led the Federal Reserve under Paul Volcker to institute a policy of
rapidly tightening monetary control, also known as the Volcker shock. As a result of Volcker's aggressive anti-inflationary policies, by 1981 the average federal
funds rate had attained a historic high of 16 percent.

While lenders and borrowers in eurodollar markets were free from US financial regulations, they were not entirely independent of US monetary policy.
Eurodollar interest rates were based on the London Interbank Offered Rate

(LIBOR), which closely tracked the Federal Reserve's policy rates. As a result, changes in US monetary policy had a direct impact on the borrowing costs of eurodollar creditors. Through a combination of domestic policy, loose money on international credit markets, and the sudden interest rate explosion, Central and Eastern European governments ended up facing dramatic rises in the costs of servicing their international hard-currency debt. As Figure 3.1 shows, Central and Eastern European foreign debt grew steadily until 1974 but then increased dramatically after the OPEC crisis. The USSR and Poland were some of the most eager borrowers on eurodollar markets. However, by the latter part of the decade, with the exception of Czechoslovakia and Bulgaria, virtually all Central and Eastern European countries were engaged in heavy international borrowing. As a result, the total foreign debt of European socialist countries increased tenfold, from about $20 billion in 1971 to over $200 billion in 1979.

The interest rate peak in 1981 led virtually all Central and Eastern European governments to curtail their borrowing on international credit markets. Poland was especially hardhit, announcing that same year that the government lacked the foreign currency reserves to service its debt. Romania faced a similar

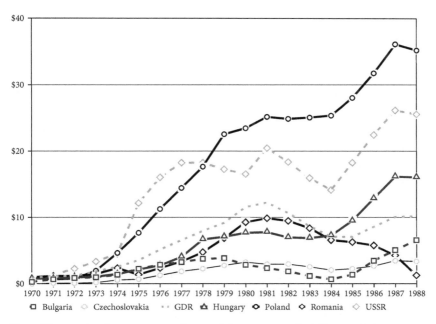

Figure 3.1. Levels of East European foreign debt, 1970–1988 (in billions USD)
SOURCE: Lavigne (1991), UNECE (1996).

challenge as the government entered negotiations with creditors and committed the country to vigorous austerity to pay down its debt (Ban 2012). The USSR also faced credit problems, though Soviet debt was more easily managed given growing commodity exports to hard-currency markets. Most Central and Eastern European countries would not return to the international credit market until 1985, when most—though not all—Central and Eastern European governments began a renewed borrowing spree. In any event, the decade of the 1970s, when borrowing was almost exclusively used to finance trade with the West, does in certain key ways represent an epochal shift for Central and Eastern European industry, as it effectively begins a period of protoglobalization. The following sections describe these critical changes.

Models of Socialist Protoglobalization

The critical structural shifts described in the preceding section form the backdrop of reforms in East Europe. East European economists and party elites were well aware of these global economic changes taking place in the course of the 1970s. They were seen—and in many occasions exploited—as opportunities not only to expand trade ties but to deepen economic ties with the Western economies. These nascent relationships were emerging through the still extensive legal barriers, protectionist measures, business cultures, and institutional incongruities on both sides. Their formation constitutes a critical period of protoglobalization that both sets the tone, as well as structures the path, of economic transformation after 1989. Protoglobalization signifies a period when socialist industry began a process of integration with Western industry in a way that went beyond ordinary trade in goods, by establishing the organizational conditions for joint production and other forms of extensive cooperation that enabled the transnational production of goods across the proverbial iron curtain.

In the course of the 1970s, ties with Western firms evolved beyond simple transfers of technology and acquisitions of turnkey plants to more complex and long-term interorganizational relationships involving collaborative research and development, joint ventures, product licensing, and the joint production of goods. To a certain extent, these changes spoke of, if not the overcoming, then the lessening of the systemic propensity to trade aversion. With trade made less dependent on planners and more on enterprises and other lower-level organizational units of the economy, direct links between firms came to assume a much more prominent role than classical trade in goods. While the period of reform socialism produced a mixed bag of results in the remaking of Stalinist planning, the policy priorities and institutional changes it introduced marked important shifts in the outward orientation of East European economies.

These changes manifested themselves differently in the various countries as engagement with the Western economies interacted with domestic patterns of institutional reform and the political goals of party elites. In general, three models of outward orientation emerged. The first is what Philip Hanson (1982) calls "import-led growth." Hanson discusses this model in the context of Poland, but it may just as well be applied to Hungary. In these cases, high-level policy goals of increasing trade with the West were combined with institutional decentralization, which enabled cooperative ties to develop at the enterprise level. The second model is the conservative model, which favored intensifying traditional trade ties within Comecon. This approach largely shunned, or was less enthusiastic about initiating, a major trade reorientation and expanding access to Western markets. Czechoslovakia and, to a lesser extent, Bulgaria, exemplify this model. The third model is the Romanian model of what can be termed "Stalinist globalization." Here, it is the high party elite that made expanded economic ties with the West a central policy goal. But ironically (and perhaps tragically), these expanded trade ties were not accompanied by significant institutional reform; in practice they functioned as alternative means to achieving the traditional goals of Stalinist industrialization.

In the import-led growth model, increasing imports of Western technology, know-how, and production techniques are complemented by a policy of financing those imports via increased exports of manufactured goods to Western markets. More than simply increasing the quantity of goods traded or acquiring Western machinery, the goal became establishing and strengthening long-term forms of industrial cooperation with advanced industry in the West. The organizational model that served as a blueprint for such "industrial cooperation agreements" negotiated at the high political level followed the model set by the agreements made between Soviet and French industry after Charles de Gaulle's visit to Moscow in 1966. The model of cooperative agreements, which ultimately required close cooperation between firms rather than governments, was intended to overcome the constraints of East-West trade, though their design reflected the asymmetries in the power and function of the political authorities entering into them. Socialist governments could negotiate and pledge resources on behalf of enterprises in their country. They also required that all trade commitments eventually reflect in national output plans.

By contrast, Western governments could at best create frameworks that could serve the interests of private business actors, without committing to quantities or compelling their firms to enter into specific deals (Lavigne 1991, 79). None of this prevented Western firms from using the cooperative agreements to search for partners in the socialist world. As a result, the number of Western firms engaging with the socialist world expanded rapidly throughout the 1970s.

During the decade the theme of industrial cooperation became very common and shared across the region. As a 1975 article appearing in Bulgaria's foreign trade journal *Vunshna Turgoviya* explained,

> Industrial cooperation is one of the forms of economic cooperation with the developed capitalist countries. . . . Production cooperation enables us to improve the organization of the production process, lower production costs, and upgrade the quality of the new goods. Its expansion is converting into an important factor in increasing trade with capitalist countries and increasing primarily the share of output in machine-building and other sectors. At the same time, it becomes a source for broadening the possibility to import complete projects and installations on a high technical level. . . . The traditional exchange of goods at the present stage is insufficient in terms of implementing the possibilities for development of mutually profitable relations between Bulgaria and the capitalist countries. (Lazarova 1975)

In the late 1970s, realizing Czechoslovakia's lag in expanding cooperative ties with Western firms, a Czechoslovak economist warned that "it is important to know what are the potential opportunities for international industrial cooperation for our mutual benefit that we have been leaving unexploited" (Nykyrn 1977, 178). And around the same time, an East German economist confidently suggested that economic cooperation was leading to "a better articulated division of labor on an international scale as well as highly diversified approaches to the utilization of the international division of labor for the benefit of national development" (Schmidt 1978, 7). He went on to argue that "neither the volume nor the structure of actual economic relations has so far reached the limits of possibilities and the needs on either side" (7). He also noted that this was not a fleeting or temporary development, but reflective of larger transformations in the world economy:

> The reinforcement and expansion of economic and techno-scientific relations with the capitalist states is considered, and implemented, as a long-term policy

by the member countries of [Comecon]. It is not subject to sudden changes of tactics or limited by short-term interests. We do not see this expansion as a "boom" phenomenon. It is rather assumed that favorable conditions exist for a continuing process of consolidation and expansion of economic relations and, consequently, the international division of labor between the socialist states and the capitalist industrial countries, and that those favorable conditions stem from a number of new trends in the world economy and in world politics. (8)

In Western Europe, it was—ironically—deepening trade integration within the EEC that turned economic cooperation agreements into one of the few institutional means to trade with socialist economies. Given changes to the EEC treaty starting in 1973, EEC members were prohibited from signing or renewing bilateral trade agreements with third countries. This led to the collapse of existing bilateral trade arrangements with socialist bloc countries. However, economic cooperation agreements were exempt from this prohibition, leaving them among the few legal mechanisms that enabled the continuation of economic ties of EEC states with socialist economies. As Marie Lavigne points out,

A convergence of political interests occurred between Western governments and socialist states. Western EC [European Community] members wanted to retain a margin of maneuver in such a politically sensitive area as trade with the East. Socialist countries were eager to remain in a bilateral framework of negotiation. As the bilateral framework could only be retained, according to EC rules, in the field of cooperation, commercial matters were as inconspicuously as possible insinuated into cooperation agreements. (1999, 80)

From the socialist side, policymakers believed that imports of capital goods can serve the goal of industrial upgrade, a process that was to be paid for by future exports of the very products resulting from that process. Partnerships between domestic enterprises and Western firms would only help facilitate that process.

In the course of the 1970s, these partnerships were advancing beyond limited contractual agreements and arm's-length transactions involving trade in goods and wholesale acquisitions of Western technology in specific industrial areas (Maximova 1977). The early 1970s saw a rapid expansion of direct firm-to-firm agreements across the East-West divide. Between 1958 and 1968, only 23 cooperation agreements were signed between socialist enterprises and Western firms. Between 1968 and 1974, that number grew to 245 (McMillan 1977,

43). Western corporations, many of which were already or transitioning toward operating as TNCs, were the preferred counterparts for East European foreign trade and industrial ministries and enterprises (Wilczynski 1976; McMillan 1977; Lavigne 1991). There were a multiplicity of reasons for this. First, TNCs had access to and sometimes proprietary control over the technologies of production sought out by East European planners, technicians, and enterprise managers. Second, many TNCs already had extensive experience in operating in foreign countries and were knowledgeable of the risks involved in operations across national boundaries. They also saw East European economies as potentially important markets, especially in the consumer goods sector. Given import restrictions, operating with a local partner often enabled them to gain a share of the local market. Finally, the brand recognition that TNCs held certainly helped enhance the legitimacy of Western-oriented policies in the socialist world, especially in the context of the national developmental programs that parties in the region otherwise promoted. More critically, large and globally reputable firms were preferred because of certain shared organizational outlooks and dispositions between executives in large corporations and socialist planners. "Only such firms are in a position to meet large and complex orders, have a capacity for long-term cooperation and are unlikely to go bankrupt. . . . [I]n several respects [TNCs] are not unlike the Socialist states—they have to 'think big,' they engage in long-term planning and have a hierarchical technocratic outlook" (Wilczynski 1976, 32).[5] During this era, the discourse among technocrats throughout the region placed greater emphasis on the importance of scientific and technological advancement while increasingly abandoning the ideological hostility against capitalist industry that characterized party discourse in the Stalinist era. Partnering with major TNCs was described as a path toward achieving those aims, not a submission to or defeat by the imperialism of capital. In the words of a Soviet economist, "the trend in both socialist and capitalist countries towards joint production, subcontracting and agreements on specialization undoubtedly opens up much greater possibilities for mutually beneficial technological exchange between them" (Maximova 1977, 21). A number of Western observers of these developments described this as a shift toward "transideological enterprise" (Perlmutter 1969; Wilczynski 1976; Frank 1977).

As a result, the 1970s experienced not only increased trade between socialist countries and the West but also the increased involvement of TNCs in introducing new technologies, manufacturing techniques, and management styles. They also connected socialist enterprises to new markets, as in many cases their local production became geared toward both the assembly of Western parts as well as the local manufacturing of components that were shipped to the Western partner. According to a survey carried out in the mid-1970s, roughly half of all interfirm cooperation agreements across the region (including the USSR) included one of three arrangements: a socialist enterprise supplying parts or components to be incorporated into a Western product, the opposite scenario, or both (McMillan 1977, 52–53). Transnational production chains thus emerged in the crux of socialist industry. In the course of the 1970s, the presence of foreign companies became more deeply rooted as socialist governments legalized joint ventures. Countries at the forefront of reform, such as Romania and Hungary, followed the Yugoslav lead in adopting measures that eased legal restrictions that allowed domestic enterprises to establish jointly owned and operated ventures with Western partners both within and outside the country. For joint ventures operating domestically, there were still a variety of restrictions, such as mandating that the domestic enterprise control a majority stake, and workarounds for the designation of ownership stakes given legal restrictions over private ownership as well as the nonexistence of shareholder entities in the law. This problem was typically resolved through substituting legal ownership with contractual arrangements. A number of joint ventures were set up in the early 1970s, with their number growing in many countries, particularly in Yugoslavia, Hungary, and Romania in the course of the decade and continuing through the 1980s.

How did joint venture partnerships operate? In the early 1970s, under the auspices of the Canadian Economic Policy Committee, Carl McMillan and D. P. St. Charles carried out a comparative study of joint ventures in Romania, Hungary, and Yugoslavia. Among the case studies they report is the entry of US-based Control Data Corporation (CDC) into Romania (1973, 31–37). In 1970, following the Romanian Party's decision to forego participation in a Comecon project for shared specialization in the computer industry, the Romanian government sought to build a domestic computer industry by drawing on the resources of Western firms. After being rejected by IBM, an official of the Romanian Ministry of Heavy Machine Building was steered, via an intermediary connection (the Corning Glass factory in New York, which he had visited to discuss the production of glass for television sets) to leading members of CDC. At the time, CDC was the fifth largest computer maker in the world. To Romanian officials, CDC seemed a worthy substitute for IBM, while CDC, which had no prior experience in Romania, saw the cooperation as an opportunity for gaining a foothold in Romanian and Comecon markets. In 1973 CDC, the Romanian government, and the Romanian Industrial Central for Electronics and Vacuum Technology (CIETV) agreed to establish a joint venture called Rom Control Data SLR, in which CDC held a 45 percent interest. The agreement called for CDC to contribute $1.8 million in technology and know-how to the venture while CIETV would provide the facilities and labor. The investment plan foresaw Rom Control Data producing peripheral computer equipment, such as card readers, card punchers, and printers. The five-year agreement committed CDC to purchase 85 percent of Rom Control Data's output, to be marketed through CDC's sales network, both in the West and in Comecon markets. The remaining output would be marketed directly by Rom Control Data. While the Romanian party's interest in constructing an advanced domestic sector is clear, why did CDC enter into such an unconventional arrangement? According to McMillan and St. Charles, CDC had a number of reasons to enter Romania. First, CDC gained a foothold in the Romanian market, where the regime had heightened its emphasis on computerization of the economy. Second, production in Romania was seen as supplementing CDC's other manufacturing activities in Europe, where CDC already had an established clientele (and where CDC competed directly with dominant players like IBM). From this perspective, production in Romania provided significant cost advantages. The improvement of Romania's relations with the United States undoubtedly helped seal the deal. The US government included Romania in the Overseas Private Investment Corporation (OPIC) list of supported countries, and its involvement in the agreement through financing and investment insurance helped mitigate some of the uncertainties involved in the undertaking.

Access to international credit markets and greater openness toward close collaboration with Western TNCs was accompanied by a number of institutional changes that made a general deepening of ties of socialist enterprises with Western firms possible. These institutional changes mainly affected the area of foreign trade. Decentralization of planning authority and enterprise autonomy, which, as was pointed out, led largely to the consolidation of intermediate industrial associations, was accompanied by the greater devolution of foreign trade authority away from central ministries to smaller organizations. Foreign trade authority was the responsibility of FTOs, which, in the classical model, were implementing agencies of the Ministry of Foreign Trade (Wolf 1988). The amalgamation of enterprises into large associations was also accompanied by their closer association with branch FTOs. In some instances,

particularly in Hungary, foreign trade authority was devolved directly to enterprises, as was access to foreign reserves, and the right of industrial associations
and enterprises to retain hard-currency earnings (which were used to acquire
future imports) (Granick 1975). While the move toward currency convertibility
remained politically off limits, the introduction of new price formulas standardized export and import prices. In effect, import prices paid by enterprises
would be equivalent to those of the domestic market. An arrangement of this
sort was introduced in Hungary and Poland. In both countries, world market
prices were made the baseline for domestic prices of exports and imports. Enterprises with high production costs and whose goods would not be competitive in the world market were given price subsidies. This made trade feasible
not only for competitive enterprises but also for inefficient industries (Adam
1989, 84).

At the political level, industrial upgrade emerged as a priority for economic
policymakers. Certainly, acquiring and imitating Western technology had been
a long-standing goal of Soviet planners since the 1920s. But by the late 1960s
and early 1970s, the goals of the technostructures of the USSR and its Comecon
allies turned toward the adoption and development of complex automation,
information technologies, and cybernetic systems (Sutton 1968; Wilczynski
1975). In 1969 the USSR produced its first integrated circuit computer. Given
the perceived backwardness in this domain (the United States began producing integrated circuit computers in 1964), accessing Western technologies in
these high-technology spheres was seen as critical for the ability of the socialist
economy to keep up with technological developments in the capitalist world.
These goals partly served as the justification for institutional reform in the conduct of foreign trade. Additionally, as socialist states increasingly assumed the
financial risks of trade, both through the provision of subsidies that maintained
price stability in the face of changing world market conditions and by taking
on the hard-currency loans to finance imports, trade with the West took off
dramatically.[6] These processes became most apparent in Poland and Hungary.

Import-Led Growth: Poland and Hungary

The economic reorientation in Poland was in part an outcome of domestic political turmoil. In the winter of 1970, shortages of basic goods and dramatic consumer price increases led to a major protest in Gdańsk which quickly spread
to other industrial centers. The upheavals were eventually crushed through a
brutal military intervention, but dissatisfaction with the regime's handling of

the protests and the policies that had led to them resulted in the downfall of long-time Communist leader Władysław Gomułka from the party leadership and his replacement by the young and energetic Edward Gierek. Gierek soon announced sweeping economic reforms, marking the beginning of Poland's industrial transformation during the 1970s through import-led growth.

The Polish reforms produced what seemed like an economic miracle. In the period 1971–1975, Poland recorded one of the highest growth rates in the Comecon area, and the highest since the end of World War II. Its official net material product (NMP) growth was a staggering 9.8 percent, a figure that outdid the USSR's own massive rate of growth in 1956–1960. Industrial output grew at 10.5 percent, a figure unseen since the 1950s. Investments in the economy grew to 17.5 percent, a dizzying figure when compared to the Comecon average of 6 percent. Moreover, Poland managed to achieve this growth while maintaining employment and making important gains in productivity.

Import-led growth was central to Poland's new developmental policy. The government sought to use Western imports, financed by international borrowing, to spur intensive growth—a policy of industrial upgrade in which productivity and quality of goods increased. Import-led growth included not only the import of Western capital goods but also licensing of products. In 1971 Poland spent more on the acquisition of licenses from Western firms than it had in the entire period of 1945–1965 (Fallenbuchl 1983, 45). Licensing involved arrangements whereby socialist industry would produce goods under license, either to supply the domestic market (as a form of import substitution) or, as was more common, to supply the domestic market and to resell a portion of the goods back to the licensing firm. Western firms seized the opportunity to capitalize on intellectual property such as brand names and proprietary technology while outsourcing production in part or in whole to economies that offered cost advantages.

Over the long run, import-led growth, it was believed, would allow an increasing share of Polish goods to be sold in Western markets. And indeed, Polish exports to the West, especially of manufactured goods, soared between 1971–1975, outdoing all other East European economies. But while the idea seemed sound, it proved too ambitious—investments were mismanaged and world economic conditions changed unfavorably after 1979. Economic growth came crashing down by the latter part of the decade, leading to a major economic crisis in 1981, one of the worst experienced by a postwar European socialist state.

Does this mean that Poland's import-led policy was a complete failure? The economist Kazimierz Poznanski (1996) argues that, seen in retrospect, the period of high investment and export growth instigated important structural changes in the Polish economy. He challenges such arguments as short-sighted that claim import-led growth failed because of Poland's economic slowdown in the second part of the 1970s. Poland's economic crisis, culminating in strikes and high debt in 1980, was the result of a perfect storm of international and domestic factors. Internationally, US monetary policy led to a credit crunch and rising interest payments. The 1979 oil crisis pushed Western economies into a recession, significantly contracting OECD demand and directly affecting East European, including Polish, exports. Domestically, the Polish Party's post-1970 political pact with workers included wage increases and a deflationary policy on consumer goods. As a result, both wages and consumption rose dramatically during the first half of the decade. In addition, economic decentralization had strengthened the influence of vested interests within the industrial associations, seizing from central planners the ability to orient investment and growth in accordance with national priorities. This influence also led to industrial associations proposing overambitious investment plans, imports of capital goods, and license acquisitions (many of which remained unused), but which were nonetheless underwritten by the government and the ample hard currency it secured in international credit markets. Both these commitments came into conflict in the second half of the decade. Rising interest rates were making hard currencies more expensive to obtain, while export earnings could not keep up with ever larger debt payments. At the same time, after 1978, as a result of shortages, wages could no longer keep up with rising prices of basic goods, and popular dissatisfaction with the regime, already on the verge, exploded in widespread episodes of worker unrest in 1979–1980. Industrial conflict only worsened Poland's economic conditions, as work stoppages led to production shortfalls and greater economic difficulties. The epilogue of Poland's short-lived economic miracle was Gierek's removal, the institution of martial law, and the introduction of draconian austerity measures, including the near total halting of Western imports to muster resources necessary to service Poland's $25 billion debt, the largest in East Europe.

In the long run, however, Poznanski argues that the policy of high investment, increasing exports, and industrial cooperation with Western firms did introduce significant changes in the structure of Polish industry.[7] From 1970 through 1979, Poland increased its exports to OECD markets fivefold and became by far the largest East European exporter to the OECD. Moreover, after 1975 Poland displaced Czechoslovakia as the largest East European exporter of manufactures to the OECD, a lead retained during the crisis years 1981–1983. While a variety of factors influenced Polish export growth, the dramatic increase in competitiveness in Western markets is remarkable for what was a historically underdeveloped economy. Import-led growth cannot but account, at least partially if not in whole, for this dramatic transformation of Polish industry.

While Poland's economy shined in the first half of the 1970s, Hungary, in many ways, had been at the forefront of import-led growth in a policy shift that unfolded over a longer period and in institutionally more comprehensive ways. Two features distinguish Hungary's import-led growth model from that of Poland. First, the goal of policy lay more with the establishment of long-term industrial cooperation ties than short-term acquisitions of technology. Second, and most importantly, Hungary's gradual openness to Western markets was among the fundamental aims of the NEM reforms. These took the form of both increased reliance on world market prices as bases for domestic producer prices and subsidies encouraging foreign trade, discussed earlier. They also involved the NEM's comprehensive institutional decentralization, which liberalized contacts between Hungarian enterprises and Western firms and gave greater room to the former to independently initiate economic cooperation (Marer 1986). A key development in this regard came in 1968 with the establishment of Intercooperation, a specialized FTO whose chief mandate was to organize and facilitate economic cooperation between Hungarian enterprises and Western firms. In its first year of operation, Intercooperation was quickly able to secure cooperation agreements with Great Britain's Imperial Chemicals, the FRG's Siemens, and Italy's Fiat Works, paving the way for Hungarian enterprises' increasingly growing ties with large Western industrial corporations. One of the results of the government's establishment of Intercooperation in the context of decentralized trade authority may have been—probably inadvertently—to compel other FTOs to become more aggressive in closing deals with Western firms in fear of their marginalization by Intercooperation's dominance in the field of trade with the West (Huszti 1969). This interorganizational competition alongside a relatively liberalized foreign trade regime accounts for Hungary's success in rapidly taking the lead in the number of interfirm cooperation agreements in the entire socialist bloc. By 1981, while economic crises were pushing governments like those in Poland and Romania to recentralize authority and pull back from trade and investment commitments, Hungary deepened its reforms in foreign trade, creating smaller enterprises that were fully independent in the conduct of foreign trade and economic cooperation agreements. Economic cooperation agreements in Hungary also became more concentrated in light industry (including agriculture), in contrast to traditional sectors such as transportation and machine building favored in Poland. This had important consequences in strengthening Hungary's long-term competitiveness in the world economy, as it began diversifying its industrial structure away from traditional heavy industry sectors.

The Hungarian government borrowed on international credit markets to finance its import-led growth policy, but the pace of borrowing was much lower than that of Poland. A reluctance to engage in heavy borrowing may account for Hungary's steadier economic performance during the 1970s, in contrast to Poland's swift boom-bust cycle. Nonetheless, just like Poland, Hungary was forced to curtail its imports beginning in 1979 as a result of the combination of the world economic crisis and growing borrowing costs. Even though facing a growing external debt burden, however, in 1979 Hungary's ratio of debt service to exports was still at a manageable 37 percent, in contrast to Poland's, which had climbed to 92 percent (Zloch-Christy 1987, 41). Indeed, Hungary's debt problems would worsen only after 1985, when Hungary reentered international credit markets to finance another cycle of import-led growth.

A measured approach to foreign debt and its ability to more successfully embed trade with the West via means of long-term industrial integration with Western firms enabled Hungary to avoid Poland's economic catastrophe after the debt crisis of 1980. Nonetheless, for the 1981–1985 period, Hungary recorded NMP growth rates were second highest after Poland. Integration with Western markets made economies at the forefront of import-led growth increasingly more vulnerable to economic shocks from the West, as the events after 1979 showed. A major problem, as one Hungarian economist observed, was that a great deal of Hungarian imports from the West were not capital goods, but intermediate products used in production (Köves 1979, 331–332). In effect, Hungarian enterprises increasingly replaced Comecon suppliers of basic commodities and other inputs with Western ones, on account of greater quality and reliability, or shifted production away from Comecon to Western markets. This was a costly strategy, however, and was unsustainable given the problem of financing hard-currency deficits it created for the government. Problems such as these led the Hungarian government in the early 1980s to ease away from the policy of import-led growth, though not as dramatically as Poland's turnaround in 1981. In the 1980s, when Polish industry was forced to cut down transactions with Western firms and the government increasingly looked to Comecon to recover from its major economic downturn, Hungarian enterprises gradually increased their integration with Western industry, with dramatic consequences for the country's economy after its second wave of liberalization in 1988.

Stalinist Globalization: Romania

Romania's turn to the West was motivated by political concerns as much as economic ones. In 1965, after the passing of the long-standing postwar Communist leader Gheorghe Gheorghiu-Dej, Nicolae Ceauşescu assumed power. Ceauşescu displayed increasing intransigence in his relations with Moscow and other Soviet bloc nations. Most famously, in 1968 Ceauşescu refused Romanian participation in the Warsaw Pact invasion of Czechoslovakia, strongly denouncing Soviet interference in the national affairs of other socialist countries. The prior year, Romania had become the first Soviet bloc state to recognize and establish diplomatic ties with the FRG. In 1969 Romania established ties with the United States by being host to a state visit from President Richard Nixon. While reasserting diplomatic ties with the United States, Ceauşescu began a tour of West European capitals. These earned Ceauşescu the reputation of a maverick, as he sought to catapult Romania into the role of a global actor, intensifying ties not only with the West but also with African, Latin American, Middle Eastern, and East Asian states. He further undermined unity in the Soviet bloc by strengthening Romanian ties with the USSR's Communist rivals China and Yugoslavia.

Ceauşescu's strategy of engagement with the West included a deepening of economic ties. In 1971 Romania adopted a law on joint ventures, in effect opening its economy to foreign investment, the second country after Yugoslavia to do so and the first among Comecon countries. The law allowed a foreign stake of up to 49 percent in a jointly set-up enterprise. That same year Romania joined the GATT and in 1972 became the first Comecon nation to join the IMF and the World Bank. While never formally abandoning the Warsaw Pact or Comecon, nor disclaiming traditional Stalinist methods domestically, the unique ties that Romania spearheaded with the West allowed a dramatic reshaping of its trade.

Ceauşescu's initiatives in the diplomatic arena were taking place as Romania was reforming its economic system. These reforms, as pointed out, were not as radical as those in Hungary and Poland, but the political goal of increas-

ments, Romanian diplomacy took advantage of the Iranian regime's isolation by the United States to secure a new trade deal. As a result, Romania secured a generous supply of Iranian crude oil, catapulting Iran into one of Romania's top trade partners. The additional advantage was that oil imports from Iran did not have to be paid with hard currency, given that trade with Iran (as with many other Third World nations) was conducted in barter. By engaging in such maneuvers, the Romanian regime was able to make up for lost domestic production and Soviet supplies and retain the status of a net oil exporter throughout the course of the 1980s, a demand made much more urgent by Bucharest's need to service its hard-currency debt to Western lenders.

Comecon Integrationists: Czechoslovakia and Bulgaria

While Hungary, Poland, and Romania spent the 1970s overcoming ideological, political, and institutional barriers toward engaging with the capitalist world, Czechoslovakia's leadership was much less open to a policy of trade reorientation toward the West, and Bulgaria's modest efforts at import-led growth were less spectacular and in the end proved less fruitful. Both countries remained deeply embedded in trade with the USSR, by choice in the case of Czechoslovakia, and by sheer default in the case of Bulgaria.

Czechoslovakia stood out as the Comecon region's politically most conservative regime. After the swift reversal of reforms in 1968, the Czechoslovak Party under Husák staunchly refused to meddle with centralized planning. It also stuck to its commitment to Soviet and Comecon trade, engaging minimally in import-led growth or other trade policies involving the West. None of these were impediments to the growth of Czechoslovakia's economy. In the 1971–1975 period, its NMP grew by 5.7 percent—a growth rate falling on the lower end of the range, but nonetheless impressive for a country that had less catching up to do than most of its socialist neighbors.

But what other countries were gaining by their "advantages of backwardness" and the import of new technology from the West, was for Czechoslovakia a loss of competitiveness in its leading sectors, especially engineering. The USSR and the GDR remained Czechoslovakia's largest trading partners, but in the course of the decade, Czechoslovakia's historically positive trade balance with these and other Comecon partners was turning increasingly negative (Holesovsky 1977, 710). Demand for Czechoslovak manufactures fell, as they entered into competition against West German, British, or American products. In the course of the 1970s, Polish, Hungarian, Romanian, and even Bulgarian products also improved in quality and could match the quality of Czechoslovak products. Another factor working to the disadvantage of Czechoslovakia were rising prices of Soviet commodity imports.

Changes in the Comecon pricing regime affected resource-dependent economies like Czechoslovakia. The fact that Soviet commodities exported to Comecon members were underpriced was something that Soviet officials had been aware since at least the 1960s. The 1973 oil price shock gave impetus to Soviet demands to revise Comecon price formulas. While the prices of many goods were determined on a bilateral basis, the price of a number of commodities were indexed to a reference world market price. Until 1975, these followed the so-called Bucharest price formula. This formula set price levels at the beginning of the five-year period. Price levels were determined by using average world market prices during the previous period, which would then remained fixed until the next five-year period. The rapidly rising prices of oil and other raw materials in world markets put the USSR at a disadvantage. Eventually, Soviet pressure led to the adoption of a new price formula that determined Comecon prices on the basis of an annual rolling average. The standard formula was planned to include the previous five years, but for the first new price revision in 1975, prices were averaged for only three years, thereby increasing the weight of the oil-price hike of 1973. The enactment of the new price formula in 1975 meant that Central and Eastern European economies would be abruptly burdened with significantly higher prices for Soviet oil and other commodities (Zwass 1989, 97–99).

This policy hurt Czechoslovakia in particular, as 90 percent of its oil and most other raw commodities were imported from the USSR. After Poland, Czechoslovakia was the bloc's largest importer of Soviet oil. As a result of Comecon price revisions, between 1974 and 1975 the price Czechoslovakia was charged for oil more than doubled (Trend 1976, 4). In addition to the higher prices for oil and other commodities, Soviet officials were also unhappy and more vocal in their protests against the price and quality of manufactured goods they were importing from partners like Czechoslovakia. Hence, while the prices charged for Soviet commodities increased, the prices of Central and Eastern European exports remained largely unchanged. This led to some controversy. Czechoslovak representatives raised price issues at the 34th Session of the Comecon Council in 1980 and continued to complain that their exports were undervalued. They also raised concerns for the largely limited success in Comecon specialization and were not shy to point out that Czechoslovak industry could manage well without it (RFE/RL 1981). But while this claim may have been valid in the 1950s, it was becoming increasing questionable in the 1980s, as Czechoslovakia's declining competitiveness and rising import bill would force the Czechoslovak Party, having embraced in a much more limited way Hungarian- and Polish-style import-led growth, to seek to intensify cooperation within Comecon. The Czechoslovak party also pursued an independent path in trying to achieve goals of technological upgrade. In 1980 the party authorized the establishment of the Ministry of Electrical Engineering and Electronics in an effort to direct and encourage endogenous technological research and development. In 1984, the party endorsed a "Long-Term Complex Program for the Electronization of the National Economy up to 1995" with the goal of both increasing the domestic production of computers and increasing their use across economic sectors (RFE/RL 1985). The shaking up of economic policy in the 1980s by no means approached the radical reforms of pre-1968, but they signaled the Czechoslovak leadership's growing awareness of the country's economic lag. More importantly, they would start the economic reform ball rolling again in Czechoslovakia, with a series of important policy changes implemented in the late 1980s.

How Effective Were Import-Led Growth Policies?

The entire premise of import-led growth was that socialist economies would make efficiency gains and improve product quality by importing Western technology. This premise both drove policymaking in East Europe in the 1970s as well as informed Cold War analysts on the other side of the iron curtain. Indeed, the evidence that imports of Western technology led to increased efficiency is partial at best. They were not ultimately responsible for either increasing output or improving the country's export position in relation to the West. While imports of Western technology seemed to correlate with increases in labor productivity, on closer examination this process ultimately seems to be driven by endogenous factors. This section analyzes investment and output data from the key period of import-led growth to show the limited impact of Western technology in efficiency gains in East Europe. The reasons for this are chiefly institutional.

In a classic study, Morris Bornstein (1985) cites three main challenges in the importation of Western capital goods by the European socialist nations. First, there was the familiar problem of Western export controls, which limited exports of high-end technologies to Communist states. The second was the problem of financing imports. As Chapter 2 shows, imports of Western technology and other goods were limited by access to hard currency. Finally, the effectiveness of Western technology imports was also constrained by the ability of East European industries to assimilate and diffuse new technologies, given the presumed incentives against innovation under central planning. These favored quantity over quality and reliance on tried and tested ways of doing things as opposed to risky experimentation with novel techniques. The same incentives made socialist industry less eager to introduce new products.

The decade between 1970 and 1980 is a useful demarcation for examining the impact of Western technology on economic change because a number of the obstacles cited by Bornstein are eased. In this section I leverage economic performance data to examine the impact of Western capital goods imports across the East European economies during the crucial transformative decade of the 1970s. The section examines the effectiveness of the strategy of import-led growth on the East European goals of intensive development: improving efficiency and quality and expanding export shares in Western markets. Clearly, the latter goal was not shared evenly across all the East European party-states, as the preceding discussion shows. Poland, Hungary, and Romania were at the forefront of embracing and implementing extensive import-led policies, though within distinct institutional settings and distinct aims. These policies were less pronounced in the USSR and Czechoslovakia, while there were moderate attempts to increase Western exports in Bulgaria. Nonetheless, trade with the West increased significantly during the period, and did so across the board for all the Comecon nations. It also declined after 1980, when a variety of factors reduced the export of East European goods to the West. Hungary, Romania, and Poland made the most impressive gains in exports, and also lost market share most severely during the first years of the 1980s debt crisis. While growth fell sharply at the turn of the decade, standard deviations show that changes *between* sectors varied tremendously, as some sectors lost more market share and/or reduced imports of Western capital goods more dramatically than others (see Figure 3.4). With the exception of Poland, where OECD exports fell across the board, the picture in other countries is much more mixed. The fall in imports of Western goods is more striking and no doubt influenced by the impact of the debt crisis in the beginning of the 1980s. Romania and Poland greatly reduced the importation of Western capital goods, and they did so across industrial sectors. But the picture is more varied in Hungary, while

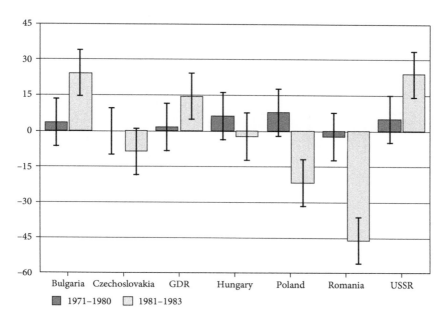

Figure 3.4. Growth of East European exports to OECD in 1971–1980 and 1981–1983
NOTE: Bars show average annual percentage change across sectors while lines show standard deviations.
SOURCE: Author's calculations from OECD data reported in *East-West Technology Transfer* (Wiener and Slater [1986]).

Bulgaria and the USSR increased their imports in the early 1980s. This indicates that economic policy in the 1970s and changes caused by events in 1980 and after varied in their impact not only across states but also across industrial sectors.

An analysis of data from the OECD, a source that includes data originating from Comecon countries, shows that the impact of Western capital goods is limited (see Figure 3.5).[10] Two analyses have been carried out. The first examines the impact of Western capital goods on the growth of exports to OECD countries, on overall growth of output, and on labor productivity. The second examines the overall impact of foreign debt on industrial performance and exports.

The growth of exports to OECD countries, which was significant during the 1970s, would indicate successful penetration of Western markets. It would also suggest concomitant increases in product quality, given the competitive nature of Western markets. A portion of this quality improvement could be

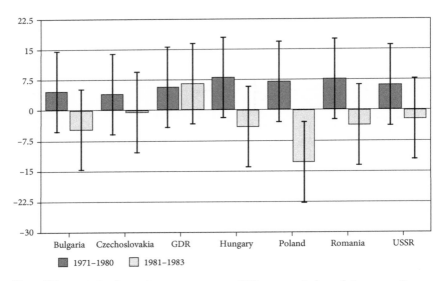

Figure 3.5. Growth of East European imports of Western capital goods in 1971–1980 and 1981–1983

NOTE: Bars show annual average percentage change across sectors while lines show standard deviations.

SOURCE: Author's calculations from OECD data reported in *East-West Technology Transfer* (Wiener and Slater [1986]).

attributed to the greater employment of Western technology and innovative production techniques introduced exogenously into the domestic economy. On the one hand, it would appear that the import-led growth strategy successfully employed new technology to improve the market share of the nation's output in rich country markets. On the other hand, the impact of Western capital goods could be claimed to lie mainly in improvements in domestic production, resulting in higher output growth. Finally and most crucially, Western technology could be seen to help socialist countries succeed in their drive for improvements in labor productivity through the introduction of time-saving technologies and techniques of production that more advanced Western technology enabled. These claims are examined through average growth data across ten industrial sectors for the periods 1971–1975 and 1976–1980 for all seven Comecon countries.[11]

Table 3.1 presents the results of an ordinary least squares (OLS) regression analysis. The analysis finds that increases in imports of Western capital goods had a very small and insignificant impact on exports to the OECD. This holds

Table 3.1. OLS regression analysis examining the impact of capital goods imports, investment, employment, and labor productivity growth on growth in exports to the OECD

Variables	Model 1	Model 2	Model 3	Model 4	Model 5
Capital goods imports	0.01	−0.02	0.01	−0.01	0.19
	(−0.046)	(−0.058)	(−0.059)	(−0.062)	(−0.129)
Investment		0.08	−0.04	−0.02	−0.01
		(−0.113)	(−0.123)	(−0.124)	(−0.123)
Employment			0.86***	0.81***	0.79***
			(−0.391)	(−0.396)	(−0.393)
Labor productivity				0.34	0.57*
				(−0.362)	(−0.383)
Capital goods imports* Labor productivity					−0.04**
					(−0.023)
Constant	6.13***	5.75***	5.24***	3.57**	2.83
	(−0.8)	(−0.963)	(−0.998)	(−2.055)	(−2.083)
Observations	128	128	126	126	126
R-squared	0	0	0.04	0.05	0.07
Adj. R-squared	−0.01	−0.01	0.02	0.02	0.03

NOTE: Standard errors in parentheses. *** $p < 0.05$, ** $p < 0.1$, * $p < 0.15$

even when controlling for growth in domestic investment. There is a correlation between growth of exports to the OECD and growth in employment, which may be the result of either employment policy at the national level or of industrial associations in high-exporting sectors using their growing leverage over export earnings to successfully push for increases in employment. I comment on the relationship between investments, employment, and labor productivity later.

The growth of imports of Western capital goods has a statistically significant relationship with growth in overall output. This relationship holds when domestic investment is introduced in the model, but the impact of domestic investment on output growth is higher than that resulting from the introduction of Western technology. This may be an expected outcome, given the traditional role played by domestic investment in output growth in the centrally planned economies. However, the effect of investment turns negative (though statistically insignificant) when a third variable, employment, is added to the model. Growth in employment emerges as the primary driver of the growth in overall levels of production when controlling for Western capital goods imports. This suggests that production levels may have improved as a result of a combination of growth in employment and (presumed) increasing application of Western technology. The dramatic rise in the predictability level (the value of R^2) of the three-variable model demonstrates the long-observed relationship between production and employment in socialist economies.

If employment growth lies at the foundation of growth in output, what role did Western capital goods play? Growth in the importation of Western capital goods is positively correlated with growth in labor productivity. Indeed, the impact on labor productivity is positive even when controlling for investment and employment. So while Western capital goods may not have been extremely effective in increasing exports to the West, they did create marginal gains in labor productivity.

These patterns prompt a closer examination of the relationship between Western capital goods, employment, labor productivity, and exports to the OECD. Were Western capital goods effective at increasing labor productivity, as these findings suggest? There is no systematic evidence on the levels of absorption of Western technology by socialist industry—that is, their effective use in the actual production process. But the existing data may provide some clue as to whether the combination of Western capital goods and improvements in labor productivity contributed to each country's position as an exporting nation vis-à-vis OECD markets. Model 4 in Table 3.1 adds the impact of labor productivity to exports. Its effects do not show statistical significance. However, this changes when an interaction term between Western capital goods and labor productivity is added to the model (model 5). The impact of labor productivity is now statistically significant and positive on growth in exports, but the impact of the interaction term is negative. This suggests that labor productivity may be improving as a result of processes *other than* the importation of Western capital goods. A similar pattern obtains with production levels, as employment and labor productivity are strongly correlated with rising output, while the effects of Western capital goods and domestic investment are virtually reduced to zero. While it is difficult to confirm such a statement given the limitations of the current data, the claim that Western capital goods helped to improve labor productivity, which then led to greater exports to the OECD, or growth in domestic output, is put in serious doubt.

Why did Western technology have such a limited impact on socialist industry, since even in the heyday of import-led growth, actual growth seemed to have been still mainly determined by the traditional factors of the centrally planned economy—investment and employment? Moreover, what explains the gains in labor productivity if they are not determined simply by the use of more efficient techniques being introduced from the West?

As pointed out earlier, most imports of Western capital goods consist of low-end technologies. Socialist countries were not importing advanced technology, many of which remained on Western lists of banned export goods. This suggests that the impact of such capital goods is expected to be minimal, since socialist planners and industrial managers used Western imports to add to or replace existing machinery with similar technology, as opposed to exchanging them for more advanced technology. The latter would be problematic from a structural perspective as well. As Karl Marx recognized in his distinction between fixed and variable capital, capitalist technical advances in production, transforming what Marx called the organic composition of capital, are introduced mainly because of their labor-saving value. This was anathema to socialist industry, where both national policy of full employment and the tendency of industrial managers to hoard labor worked against optimizing capital and worker productivity. Labor-saving techniques would create employment redundancy. This would create a direct problem at the enterprise level, as well as an issue for national economic planning. The fetishizing of advanced technology by both Cold War economists in the West and by East European socialist reformers seemed to neglect the fact that capitalist labor-saving technology was not always compatible with socialist labor-maximizing industry. Socialist industry was not in the habit of replacing workers with machines, nor did it operate under the same cost considerations of capitalist technological innovation, which was all about reducing labor involvement in the production process.

The other part of the explanation is institutional. The aim of import-led growth was never increasing exports to the West alone. Romania's Stalinist globalization offers an exaggerated view of the socialist economies in the 1970s, in which debt-financed investments are channeled throughout legacy sectors and do not necessarily favor sectors with high export prospects. Western capital goods were just as crucial for legacy industries in metallurgy and fuel as they were for the apparently more competitive light industries like food processing, textiles, and wood and paper, which seemed to have greater success in establishing a foothold in Western markets. As socialist states incur debt in order to finance the acquisition of Western capital goods, these goods are just as likely equipment and machinery intended for oil refineries and steel mills as they are for light industry. These domestic imbalances contribute to the limited utility of

Western capital goods as they are not channeled toward sectors in which they might produce the greatest improvements in efficiency and product quality.

There are distinct sectoral patterns within countries, however. And it is in the divergence after 1980 that a more sustainable form of export specialization emerges in Central and Eastern Europe, in which the region's future (post-1989) global industries take shape.

An analysis of country-level sectoral averages reveals that some countries were more successful in leveraging Western capital goods for expanded exports than others. A sectoral analysis shows that the economies at the forefront of import-led growth exhibited the highest within-country cross-sectoral impact of Western capital goods imports on exports (Figure 3.6). The impact on exports of Western capital goods is highest in Hungary, the GDR, Romania, and Poland, and the correlations are statistically significant. The data covers the period 1971–1983. The data may thus indicate the long-term impact of Western capital goods imports on the world competitiveness of individual sectors within specific socialist economies, even as domestic and world economic conditions took a turn for the worse after 1980.

Important variations emerge at the cross-sectoral level as well. Interestingly, the most robust correlations between Western capital goods and

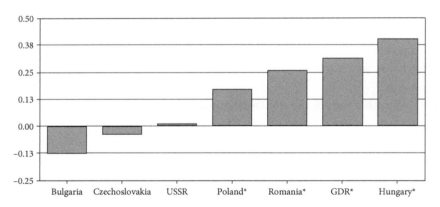

Figure 3.6. Graphical representation of OLS regression coefficients indicating the predicted impact of the growth of imports of Western capital goods on growth in exports to the OECD, across sectors and by country, for the combined observational periods 1971–1975, 1976–1980, and 1981–1983

NUMBER OF OBSERVATIONS: Bulgaria (27), Czechoslovakia (30), the GDR (23), Hungary (25), Poland (29), Romania (28), USSR (29).
NOTE: An asterisk (*) denotes statistical significance at the $p < 0.10$ level.

increased exports emerge in the fuel, metallurgy, and food sectors. The significance of fuel (including oil refinery and natural gas production) may partly reflect a bias of the USSR, where a great deal of imports of Western equipment went into the energy sector. When individual country control variables (in the form of dummy variables) are introduced in the sectoral models, the USSR is very strongly associated with export increases in the energy and fuel sectors. By contrast, other East European states are more strongly associated with increases in exports (as predicted by the larger imports of Western capital goods) in the food and metallurgy sectors. The dummy variable for Hungary captures a great deal of the variation in food exports, being strongly associated with higher exports in that sector, while Poland is associated with a negative tendency in exports of chemicals. Romania is positively correlated with increases in all sectors except wood and paper, but the analysis does not warrant definitive claims as these are statistically insignificant, with the exception of the areas of production classified as other light industry. What is suggested here is that the benefits of Western capital goods differed not only across countries but also across sectors, as export specialization was taking shape. The USSR was carving out its long-term specialization as a fuel exporter, and Hungary was increasing its specialization in light industry, while Poland and Romania were increasing specialization in heavy and intermediate industries.

What overall judgment can be passed on the effectiveness of the policy of debt growth on the industrial and export performance of socialist countries? The answer involves examining aggregate macroeconomic rates of growth as opposed to the sectoral ones analyzed in the preceding discussion. Interestingly, the overall impact of debt growth is negatively correlated with exports, when controlling for imports of Western capital goods and domestic investment. Indeed, debt growth is not correlated strongly with increases in the imports of Western capital goods, which suggests that a good deal of the borrowing, as some East European economists of the era pointed out, was used to finance ongoing transactions (such as purchases of intermediate goods) rather than acquisitions of capital goods. At the same time, there is no consistency in the relationship between growth of debt with growth in overall output, suggesting no strong pattern in the use of debt financing for the purposes of economic growth. These results change when the latter period of 1981–1983 is included in the analysis. For the entire period, we find that debt is positively associated with output growth, but virtually nonexistent for growth in exports.

These findings highlight the fact that despite purported upgrade goals, debt financing in East Europe could not overcome the existing institutional limitations of central planning. The macroeconomic inefficiencies of the planning system, as well as entrenched interests within the large and established industrial associations, made it an inflexible system to take full advantage of the opportunities provided by the relative opening of Western credit and product markets in the 1970s. This led to investments producing marginal gains in output, but not in the ability of East European enterprise to establish permanent footholds in Western markets. The socialist countries turned valiantly to the capitalist world economy with the aim of, if not conquering it, at least exhibiting their competence in competing in it with their productive capabilities and technical knowledge. In the end, they turned out to be ineffective actors in that world and were ultimately run down by the forces they unleashed on themselves.

The above analysis shows that policies of industrial upgrade in the 1970s would become important not so much for turning socialist countries into major export players, but in the organizational transformations they would generate internally, and especially the legacy of ties the period left behind between socialist industry and Western transnational enterprise. Chapter 4 discusses this in greater detail.

Conclusion

Reform socialism, whose political and intellectual roots lay in the late 1950s but which officially commenced with the Hungarian reforms of 1968, ushered in an era of institutional reform in East European economies. While motivated by domestic concerns over socialist economic performance, these reforms temporally intersected with upheavals in the world economy that gave these measures a particular (and originally unintended) direction. Those events included the 1973 oil shock and the beginning of economic recessions in the capitalist world, and the ensuing dollar glut that vastly expanded hard-currency credit in international markets. In themselves, these developments were not of direct consequence to the socialist economies, but they created a set of structural opportunities and strains that would begin to reshape organizational patterns in East European industry.

The strain, of course, stemmed from the rising price of oil and other commodities, which had direct impact on the USSR. As the USSR pressured its Comecon trade partners to accept new pricing arrangements that were more directly reflective of world market prices, the process ultimately led to changing terms of trade that gradually brought the era of cheap Soviet commodities to a close and forced Central and Eastern European economies to find new ways of covering growing trade deficits. The opportunities came as a result of the expansion of international dollar markets that allowed profuse flows of cheap money into socialist economies. These monies provided the means for socialist economies to, in the course of the 1970s, temporarily overcome one of the key obstacles to East-West trade, engage in a major cycle of investments, and begin creating interorganizational ties to emerging world market players, TNCs. This growing export orientation was combined with domestic institutional reforms that increasingly devolved trade authority from a political matter decided by central ministries to a set of commercial decisions made by FTOs, enterprises, and industrial associations.

The debt crisis of the 1980s, whose origins are linked directly to the contractionary interest rate policy of the US Federal Reserve, brought the era of import-led growth to a dramatic halt. East-West trade was already cumbersome given extensive political and legal barriers, but near impossible without access to hard currency. Furthermore, the efforts of these nation-states to gain permanent shares in Western export markets were proving a failure; the importation of Western capital goods was not proving to be the panacea for socialist industry, as promised by reformers. Indeed, output and export growth was still mainly accounted for by factors that were endogenous to socialist economies, although individual countries benefited from the import-led model more than others, mainly as a consequence of internal reforms. However, in the 1980s, as socialist countries diverted more of their hard-currency earnings to finance debt service, overall trade with the West floundered.

But the period of import-led growth provided important organizational ties that would prove key in the remaking of Central and Eastern European economies when a new opportunity for institutional reform arrived after the fall of Communist Party rule across the region in 1989. The legacy of this period would provide the essential organizational means for industrial restructuring and renewal, based on an entirely new institutional model, the market economy. How these organizational links were mobilized and how they transformed the path of Central and Eastern European industry in the context of massive political upheaval is discussed in Chapter 4.

Socialist Protoglobalization and Patterns of Uneven Transnational Integration After 1989

4

> What we need, in effect, is a form of structural history that is rarely practiced, which finds in each successive state of the structure under examination both the product of previous struggles to maintain or to transform this structure, and the principle, via the contradictions, the tensions, and the relations of force which constitute it, of subsequent transformations.
>
> —Pierre Bourdieu, *An Invitation to Reflexive Sociology*[1]

Chapter 3 examines patterns of economic reform and trade orientation during the reform socialist period and their consequences for East European industrial development. The discussion in this chapter turns to economic policy after the unravelling of Communist Party rule in 1989 and the beginnings of the making of the region's transnationalized economies. In particular, the chapter looks at the rise of FDI both as a new policy orientation and as a process of capital flows with institutionally transformative consequences in postsocialist economies. While the previous chapters focus largely on political elites and macro-institutional change during the late socialist era, this chapter shifts attention to the impact of institutional change and organizational processes at the firm level during the immediate postsocialist period in driving the transition toward globally integrated postsocialist industries. This chapter seeks to trace the process of what can be called socialist protoglobalization—that is, the expansion of organizational ties between socialist enterprise with TNCs in the course of the era of reform socialism and its causal significance for regional patterns of economic transnationalization after 1989.[2]

If socialist protoglobalization of the 1970s mattered at all for the reconstitution of postsocialist economies after 1989, it is in the context of the great uncertainties of the early transition period that we should observe the importance of continuities and the strongest impact of legacies. This chapter demonstrates continuities between socialist protoglobalization and postsocialist FDI. It identifies organizational mechanisms that enabled the regionally uneven integration of local industrial assets inherited from the socialist era into a post-1989 transnational production regime. These organizational resources operated in ways that privileged some economic actors and states over others in the ensuing process of economic restructuring via FDI. In other words, the chapter offers an alternative explanation for patterns of FDI in Central and Eastern Europe during the immediate postsocialist period to those that account for uneven flows based solely on the relative distribution of costs, policy differences, cultural variables, or overall levels of industrial advancement.

This chapter examines the changing organizational vehicles of TNC involvement in the Central and Eastern European economies from pre-1989 to post-1989. During this time integration based on symmetrical contractual arrangements of collaboration and cooperation with local actors was increasingly replaced by direct and asymmetrical organizational control of local assets by TNCs. TNC strategy went through a transitional period in which the mode of local operation shifted from establishing partnerships and joint ventures with local partners to direct acquisition of local assets. Against conventional views that TNC entry into the postsocialist economies was a novelty of the post-1989 liberalization era, this chapter reveals evidence of systematic continuities in that process.

Chapter 4 is organized into eight sections. First, I discuss the political and policy context of postsocialist reform after 1989 and the reasons for the turn of policymakers toward FDI as a postsocialist developmental strategy. Next, I describe limitations in existing explanations for East Europe's uneven transnational integration after 1989 and develop this book's alternative explanation by identifying and defining the role of what I call transnational organizational capital. In the third section, I trace the origins of transnational organizational capital in the era of socialist protoglobalization in the 1970s, while in the fourth section, I provide empirical support for the continuities argument through an analysis of correlations between the regional diffusion of transnational organizational capital before 1989 and the distribution of FDI after 1989, as well as patterns of transition from joint ventures to direct control immediately before and after the political revolutions of 1989–1990.

The fifth section provides additional support for the continuities argument by showing how transnational integration could and did proceed without FDI, particularly in sectors that had proven most successful in accessing Western markets during the import-led growth era of the 1970s. Then, I devote attention to the Czech case, explaining its apparent divergence from patterns of transnational integration observed elsewhere in the region. I return to the question of continuities from a different angle in the seventh section, demonstrating that immediate gains during post-1989 globalization—at least in the early era of reform—were unevenly made by economies that had been at the forefront of import-led growth in the 1970s. Finally, in the conclusion I summarize this chapter's analyses and findings.

The Policy Context of Postsocialist Reform: FDI as a Solution

Chapter 3 illustrates the debates unleashed in the course of the 1960s over the plan and the market in East European socialism. Just as conservative party backlashes after 1968 put an abrupt end to radical visions of market socialism, the political revolutions of 1989 also decisively settled the debate against the plan in favor of what Czech economist and post-Communist politician Václav Klaus called a "market economy without adjectives" (*Economist* 1990).

No justice is done here to the diversity of actors and fierce debates over the ideas, goals, strategies, and package of concrete reform policies that governments across the post-Communist world devised and implemented with the goal of constructing market economies (Kornai 1990; Sachs and Woo 1994; Gowan 1995; Orenstein 2001; Appel 2004; Åslund 2007; Frye 2010; Bohle and Greskovits 2012; Ban 2016). This chapter instead speaks of a general and broadly constituted marketization project, whose shared aims were to transition state socialist economies from the plan to the market. From the perspective of post-Communist governments, the marketization project consisted of two key pillars. The first was economic liberalization, which involved the dismantling of central management of domestic production and distribution through the corporatization of enterprises, the liberalization of prices, and the introduction of exchange rate convertibility to facilitate foreign trade. The second pillar was privatization, which took the next step of divesting the state of ownership of industry and other assets. Though intricately related, both sets of policies followed separate timings and institutional tracks (Lavigne 1999).

These policies were followed under the guidance and advice of the IMF and Western economists who took up key advisory positions in postsocialist governments (Wedel 1998). Among the policies advocated by Western advisors and domestic reformers to address the region's structural difficulties in economic transformation and the need for trade reorientation was for East Europe to fully liberalize domestic FDI regimes. Some of the early reformers, including radical neoliberals like Klaus, had an uneasy relationship with FDI (Klaus 1997; Drahokoupil 2009). FDI was advocated as a solution that simultaneously addressed multiple structural problems in the postsocialist economy. FDI generates renewed investments in industry, upgrades domestic technology, enables rapid firm restructuring, and expands exports to Western markets, all while replenishing the drained coffers of postsocialist governments. FDI would thus not only help facilitate the process of property transformation, its contribution to rapid industrial upgrade and connectivity with Western markets would also increase the chances of capitalism's success. On the political side of the ledger, foreign owners would also help keep so-called red managers (leading technocratic cadres of the socialist era) in check by preventing the rise of a new nomenklatura capitalism. Considering the alternatives, the temptation of FDI as a policy instrument was irresistible. While international financial institutions enthusiastically endorsed FDI, publics became leery of what were described as sinister "foreign takeovers" of the local economy (Lankes and Venables 1996; Drahokoupil 2009; Bandelj 2009). But FDI enjoyed a strong constituency among reformers. Even those who were not enthusiastic about FDI did little to push back (Myant and Drahokoupil 2011).

Another source of pressure to embrace FDI came from the collapse of the trade structure of international socialism with the dissolution of Comecon. In 1990, at Moscow's insistence, the 45th Session of Comecon decided to shift all internal bloc trade to world market prices. It also abandoned the convertible ruble in favor of dollar trade. With these measures effectively destroying the institutional rationale for Comecon, the organization itself was dissolved the following year. The dismantling of international socialism deeply disrupted industrial trade patterns that had evolved since the end of World War II. This disruption helped create part of the dire economic conditions under which reforms were formulated in 1990 and after. Indeed, some economists saw the dissolution of Comecon as one of the chief causes of the region's dramatic decline in output after 1990 (Rodrik 1992). Trade reorientation became one of the key challenges of postsocialist industry, as the once secure Comecon markets for East European producers evaporated overnight and expanding presence in Western markets became a top priority for both policymakers and firms.

As a result, after 1989, many of the constraints on foreign investment were lifted and trade and foreign exchange policy liberalized. Domestic reforms to liberalize and open up economies were paralleled at the international level by European Union (EU) efforts to commence a process of economic integration via trade and investments in the wake of Comecon's demise. By 1992, the EU had signed association agreements liberalizing trade with virtually all states in Central and Eastern Europe. While economic cooperation agreements of the 1970s and 1980s were in principle partnerships of equals between TNCs and local actors, the dramatic institutional changes beginning in the late 1980s and early 1990s created the opportunity for new forms of TNC control. With the lifting of restrictions on trade and foreign ownership, foreign investors could now begin to exercise direct control by establishing local subsidiaries and acquiring local assets. For many local firms, foreign investment represented a clear opportunity for technological upgrade and access to new markets, but more importantly, the chance for organizational certainty in the context of uncertain institutional reform and declining demand from traditional clients. In other words, changing international and domestic institutions combined with growing TNC interest to produce a radically new FDI *regime* for Central and Eastern Europe.

In the course of the early 1990s, FDI not only represented the largest type of capital inflow in the reforming economies but also a central force in the restructuring of Central and Eastern European industry (Myant and Drahokoupil 2011; Bohle and Greskovits 2012). Leading TNCs with major investments became prime agents in restructuring existing industries, and they expanded into new sectors by bringing in new investment as well as upgrading capital equipment and rapidly linking Central and Eastern European production with transnational networks and export markets in the West (Berend 2009, 108–133). As Table 4.1 shows, FDI inflows into Central and Eastern Europe were highly uneven. In the 1990s, Hungary, Poland, and the Czech Republic became the prime recipients of FDI, with Hungary in particular standing out as the dominant destination. By contrast, Bulgaria, Romania, and Slovakia—not to speak of post-Soviet Russia—quickly fell to the bottom of the list. The high-FDI countries also proved the most effective in expanding trade with the West (Lankes and Venables 1996). Between 1989 and 1991, Hungary received roughly half of all FDI inflows in *all* former socialist economies (Young 1993). By 1995, Hungary had accumulated an FDI stock of roughly $11 billion. Within a few short years of liberalization, Hungary came to accommodate an FDI stock equivalent to over a quarter of its GDP. Only Poland and the Czech Republic came close. Other countries attracted less impressive amounts. Russia, with a much larger (and exceedingly more resource-rich) economy than Hungary's, attracted only half of Hungary's level. In terms of GDP, by 1995, overall FDI *stock* in Russia represented a mere 2 percent of its GDP.

Table 4.1. FDI stock in select years

	FDI stock in 1989 (in millions USD)	FDI stock in 1995 (in millions USD)	FDI stock as a percentage of GDP in 1995	Per capita FDI stock in 1995	FDI stock in 2000 (in millions USD)	FDI stock in 2010 (in millions USD)
Hungary	0	11,304	28	1,097	22,870	90,777
Poland	0	7,843	6	203	34,227	201,003
Czech Republic (after 1992)	—	7,350	14	714	21,644	128,504
Slovak Republic (after 1992)	—	1,297	5	240	4,762	50,284
Czech and Slovak Republics combined (Czechoslovakia before 1992)	1,479	8,647	11.2*	551*	26,406	178,788
Russia (USSR before 1991)	4.76	5,601	2	38	32,204	490,560
Romania	0.01	821	2	36	6,953	70,264
Bulgaria	108	445	<1	53	2,704	46,874

SOURCE: UNCTAD, World Bank Development Indicators, and author's calculations.

NOTE: An asterisk (*) indicates means are weighted by GDP.

A great deal of FDI in the early 1990s resulted from the acquisition of existing firms by TNCs (Artisien and Rojec 2001). While the service sector became
a significant target of FDI, most FDI poured into traditional manufacturing activities (UNECE 1996). The EBRD (1994, 123) estimated that between 1991 and
1994 nearly two-thirds of all FDI inflows in East Europe went into manufacturing. The effects of industrial transformation in some countries were dramatic.
By 1995, in Hungary the output of foreign-owned firms amounted to 40 percent
of the total value added in manufacturing (the average regional level was less
than 8 percent). That is, it took no more than a few years from the demise
of Communism for TNCs to become dominant actors in Hungarian industry.
FDI proved critical in the rapid structural transformation of Central and Eastern European industry, no matter that the region's admittance into the EU was
uncertain and still years away (Berend 2009; Bandelj 2010).

The existing literature offers several explanations for this highly uneven
global economic integration via FDI during the early era of reform. In economics, standard explanations have relied on neoclassical frames to explain
patterns by focusing on marginal cost differences across economies. Another
set of approaches has focused on policy differences between countries. A recent
wave of literature has taken a more contextual approach, looking at cultural
ties and industrial legacies. The following discussion evaluates these explanations and demonstrates the importance of past organizational capacities in
interpreting the region's global integration and its patterns during the immediate postsocialist period as a direct consequence of the legacy of 1970s socialist
protoglobalization.

Existing Explanations of Uneven Transnational Integration in the 1990s

Early analyses of Central and Eastern Europe's global economic integration explained the divergences between countries like Hungary and Poland, on the
one hand, and Russia and Bulgaria, on the other, by emphasizing differences in
policy factors, in particular the pace and depth of postsocialist market reform.
In this view, FDI inflows were a reward for states that reformed most extensively; so the more resolute and comprehensive the market reform, the more
foreign investment flew into economies (Artisien, Rojec, and Svetlicic 1993;
Fish 1998). The EBRD suggested that "successful" market reforms resulted in
"stable macroeconomic conditions and predictable government policies [that]
have doubtless been decisive in explaining the initial success of the principal

FDI destinations" (1994, 141). This view has two problems. First, while economic reforms began earlier in Hungary than elsewhere, it is not clear why equally radically reforming countries like Slovenia, which emerged as one of the region's most stable economies after its secession from Yugoslavia in 1991, lagged behind Hungary in comparable levels of FDI. Second, this view does not explain behavior on the supply side. Namely, if states are at comparable stages of reform, and if marginal cost considerations are key, what drove TNC decisions to invest in countries like Hungary, where costs of doing business were higher, than in places like Poland and Bulgaria? The view that reforms improve domestic market conditions, which then result in greater levels of FDI, is premised on the belief that TNCs operate as rational actors in a locational FDI "market," choosing investment locations strictly on the basis of comparable cost considerations. Research shows, however, that global FDI patterns do not reflect such a logic, given distinct patterns of regional concentration that cannot be accounted for by locational advantages distributed according to marginal cost differences (UNCTAD 2007, 2015). A number of economists concede that a country's attraction as an FDI destination depends not only on purely market considerations but also on the nature of domestic institutions. Investment decisions are also constrained by regulatory and policy frameworks—that is, what some term the "investment climate" (Kostevc, Redek, and Rojec 2011, 156). These variables include trade, taxation, and labor and product market regulation as well as less tangible public goods such as "economic, political, and social stability." In the postsocialist economies, privatization policy—and the extent to which it favored or even actively sought foreign buyers of domestic assets—was also a key determinant of the initial wave of FDI.

Neither pure market considerations nor institutional stability nor reform nor specific policies favoring FDI sufficiently explain patterns of FDI in Central and Eastern Europe. From a constructivist standpoint, Nina Bandelj (2008) argues that previously existing social and cultural ties connecting investors with recipient countries were the key to facilitating entry of FDI into Central and Eastern Europe. In this view, it is not institutions and comparative market conditions that explain FDI patterns, but relational social and cultural ties, such as those shared through linguistic ties and the existence of diasporas and ethnic minority communities between investor and recipient nations. These features and other forms of "cultural match" between investor and recipient were critical in establishing the social relations necessary to conduct foreign transactions on a large scale and within institutional contexts laden with uncertainty.

Bandelj calls these "multiplex social ties" that mediate between actors involved in transnational market exchanges. By contrast, Dorothee Bohle and Béla Greskovits (2012, 87–91) emphasize the importance of socialist industrial legacies in determining FDI-driven postsocialist industrial transformations. Bohle and Greskovits's conception of legacies is macrostructural and relates to the overall industrial profile of the recipient economy. They rely on Vernon's (1971) product-cycle theory to suggest that FDI patterns in postsocialist Eastern Europe reflected variance in levels of complex industrial development in the region. Bohle and Greskovits argue that, while partly conditioned by policy factors such as liberalization and openness, initial FDI flowed to economies with the most complex industries as measured by the sophistication of sectoral mixes of technology, skill, and product diversity (Greskovits 2004, 2014). Given their already advanced industrial and technical development, Hungary, the Czech Republic, Slovakia, and Poland naturally attracted most investments and maintained their lead as FDI destinations in the 2000s and beyond.

While similar to the argument presented here, this view is not without some issues. First, it is doubtful that industrial complexity at the sectoral level alone accounts for the early advantage in investments. There are few indications that Hungarian industry, while larger in overall size, was more complex than sectors of Bulgarian industry in the 1980s. However, Bulgaria fell far behind in attracting comparative levels of TNC interest. Indeed, Greskovits's (2014) own measures of industrial complexity show that in the mid-1990s, Hungary and Romania differed little in terms of the sophistication of their industry, yet differed widely in the speed and depth of the TNC-led transnational integration of their respective manufacturing sectors. In the 1980s, one of Comecon's largest and most technologically advanced industries, the production of computer hardware, was based in Bulgaria, yet it was nearly wiped out after 1989 (Judy and Clough 1989; Rosenbaum 1990). The question is thus not simply one of industrial complexity, but why some sectors became more likely to make rapid transitions to transnational production than others.

The issue, then, is about the origins of industrial complexity and particularly the *kinds* of complexity favored by foreign investors. Clearly, industrial complexity has multiple determinants. As Alice Amsden (2001) argues, industrial complexity depends not only on the sectoral structure of a nation's industry but also on the quality of its human capital, the breadth and depth of its industrial legacy, the investments made in the reproduction of skills, and the maintenance of a technological lead through investment in research and development. On this count, as well, Chapter 3 shows how, from the 1960s on, the initial differences between the countries of East Europe become increasingly blurred. Economies like Czechoslovakia maintained an advantage over regional competitors given a longer industrial tradition. However, the period witnessed the remarkable industrialization of Bulgaria and Romania. Even within Czechoslovakia, the once predominantly agricultural Slovak lands became increasingly industrialized. Investments in human capital formation also expanded relatively evenly across the region, and the diffusion of technical expertise meant that no country would enjoy an absolute advantage in any particular area for very long. While certain comparative advantages and specializations developed within Comecon over the years, the striking feature of East European economies outside of the Soviet Union is their relative similarity, rather than diversity. As Chapters 2 and 3 explain, there were institutional reasons for such homogeneity. The crucial advantage, from an industrial development standpoint, is thus not a state's overall industrial profile, but the types of organizational capacities developed in relation to the TNC sector during the socialist era. Chapter 3 demonstrates the impact transnational production had on socialist industry beginning in the 1970s. The question here is whether the experience of that era had any causal relevance for patterns of industrial transformation after 1989. The following section defines the *organizational* legacy of that experience and its mobilization during FDI-led transnationalization in the 1990s. It shows that comparative levels of transnational integration in the 1990s were for the most part proportionate to the depth of industrial protoglobalization in the socialist period.

The Socialist Origins of Transnational Organizational Capital

As Chapter 3 indicates, during the socialist period, industrial links with Western firms were significant in two ways: They enabled trade with Western economies as well as facilitated technology transfer during the import-led growth period of the 1970s. For East European countries, the policy of import-led growth caused rapid (though temporary) gains in their share of Western import markets. While the disruptions of the 1980s diminished politically the importance of this export-oriented developmental policy—whether in the form of Hungary's and Poland's import-led growth or Romania's Stalinist globalization—they created an important organizational legacy that became especially crucial during the liberalization era. This legacy was found *within* particular

industrial sectors that had adapted not only technological capacities (and therefore human capital capabilities) but also the extensive organizational processes
involved in working and negotiating with actors operating in Western markets.
That is, it was not industrial complexity *per se* that put particular countries at
an advantage, nor were multiplex social connections and cultural affinities with
the outside world alone important. What were important were the *organizational capacities* needed to operate successfully in transnational manufacturing
chains. In the context of an emerging regional market for FDI, this experience
functioned in the form of what, following Bourdieu (1986, 1993), we can term
transnational organizational capital.[3] Possession of such organizational capital
at the firm and sectoral level gave organizational actors an advantage over competitors in terms of technology, human capital, and organizational skills that
enabled them to interact effectively with the organizational culture of TNCs.
The distribution of such organizational capital across the region became, I
argue here, important in a critical area of the transition from socialism, that of
attracting, accommodating, and integrating TNCs as part of the new postsocialist economic landscape.

What did these organizational capacities consist of? These capacities were
cultural, technical, and organizational. First, this organizational capital involved the capacity of actors, especially at the managerial level, to "speak the
language" of international business by knowledge of the codes, norms, and organizational imperatives of Western counterparts (Bandelj 2008). Second, it
involved capacities to align local priorities and production programs with TNC
expectations and performance metrics. This included the technical and technological capabilities to produce goods of quality standards that were satisfactory
to the needs of large, Western-based producers operating in cost-sensitive markets. Lastly, it involved the overall organizational capacity to see a transaction
through to completion. That required not only effective managerial oversight
over the production process but also the ability of management to ensure the
reliability of supply chains in order to predict and resolve potential delays and
deliver goods at agreed-upon schedules. In the late socialist economy, where
quality and production schedules were continuously negotiated between enterprises and where one's ability to impose bottlenecks by controlling valuable
resources could improve one's bargaining position in the supply chain, these
kinds of organizational capacities were in short supply (Kornai 1991). The partial bridging of technological gaps during the era of import-led growth also
meant the lowering of adaptation costs as goods and production processes be-

came increasingly standardized and technically comparable across Cold War frontiers.

An empirical illustration of how such organizational capacities were constructed at the firm level is in order. The formation of long-standing interfirm networks through cooperative arrangements are an obvious way connections between actors were established and maintained. But this was not all of it. The introduction of (often proprietary) technology transformed not only the capital basis but also the skill level of employees in the socialist enterprise. Moreover, TNC involvement also remade management styles and aided in the reorganization of labor processes that mimicked more closely those found in the Western firm's home base. A case study from the role of a TNC's intervention in the reorganization of a Hungarian textile producer in the mid-1970s illustrates this process:

> While the Western firm operated 20–22 machines with 91 percent use of capacities, in Hungary 10 machines ran three shifts using only 78 percent of capacities. The Western firm thoroughly examined the production, organization, structure and management of the Hungarian firm, and suggested ways of improving the existing production pattern, how to develop a new product pattern and what fashion service (know-how) was necessary. For quality control, the foreign firm proposed a completely closed system in which the Hungarian partner would have to carry the consequences of deterioration in quality. The technology, which both improved productivity and quality, and the corresponding know-how, were used principally for the manufacture of cotton and cotton-synthetic mixture products but could also be applied to the whole of the firm in a comprehensive manner (and for this reason is treated as confidential). The Hungarian firm pays a fixed annual fee which includes the costs of instruction. The Western partner has agreed to take a fixed quantity of the new product manufactured with the help of its technology and know-how, over a five year period. The Western partner either sells this without further processing (using its own trademark), or first produces garments from it. The two partners have maximum confidence in one another; one sign of this is that the contract does not stipulate sanctions for delayed shipments. (Bojkó 1977, 160)

This descriptive paragraph captures the key elements of how organizational capacities were constructed: the introduction of organizational patterns of production and management from TNC to socialist enterprise, the diffusion of technology and embodied techniques of production, the growing integration and codependence of the parties in the overall production process, and, most crucially, the enhancement of trust between leading actors that contracts will be honored and standards of quality upheld. As Béla Bójko observed in the 1970s, the "progressive deepening of mutual confidence can not only overcome the handicaps of bureaucracy on both sides, but can also become one of the most important factors in the efficiency of cooperation" (1977, 160–161). This is partly a consequence of the time investment by TNCs in identifying and nurturing relations with local actors. Reporting on the activities of his firm in Poland in the 1970s, a German director advised that the investment of time in getting to know the local environment and its actors is key for a successful cooperative relationship with socialist enterprises: "While it is relatively simple to pick the right foreign trade enterprise, much care must be taken to study all the manufacturers. At this stage it is necessary to talk to as many people as possible, at all levels and within every organization concerned, so as to get a true picture of the capabilities, the expertise, the ambitions, the plans and the past record of success and failure" (Hardt 1977, 167). On the nature of orga- nizational cooperation in the implementation stage, the director pointed out that "there are direct operational links between the various departments and services (design office, quality control, purchasing, spares store etc.)" (169). And on the learning experience during cooperation, he wrote that "especially at the beginning of our agreement, we were confronted with a lack of apprecia- tion for some of our requirements (for constant high quality, good appearance, punctuality, availability of spares, accuracy of spares and service literature, etc.) which our partners obviously thought had been invented by ourselves—typical grumbling German 125-percenters—until we got them to meet our custom- ers, made them conscious of our competitors, and got them to understand the laws of the market" (169). The totality of these organizational processes—an initial familiarity leading to continuous interpersonal relationships, the dif- fuse intra-organizational nature of interorganizational collaboration, and the organizational learning transforming processes (and eventually outputs) of the production process—are the temporally formed structures embodied in the concept of transnational organizational capital. Such organizational capital found in East European firms was cumulative (it was formed over long years of experience) and also uneven (since not all firms experienced close relations with Western TNCs). That this process was widespread is shown by Carl Mc- Millan's survey from the mid-1970s, which finds that, with the exception of the GDR and the USSR, nearly half or more of interfirm agreements involved, in addition to subcontracting and coproduction, the training of personnel by the Western partner (1977, 52–53).

If the existence of transnational organizational capital mattered *causally* after 1989, we ought to observe that patterns of FDI in the early reform period closely follow the availability of these capacities found in individual postsocialist economies. This claim follows the logic of an ecological argument—in an organizational *environment* (a national economy) characterized by a legacy of dense past ties with TNCs, organizational capacities for transnational production are likely to be more diffuse. Diffusion expands the constituency of likely investment (FDI) targets. Legacies of import-led growth create an environment in which potential investors, even those not directly connected to local actors, may find access to reliable information, while the organizational background of the target firm, given its previous experience in transnational production, ensures the investor that the target firm is "up to the task" of the investor's production program and corporate strategy. In other words, where socialist protoglobalization went deeper, rapid postsocialist globalization was more likely. Let us now examine this argument empirically.

Legacies of Socialist Protoglobalization and FDI: Empirical Relationships

How do we uncover the relationship between socialist protoglobalization (which, as is hypothesized here, established and enhanced organizational capacities for transnational production) and flows of FDI after the post-1989 liberalization of East European economies? More specifically, how do we determine that this relationship is also a causal one? There is no systematic and comparable firm-level data on postsocialist firms acquired by foreign investors (TNCs) that would allow the direct analysis of the correspondence between transnational organizational capital as legacies of socialist protoglobalization and foreign acquisitions.[4] Lacking such firm-level data, the analysis turns to macrolevel data and the correlations between socialist-era interfirm agreements and FDI after 1989. Interfirm agreements can serve as a proxy measure for the distribution of organizational capacities for transnational production within an economy. As a reminder, the hypothesis proposed here suggests that economies that developed denser ties in the 1970s generated greater transnational organizational capital, a legacy that then increased the appeal of those industries as a potential target of acquisition by foreign investors—most typically TNCs—in the 1990s. We should, therefore, *ceteris paribus*, see more FDI in countries that inherited denser ties from the era of socialist protoglobalization, and thus the legacy of 1970s protoglobalization ought to map directly onto patterns of FDI in the 1990s.

One general correlation between protoglobalization legacies and foreign investment is illustrated by Figure 4.1, which plots cumulative interfirm agreements operative in 1984 with total FDI stock in 1993. While not a perfect pattern, when plotted against a linear regression line, we observe an overall positive correlation. The timing of FDI openness can partly account for Hungary's lead and Russia's great lag. Hungary's early openness drew large inflows into the country, accounting for its dominance in 1993. But FDI inflows into Hungary slowed after 1995, and by the early 2000s the country lost its status as leader in the attraction of FDI inflows. The Russian case can be explained by the reverse—that is, the lateness by which it entered the new FDI regime. Especially in 1990–1991, as the USSR faced great political uncertainty and crisis, foreign investors proceeded more cautiously. In 1992, Russia emerged as an independent nation and implemented its economic reforms. The Czech case is distinct and the reasons for its outlier status are discussed in a later section.

Figure 4.2 plots past ties against FDI stock in 1995. We can assume that by this point Hungary's first-mover advantage was diminishing, Romania and

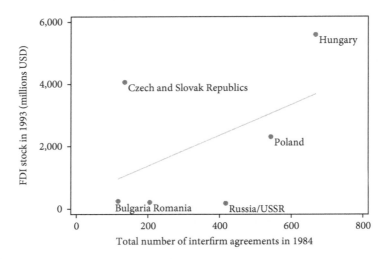

Figure 4.1. Interfirm agreements in 1984 by country plotted against their FDI stock in 1993 (in millions USD)

SOURCE: OECD data reported in *East-West Technology Transfer* (Wiener and Slater [1986]), UNCTADstat.

Bulgaria had more forcefully entered the new FDI regime, and Russia had had sufficient time to catch up with the rest. Here we observe that, with the exception of the Czech and Slovak Republics, interfirm ties in the 1980s almost perfectly correlate with FDI stock in 1995. This correlation does not conclusively "prove" the causal relationship proposed here, but it is consistent with the process-driven narrative of socialist protoglobalization operating as a legacy that paves the way for transnational integration via FDI in the 1990s.

Let us examine the relationship between FDI stock in 1995 and other common factors taken to be supportive of FDI inflows. Policy-based approaches suggest that FDI inflows are based on a favorable privatization policy (Artisien, Rojec, and Svetlicic 1993). Namely, states implementing a privatization policy that specifically aims at selling domestic assets to foreign investors has a greater chance of attracting FDI inflows than states that implement a policy that favors domestic owners. Typically, privatization carried out through direct sales has been more favorable to FDI than various insider schemes or mass privatization through distribution of privatization vouchers. With the exception of Hungary, where direct sales were the primary method of privatization, the method was also implemented in limited ways in Bulgaria, Slovakia, and Poland.[5] Yet, besides the Hungarian case, there is no consistency between the use of direct

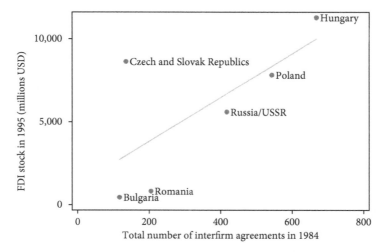

Figure 4.2. Interfirm agreements in 1984 by country plotted against their FDI stock in 1995 (in millions USD)

SOURCE: OECD data reported in *East-West Technology Transfer* (Wiener and Slater [1986]), UNCTADstat.

sales and levels of FDI. Efforts to bid assets to foreign investors in Bulgaria did not fare well, even in such advanced industries as personal computing, and in Slovakia direct sales were mainly used by the postindependence Mečiar regime to channel assets to domestic political allies (Hake 2000; Myant and Drahokoupil 2011). By contrast, domestic owners were clearly favored in the Czech Republic, which was the first to implement voucher privatization from which foreign nationals were expressly excluded. However, the Czech Republic is second only to Hungary in the amount of FDI it attracted in the early 1990s. By contrast, Romania and Russia both relied predominantly on management-employee buyouts (MEBOs) for privatization, in which firm insiders were the chief beneficiaries (Poznanski 1995; Anderson et al. 1997). Overall, there is no clear consistency between privatization policy and FDI inflows across all cases. With the exception of Hungary, where past ties combined with a privatization policy that strongly favored foreign owners (and where strong foreign interest may have partly guided the choice of privatization method), and that of Russia, where low density of ties combined with a privatization policy unfriendly to FDI, other cases exhibit a mixture of combinations between past ties and openness to FDI in privatization policy. Overall, the comparative analysis shows that differences in privatization policy do not by themselves consistently account for differences in patterns of FDI inflows in the early 1990s.

Another line of argumentation might suggest that previous trade ties were determinant of FDI patterns. In this view, economies that traded more heavily with the West, as opposed to those trading primarily with Comecon, were better positioned by these trade ties to attract FDI from the West. However, trade patterns in 1980, when pre-1989 East-West trade was at its height, show little correspondence with country-level FDI distributions in the 1990s. Indeed, the country with the largest trade with the West at that time is Romania, which in 1995 is among the countries with the lowest level of FDI stock. Other countries, like Hungary, also display similar shares of trade with the West, but Hungary's margin is not larger than Poland and even the USSR's. By contrast, Czechoslovakia traded the least with Western economies, yet experienced very high FDI inflows at the turn of the decade. In other words, while partly indicative for Hungary and Poland, there is no consistency between FDI and the volume of trade with the West. Similar nonlinear relationships emerge with other variables, such as economic structure (as measured by portion of the industrial economy consisting of complex engineering against resource extraction). Labor costs turn out to be inversely correlated, as FDI appears to be drawn to economies with *higher* labor costs. For illustration, Table 4.2 lists pairwise correlations between FDI stock in 1995 and the variables previously discussed.[6]

Support for the legacy argument is also found in the transition from joint ventures to FDI. As pointed out, in the 1980s joint ventures were the common approach taken by TNCs in establishing a local presence in East European economies. Table 4.3 illustrates the dramatic shift in the period 1988–1992, as joint ventures lost their role as the near-exclusive form in which foreign business entered East European economies in 1988, to becoming a minor organizational pattern in 1992, during which time direct acquisitions became the dominant form of entry. While the data represent only a subset of the economies, they are likely reflective of general trends in the region.

The nature of joint ventures changed as the political and institutional context of East Europe transformed. In the late 1980s, joint ventures were initiated by foreign investors with the aim of establishing a local market presence and

Table 4.2. Correlation between FDI stock in 1995 and certain variables

Pairwise correlations	
Variable	*FDI stock in 1995 (Pearson's r coefficients)*
Total number of interfirm agreements in 1980 (subcontracting and coproduction only)	0.85
Index of per unit labor costs, 1992 (excludes Russia)	0.70
Total number of interfirm agreements in 1980	0.69
Share of exports to the West, 1980	0.34
Per capita GNP in 1988	0.34
Resource extraction as share of industrial output, 1993	0.21
Share of exports to Comecon, 1980	0.09
Engineering as share of industrial output, 1993	−0.03

Table 4.3. Change of mode of foreign entry into the Central and Eastern European economies from joint ventures to direct acquisition, 1988–1992

Year	*Greenfield FDI (%)*	*Joint ventures (%)*	*Direct acquisitions (%)*	*FDI total (in millions USD)*
1988	2.5	93.3	4.1	808
1989	9.4	64.6	25.8	2,507
1990	22.2	53.8	24.0	5,150
1991	22.3	46.5	31.3	10,120
1992	31.2	30.0	38.7	15,155

SOURCE: Artisien and Rojec (2001).

gaining access to the larger region by entering Comecon trade. While some joint ventures were the outgrowth of long-standing cooperative ties with domestic firms, in the late 1980s many were "wait-and-see" type operations that were intended as a beachhead to explore potential future expansion (Gabrisch and Vale 1993). With the removal of legal restrictions over foreign ownership and the ensuing process of privatization in the early 1990s (and the collapse of the Comecon market in the interim), the role of joint ventures transitioned increasingly toward the capture of local markets and the use of local manufacturing for the supply of the EU markets (Artisien and Rojec 2001). At the same time, via privatization, joint ventures could be transformed into direct acquisitions of domestic firms. We observe at the turn of the decade an increasing shift away from joint ventures to direct acquisitions.

In retrospect, we see that joint ventures served as the organizational vehicle that enabled the entry and establishment of TNCs into East European economies. The continuity between joint ventures and FDI is shown from an analysis of the data. In Figure 4.3, we observe a close correlation between total FDI stock in 1995 and the number of joint ventures in existence in 1990. Why 1990? The year captures the number of joint ventures in existence in a country just before it became clear that East Europe would be undergoing major po-

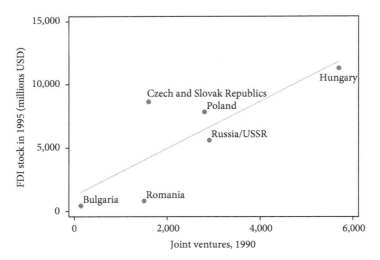

Figure 4.3. Number of joint ventures in 1990 by country plotted against FDI stock in 1995 (in millions USD)
SOURCE: UNCTADstat, UNECE (1996).

litical and institutional reforms. Until then, most foreign investors would have presumably been operating under the assumption that existing institutional frameworks, including Comecon, would continue to exist. By contrast, any joint venture established after 1990 would presumably be operating with the knowledge of Comecon's demise and awareness that economies were undergoing profound institutional changes. The opportunities and incentives those changes provided to foreign investors were, especially with privatization, of a different nature, necessitating revisions in TNC strategy. It is no surprise, then, why the number of joint ventures exploded *after* 1990. The question here is, of course, that of particular organizational continuities thriving despite such disruptive events. Figure 4.3 indicates that continuity in that the economies that had the most joint ventures in the pre-reform era were the ones to attract the most FDI in the post-reform era. The correlation is by no means perfect, but the overall pattern is clear.

One might question the degree to which the number of joint ventures in a country in 1990 reflect prior patterns of protoglobalization. Could interest by foreign firms as registered by 1990 data be independent of any historical developments in the field of industrial cooperation? While this is possible, Figure 4.4

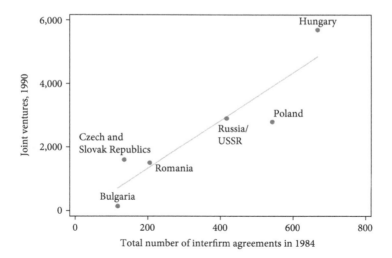

Figure 4.4. Number of interfirm agreements in 1984 by country plotted against number of joint ventures in 1990

SOURCE: OECD data reported in *East-West Technology Transfer* (Wiener and Slater [1986]), UNECE (1996).

shows that the number of joint ventures in existence in 1990 correlates strongly with interfirm ties as they stood in the mid-1980s. The general pattern is thus: Interfirm ties led to future joint ventures, and joint ventures led to future FDI, *ceteris paribus*. For the most part, then, states best situated in the early 1990s to attract FDI were not simply those that adopted specific policies in the reform era, nor those that inherited a particular industrial structure. Instead, FDI patterns reflected the uneven diffusion across economies of organizational capacities for transnational production that were created as a result of long-standing experience of collaboration with manufacturing TNCs. In general, how productive forces were shaped under socialism mattered more than the specifics of postsocialist reform in determining the competitiveness of nations in the globalizing world economy that Central and Eastern European economies were becoming rapidly incorporated into during the 1990s.

Transnationalization Without FDI: Outward Processing

Another aspect of the impact of socialist protoglobalization legacies is the distinct capacity of particular sectors with long and deep experience in transnational production to not only survive, but thrive during the immediate transition period of 1989–1993. That is, East European firms with such experience could independently pursue the intensification of involvement in transnational production, and indeed they did so, by exploiting networks established prior to 1989 to break into Western markets. Thus the experiences of socialist protoglobalization carried over into the conduct of trade after the downfall of socialist regimes and was not an exclusively FDI-led process.

The analysis in Chapter 3 shows that, in the 1980s, among the best-performing East European exports to OECD markets were those in light industry. Transnational production was probably more deeply embedded in this sector than in any other industry. Light industry, including but not limited to food and food processing, textiles and clothing, wood processing and the production of furniture and paper products, and the production of rubber and light chemicals among others, was able to flourish for a variety of reasons. These include the prevalence of subcontracting in the global garments industry and the attraction of global firms by the lower costs of labor-intensive manufacturing in developing nations. In the early 1990s, direct TNC investments in the textiles and garments sector in Central and Eastern Europe were small, yet in the short run, this is one of the manufacturing sectors that not only maintained output but was even able to expand its exports in the course of the post-1989 economic depression. The expansion of exports came primarily in the form of subcontracting—that is, outward processing trade (OPT). OPT reflects a subcontracting arrangement in which a domestic firm processes inputs supplied by a manufacturer located in a third country and then reexports the processed goods back to the country of origin.

Table 4.4 shows the patterns of exports in the textiles and garments industry to the EU and the growing share of OPT in East European exports during the early reform years. It is clear that, while all reform countries were experiencing an overall collapse in exports, the textiles and garments industry experienced

Table 4.4. East European clothing and textile exports to the EU (in millions ECU) with share of OPT (in percentage), 1988–1994

Country	1988	1989	1990	1991	1992	1993	1994
Bulgaria							
Textiles and clothing	52.4	59.5	78.9	112.9	197.7	213.6	248.9
of which: OPT share	*30.1*	*34.4*	*37.1*	*24.6*	*42.3*	*47.9*	*49.8*
Czechoslovakia							
Textiles and clothing	240.9	252.9	297.8	481.3	665.3	—	—
of which: OPT share	*16.3*	*18.6*	*19*	*31.6*	*36.7*	—	—
Czech Republic							
Textiles and clothing	—	—	—	—	—	565.2	709.2
of which: OPT share	—	—	—	—	—	*44.2*	*49.6*
Slovakia							
Textiles and clothing	—	—	—	—	—	208.2	318.7
of which: OPT share	—	—	—	—	—	*53.8*	*50.7*
Hungary							
Textiles and clothing	340.6	381.1	464.7	554.4	657.3	698.7	782.6
of which: OPT share	*64.2*	*65.9*	*66.7*	*70.9*	*67.7*	*70.3*	*69.4*
Poland							
Textiles and clothing	356.8	395.7	592.9	866.1	1112.5	1391.5	1635.3
of which: OPT share	*58.7*	*65.0*	*67.8*	*73.6*	*74.4*	*77.7*	*79.9*
Romania							
Textiles and clothing	404.5	442.8	373.9	375.1	493.8	644.3	840.2
of which: OPT share	*43.4*	*45.8*	*51.5*	*55.4*	*63.8*	*64.7*	*70.4*
Totals							
Textiles and clothing	1395.2	1532.0	1808.2	2389.8	3126.6	3721.5	4534.9
of which: OPT share	*47.2*	*49.7*	*49.9*	*60.2*	*61.3*	*70.0*	*67.9*

SOURCE: UNECE (1996).

little to no crisis in this regard. Not only did exports not decline, but within the short timeframe of 1990–1994, they more than doubled. The table also shows the role of OPT exports from East Europe to the EU, which accounts for a great deal of the rise in exports. Indeed, the growth of OPT is much higher than the growth of direct exports.

This expansion of exports took place despite the fact that the EU had not fully eased trade restrictions, nor had it opened market access to East European countries at this time. Access to the EU market in garments and textiles was limited both by specific EU protectionist policies in this sector and by the Multi-Fiber Arrangement (MFA) regime under the GATT. The MFA regime enabled the EU to selectively apply import restrictions of textiles and garments in an effort to protect domestic industry from competition from low-cost, non-EU producers. The EU had been especially vocal in introducing quota restrictions in MFA III (1982–1986), which were implemented in the context of EU external trade. These restrictions were in place until the Uruguay Round of the GATT, which foresaw the gradual abolition of quotas and the placement of textile and garment trade under the general rules of the newly established World Trade Organization (WTO) in 1995.

There was some easing of access in this market after the East European countries signed association agreements with the EU, but the trade in textiles and garments would not feel the effect of these agreements until 1992 for Hungary and Poland, and 1993 for Bulgaria, the Czech Republic, Slovakia, and Romania. (Slovenia did not sign its association agreement until 1995.) Moreover, duty-free access to the EU market in textiles and garments was granted to East European nations only in 1994, after the negotiation of a separate set of protocols governing this area of trade.

EU rules did provide exceptions, however, for OPT. OPT quotas were larger than those for direct exports, and EU-based firms engaging in OPT had fewer licensing requirements than those engaged in direct imports from Central and Eastern Europe. Moreover, importers of finished goods faced a 14 percent tariff, which did not apply to OPT. EU producers, then, had significant incentives for engaging in OPT. As a result, OPT quota utilization was tremendously higher than those of direct exports. In 1993 average quota utilization for OPT was 75 percent, whereas for direct exports utilization was only 31 percent.[7] The fact that trade rules favored OPT over direct exports until 1994 may partly account for the larger rise in OPT over direct exports, and this may have contributed to Central and Eastern European economies overtaking developing countries like

Egypt, Morocco, Turkey, and neighboring Yugoslavia as the top-ranked OPT countries for garments and textiles in the EU by market share. The capacity of the East European textiles and garments industry to seamlessly transition from socialist trade to global supplier-chain production is a sign of continuity in the conduct of such transactions through the intensification of ties that had been in existence for over two decades prior.

This pattern is observed in the data in Table 4.4. The share of OPT in textile and garment exports from Eastern Europe to the EU for Hungary, Poland, and Romania was nearly or above half of all exports already in 1988, and the share began to grow as early as 1989. In other words, these countries were already established as important low-cost, labor-intensive producers for the EU market prior to the post-1989 reforms. It is difficult to assess the variables accounting for the varied performance of the sector in individual countries after 1989, since these involve differentiating between the effects of past ties, domestic economic disruptions, sectoral FDI (especially of the small plant variety targeting low-cost textile and garment production), and unequal access to the EU market. The continuities in the more trade-friendly countries of the 1980s are apparent, however, although former Comecon integrationists like the Czech Republic, Slovakia, and Bulgaria quickly catch up.

The textiles and garments sector drove the explosion of OPT in Eastern Europe after 1989, as that sector accounted for the bulk of growth in this form of trade (Figure 4.5). The structure of OPT trade gives us some indication of the patterns of transnational production. The textiles, garments, and related industries such as footwear and leather processing were less targeted by TNC acquisition and typically conducted their transnational production operations on an independent subcontracting basis.[8] These patterns turn the industrial complexity argument on its head—it is the least complex, but already highly integrated, industries that were the first to benefit from the economic liberalization after 1989, although most of these sectors were eventually cut down by global competition.

Explaining the Czech Exception

The reader is owed an explanation of the Czech exception. The Czech case stands out because of its high comparable level of FDI in relation to the number of interfirm agreements in existence in Czechoslovakia in the mid-1980s (see Table 4.1). Indeed, as discussed in Chapter 3, the Czechoslovak Commu-

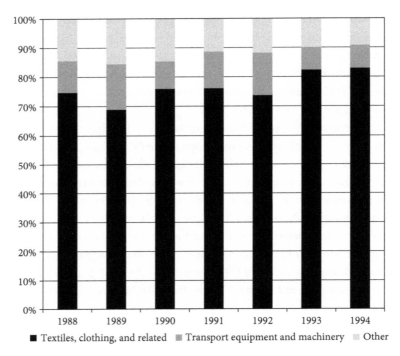

Figure 4.5. Share of textiles, clothing, and related products; transport equipment and machinery; and other products in the structure of East European OPT with the EU, 1988–1994
SOURCE: Author's calculations based on data from UNECE (1996).

nist leadership resisted fully embracing the import-led growth model. Trade with the West was minimal. Czechoslovakia's borrowing on international credit markets was also the lowest among all Comecon nations. In other words, Czechoslovakia was on many counts Comecon's least integrated country with Western industry. Yet, FDI stock in Czechoslovakia grew rapidly very soon after the country liberalized. What accounts for this dramatic turn, which does not seem to follow the general pattern laid out in the preceding discussion?

A number of contingent factors were at play in Czechoslovakia. First, the distinct Czechoslovak (and, after 1992, Czech) approach to FDI in the early years of reform—that is, before the introduction of voucher privatization—involved the government's privatization of a number of big-ticket companies to TNCs. These sales were not only situated in key industrial sectors but also drew the interest of major TNCs. One of the first such major sales—and in many ways inaugurating the era of TNC involvement in Central and Eastern Europe—was the acquisition by Volkswagen of the Czechoslovak automobile producer Škoda Auto–Mladá Boleslav in 1991. The deal committed Volkswagen to investing $4.7 billion over a four-year period in exchange for a minority stake, with ownership of the company eventually falling onto the new investor. In the first year, the deal brought a $370 million investment by Volkswagen into Czechoslovakia, the single largest investment in all of East Europe. Soon after the VW-Škoda venture, a number of other large investments arrived in Czechoslovakia. In 1991 these included the German gas company Linde's joint venture with Technoplyn, Belgian Glaverbel's joint venture in the production of sheet glass with Sklo Union Teplice, Otis Elevator's investment in Tranza Breclav, and Siemens's joint venture with Tescom. In addition to these and other large investments in construction, textiles, agricultural machinery, and pharmaceuticals, a portion included automotive suppliers that followed Volkswagen's entry into Czechoslovakia: Secheron (Switzerland), Poclain Hydraulics (France), Schweinfurt Ulbricht (Austria), Enidine (USA), and Ralston Purina Overseas Battery (USA). Each of these came in the form of joint ventures with local producers, and their entry was partly conditioned by Volkswagen's demand that Škoda Auto and the Ministry of Industry encourage improvements and upgrades in Škoda Auto's domestic supply chain (Pavlínek 1998). Big-ticket sales continued in subsequent years. In 1992 Philip Morris (USA) acquired the state tobacco monopoly Tabak for $400 million, a deal described by the *Financial Times* (1992) as "the largest price ever paid for a tobacco company in terms of its size and turnover." That same year, Nestlé (Switzerland) and BSN (France) jointly acquired a minority stake in Čokoládovny for $200 million. These large acquisitions of what major TNCs clearly considered to be high-value assets enabled the Czechoslovak government to quickly rack up large amounts of FDI. Thus, between 1990 and 1996, out of a total of $6 billion of FDI that had entered the Czech Republic, nearly half was invested in telecommunications, automotive, and consumer goods and tobacco. By contrast, much smaller amounts were invested in engineering and electronics, which had been the mainstay of Czech industry for decades.[9] Indeed, nearly 60 percent of all FDI between 1990 and 1995 was on account of only four large, heftily priced investments (Pavlínek 1998, 75).

Another important development in Czech FDI was the rise of what Petr Pavlínek (1998) describes as greenfield investments in the form of "screwdriver plants." These plants were small manufacturing operations set up mainly in labor-intensive industries like textiles, electronics, and low-end automotive components. Because of their small scale, many were not officially tracked by the Ministry of Industry or were placed in the category of negligible minor investments. These operations tended to cluster in the western border region with Germany and Austria, where the bulk of these small, foreign-owned companies and joint ventures formed. Many employed women. Pavlínek, who performed fieldwork in the region in the mid-1990s, describes them as "similar to the maquiladoras at the U.S.-Mexican border," in which "low-skilled, young female laborers assemble imported components and the finished products are then reexported to Germany" (79). There was some TNC presence in such labor-intensive industries. Pavlínek describes one plant established by Siemens that produced cables for BMW. But this case was atypical, as most firms were small operations set up on a subcontracting basis using the Czech Republic's labor-cost advantages to supply the German market. In the overall structure of FDI, these investments were marginal. But they exhibit an alternative FDI strategy that was aimed mainly at the short-term exploitation of local labor costs and geographical proximity. While overshadowed by large acquisitions, these peripheral developments played into the intensified FDI patterns observed in the Czech Republic.[10]

A number of well-placed big-ticket investments and the advantages offered by low-cost, cross-border production permitted the Czech Republic to overcome its apparent disadvantages and previous isolation from TNC production. Moreover, these advantages mainly benefited the Czechs. After the disintegration of Czechoslovakia, the newly independent Slovak Republic inherited only one-tenth of the FDI that had entered the joint state. While a number of contingencies and particularities enabled the Czechs to overcome inherited limits, the factors constraining investments were clearly at work in the former sister state.

At the same time, the apparent isolation of Czech and Slovak industry during the era of reform socialism must be qualified. Two features of Czechoslovak ties to the Western economies are important. First, while Czechoslovakia had fewer overall ties through interfirm agreements, the structure of its ties consisted of the kinds that came to matter more in the liberalization era. Figure 4.6 plots FDI stock in 1995 against agreements involving subcontracting and coproduction.[11] Unlike Romania, which had a greater number of agreements in the 1980s but which were mainly in the form of joint ventures, Czechoslovak authorities shunned joint ventures in favor of cooperation in the area of manu-

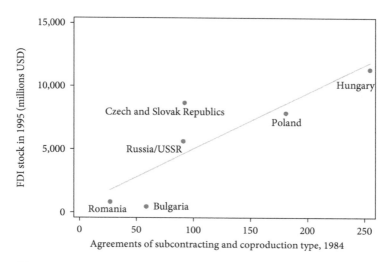

Figure 4.6. Number of interfirm agreements involving subcontracting and coproduction only in 1984 by country plotted against FDI stock in 1995 (in millions USD)
SOURCE: OECD data reported in Wiener and Slater (1986), UNCTADstat.

facturing. As a result, Czechoslovak industry was not entirely isolated from the trend of transnational production, and such capacities—especially in the machinery and electronics industries—were a draw for TNCs (Genillard 1991).

To sum up, the Czech case is explained by a number of contingencies that made FDI inflows to the country diverge from the rest. The first is the interest of a number of investors willing to pay large sums for the acquisition of a small subset of Czech industrial assets. It is difficult to assess whether TNCs' coveting of Czech assets led them to overvalue them, or whether the Czech Ministry of Industry simply succeeded in persuading investors of the high value of their market. The timing of sales was an important factor in the ability of the Czech government to exploit TNC interest to concede its market in exchange for large sums. The capacity of governments to negotiate high prices for their assets diminished over time. One can contrast the VW-Škoda deal in 1991, which brought Czechoslovakia a commitment of $4.7 billion, with $370 million invested in the first year alone, with Romania's sale of its domestic car maker Dacia to Renault in 1999 for a *total* of $270 million. The explosion of investments in small-scale, labor-intensive, export-only manufacturing, especially along its western border regions with Germany, formed a second feature of FDI in the early years of liberalization. While this feature would become prominent

across all border regions in Central and Eastern European economies, it secured a crucial inflow of greenfield FDI into the country conducted by smaller
firms and investors.[12] Overall, highly priced sales of a targeted set of industries
alongside the flow of greenfield investments in screwdriver plants were what
distinguished the case of Czech FDI and the country's rapid accumulation of
FDI stock. This more targeted and strategic entry of TNCs into the Czechoslovak economy distinguished the pattern from the depth and breadth of FDI
penetration taking place in neighboring Hungary. Moreover, the low FDI inflows in the Slovak region both during the existence of the Czechoslovak feder-
ation and immediately after independence in 1993 shows that these exceptional
factors were operative only in the Czech case. Levels of FDI in Slovakia fell in
line with patterns that would be expected from the region's relative isolation
from transnational production during the era of reform socialism, indicating
the consistency of the general correspondence between socialist protoglobalization and postsocialist FDI inflows in the early years of reform.

Assessing Relative Gains and Losses from Globalization After 1989

The increasing importance of transnationalized industries in the East European
economic transformations should be evident after the preceding discussion, as
should be the advantage possessed by countries that had been most aggressive
in expanding ties to TNCs in the era of reform socialism. The fact that the post-
1989 transition unleashed a process of deep structural transformation of East
European industry is also observed in the changing composition of the countries' exports—that is, not only in the types of goods that are being exported
but also in their constitution. The increasing penetration of transnational production in the region affected not only patterns of trade (such as the rise of
OPT) but also the manner in which economies were becoming integrated into
global value chains.

   One way to measure the extent of such transformation and adjustment is
to examine ratios between domestic and foreign value added in a country's
exports. This figure expresses the extent to which domestic or foreign value-
added components dominate a country's exports, suggesting the domestic
industry's overall higher relative standing in global value chains (e.g., in exporting domestically engineered goods), or its reliance on largely foreign value
added (e.g., foreign-engineered inputs) to supply domestic industry that serves
mainly a processing or assembly function in the value chain. While an exact

mapping of East European standing across value chains is not possible, data from UNCTAD's global value chain database enable us to observe, if not the exact global position, the *movement* of countries up and down value chains in the crucial transitional period of 1990–1995. Figure 4.7 captures overall change in the composition of the value added of each country's exports expressed as a linear vector of change in the ratio between domestic and foreign value added. A positive value represents the growth of domestic value added against foreign value added, and thus an economy's gains in increasing its share of domestic value added in its exports. When this happens, one can claim that globalization has had a positive impact on domestic industry, since it has enabled domestic production to rise up global value chains—that is, domestic industry becomes capable of exporting ever more sophisticated goods. A negative value would suggest that globalization has downgraded the role of domestic production, as domestic industry becomes increasingly reliant on value-added goods (raw materials, components, and other inputs) that are imported from elsewhere. That is, while the economy might export more sophisticated goods, those are

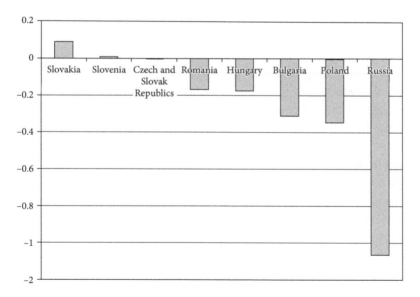

Figure 4.7. Coefficient of change in domestic and foreign value added in each country's exports in the period 1990–1995

NOTE: The figures capture the economy's direction of adjustment in global value chains.
SOURCE: Author's calculations based on the UNCTAD-EORA GVC database (Lenzen et al. 2012; Lenzen et al. 2013).

made from technologies and components imported from another country, in which domestic industry performs lower value-added tasks such as their assembly into final products. The figure reveals an interesting though largely expected pattern, as virtually all countries with the exception of Slovenia and Slovakia experience a rise of foreign value added in their exports. This suggests, as one would expect, that East European countries were becoming more reliant on foreign imports to maintain the complexity of their exports, thus relegating domestic activities to a lower value-added activity. But this drop is particularly large for Russia, which is unsurprising given the country's transition toward a more simple commodity exporter. Declines on this account are also experienced by the other countries, but these are less dramatic, suggesting a differentiated capacity for maintaining the sophistication of exports against the threat of increased world competition. Slovenia's position remains largely unchanged, reflecting the country's inherited export-based manufacturing and its capacity to preserve the growth of domestic value-added activities even as its reliance on foreign value added was growing.[13]

Figure 4.8 suggests a differentiated capacity of some countries to maintain the complexity of domestic inputs in exported goods despite the massive economic disruption of the early 1990s. The figure disaggregates differences between growth in domestic and foreign value added and shows average rates of change in each category in the period 1990–1995. Here, we observe that virtually across the board, the dramatic rise of foreign value added makes East European exports increasingly reliant on foreign complex inputs. But an interesting pattern emerges in relation to change in domestic value added. The highest levels of growth in domestic value added occur in the countries that in the 1970s had been at the forefront of import-led growth (Hungary, Poland, and Romania). By contrast, in the former Comecon integrationists like Bulgaria and the Czech Republic, the capacity of domestic industries to increase their value-added contribution to exports is less impressive. In Russia, with the least extent of protoglobalization (relative to the size of its economy), domestic value added fell precipitously. Clearly, in all economies growth in the contribution of foreign value added in exports outstrips any gains in domestic value-added activities. For Hungary, the reasons for this are obvious, as the country was quickly integrated into TNC-based transnational production by large inflows of manufacturing FDI. In Poland and Romania, this is reflective of patterns of globalization that are not entirely reliant on FDI, indicating the importance of the expansion of domestically driven globalized production (such as the textiles and garments industry discussed earlier). Slovenia is the only economy to experience growth in domestic value added that is slightly higher than foreign value added, suggesting that the postsocialist era brought an improvement in the economy's overall position in global value chains. In other words, in the early period of openness, Slovenia performed best as a postsocialist globalizer. With the exception of Russia, the rest also improved their lot, but largely as a result of greater reliance on higher value-added imports in domestic production. At the same time, the greatest gains in domestic value added—and thus, a relative improvement in the global value chain position of their domestic industries—were experienced by countries at the forefront of socialist protoglobalization. With the exception of Slovenia, all countries lost ground to globalization. But the relative gains *within* globalization are uneven: The more globally integrated these countries were as socialist economies, the greater their relative gains after 1989. In aggregate, it was industrial transnationalization over the long run, and particularly the experience of socialist protoglobalization, that determined the capacity of postsocialist industry to successfully gain from globalization after 1989. Postsocialist industrial integration with the global economy was path dependent and derives its structure and patterns from legacies of socialist reform in the 1970s.

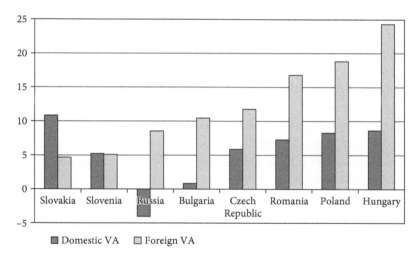

Figure 4.8. Average annual growth (in percent) of domestic and foreign value added (VA) in exports for the period 1990–1995

SOURCE: Author's calculations based on the UNCTAD-EORA GVC database (Lenzen et al. 2012; Lenzen et al. 2013).

Conclusion

Prevailing accounts portray the arrival of FDI and its uneven flows into the postsocialist East European economies as reflecting country-level differences in policy factors, economic profiles, and social and cultural ties with the West. This chapter challenges these perspectives by making the case for a continuities argument in socialist to postsocialist patterns of transnational economic integration. The chapter shows that pre-1989 patterns of transnationalization can account for a great deal of the patterns of FDI inflows across the region during the early years of reform.

More precisely, uneven patterns of transnational integration in postsocialist East Europe are accounted for by the uneven distribution of organizational capacities for transnational production. These organizational capacities, here called transnational organizational capital, were generated during the era of reform socialism, particularly in countries that spent the 1970s pursuing policies of import-led growth. While Chapter 3 shows that the policy of import-led growth had marginal and even negligible impact on achieving the manifest economic policy goals of East European economic planners, their byproduct was to create a critical experience for local actors to operate competently in organizational contexts of transnational production. Using data on interfirm agreements in existence during the 1970s and 1980s, the chapter shows that, taken as proxies for the distribution of organizational capacities for transnational production across the region, they correlate very strongly with patterns of FDI in the early 1990s. Patterns of FDI also correlate strongly with patterns of joint venture formation in the critical and uncertain period 1988–1990, establishing a general pattern of TNC accommodation that begins with interfirm agreements enabling arm's-length collaboration with domestic actors, then joint ventures, then direct acquisition of local assets. While this pattern does not hold in absolute empirical terms across all cases, it is sufficiently typical to demonstrate the importance of path-dependent developments in FDI and economic transnationalization, in strong distinction to perspectives emphasizing short-term policy factors, economic profiles of recipient countries, or broadly defined cultural ties to the West.

The chapter also shows that the deepening of transnationalization in domestic manufacturing did not take place solely through FDI. Transnationalization was also self-propelled by domestic actors, especially in labor-intensive industries such as textiles and garments, which expanded *existing* transnational production operations after 1989 by increasing participation in OPT. At the same time, the chapter demonstrates the impact of socialist-era experience of transnational production on the benefits of post-1989 globalization. The chapter shows that while absolute gains from globalization were positive overall (with the exception of Russia), *relative* gains were disproportionately captured by countries that had been at the forefront of import-led growth in the 1970s, such as Hungary and Poland, and early globalizers like Romania and Slovenia. In the Czech Republic, a set of unique contingencies, including the willingness of foreign investors to pay large sums in exchange for a small number of companies, enabled the Czech Republic to amass disproportionate stocks of FDI and break from its historical pattern of relative isolation of its domestic industries from Western TNCs. However, Czech relative gains from globalization were less impressive, and this is consistent with patterns of socialist-era openness to the West.

What patterns of FDI in post-1989 East Europe reflect, thus, are not competitive advantages in the scale and depth of reform or inherited industrial profile, but *cumulative advantages* (Merton 1988) gained as a result of a particular pattern of development of productive forces as a consequence of economic policy undertaken by socialist governments since the 1970s. Those policies appeared marginal to the overall economic goals of socialist regimes, who at the time spoke of cooperation with Western capitalist countries as a means of technological progress and improved productivity. They proved determinant, however, when the unexpected political events of 1989 opened economies to external capitalist investment and made globalization virtually inevitable. In this context, it turned out that, in terms of FDI, the nature of socialism proved critical for postsocialist industrial transformation. This is not to say that reform policies, domestic economic conditions, the changing international context, and other factors did not matter at all. What this does mean, however, is that the likelihood of reform policies favoring FDI becoming effective grew with the increased concentration of organizational capacities for transnational production. The causal relationship between policy and economic outcome can also be reversed to claim that particular reform policies were effective because they came to embody the interests of concrete actors who had a stake in their effective implementation (Hoff and Stiglitz 2004). While this chapter does not adjudicate between these competing perspectives, it does suggest that the latter view requires serious consideration in the explanation of postsocialist developmental patterns.

Transnational Integration and Specialization in the 2000s

Diverging International Market Roles

5

The narrative of the previous chapters would seem to suggest that paths of global integration in post-1989 East Europe were already prefigured in the industrial development strategies of the late socialist era. In states where socialist-era reform policies deepened the process of integration with transnational production networks, rapid globalization had a better chance of occurring and policies of adjustment to external economic pressures via FDI more likely to succeed. By contrast, states whose economic sectors remained isolated from transnational production networks would be more likely to face deeper structural problems and their business enterprises greater difficulties in responding to world market pressures. This account is only partly true. This chapter completes that account by examining patterns of structural transformation and how these cumulatively led to new international roles in world market integration during the 2000s. In this process we see that, over time, legacy factors seem to matter increasingly less while the politics of adjustment begin to matter much more. Put differently, while legacy factors were important to the extent that they constrained the choices of postsocialist policymakers by increasing or decreasing the likelihood of success of particular economic reform strategies, the politics of reform were important in determining just how industrial legacies were mobilized toward future economic goals.

This chapter uses comparative data to trace patterns of structural transformation leading states toward one of the three distinct roles in international market integration, which are developed as theoretical types. The international market integration of small, developing states in a globalized economy is defined as the structural location that the nation's industry assumes within global production networks. The concept incorporates both the specialization of national industry as it intersects with and participates in global value chains (Sturgeon 2001) and the associated (national) political economy or institutional framework within which the organization of industrial activity takes place (Hall and Soskice 2001). As outcomes, such roles represent distinct combinations of structural and institutional features within individual states, including the centrality of FDI to the economy, the role of domestic skill and technology in exports, and the degree of the economy's overall export specialization. Examining variations across these and other dimensions, the chapter distinguishes between three such roles for Central and Eastern European states: assembly platform, intermediate producer, and combined.

This chapter does two things. First, it shows why, among other alternatives in the 2000s, production network integration strategies in Central and Eastern Europe ultimately converged on FDI. This shared policy orientation became a defining feature of the region's approach to global economic integration, with important consequences in patterns of postsocialist industrial development. Second, it compares structural differences between states in their patterns of postsocialist world economic integration by examining individual economies in the areas of FDI, export markets, technological dependence, and the size of domestic TNC sectors. These differences are used to develop the three distinct international market roles previously highlighted.

The Convergence Toward FDI

Production network strategies reflect the combined choices of political and economic actors of the particular mode of integration of a nation's industry in global value chains (Sturgeon 2001; Gereffi, Humphrey, and Sturgeon 2005; Yeung 2016). At least four such strategies were in use during the postsocialist era: direct exports, OPT, joint ventures, and FDI. Chapter 4 shows how, in the course of the 1990s, OPT and joint ventures became increasingly marginalized in favor of FDI. By the 2000s, FDI became the dominant production network integration strategy in Central and Eastern Europe, in the form of granting leading global firms in transnational production networks (manufacturing TNCs) control over domestic industrial assets. At least three factors led to the convergence toward FDI as the dominant production network strategy. First, recessions and credit crisis across the region in the late 1990s left FDI among the few stable sources of investment. Hungary pursued an FDI strategy most intensely and consistently after the launch of market reforms in 1990. By contrast, other states initially pursued internally based strategies of restructuring, using privatization and industrial policy with the aim of retaining domestic ownership of industrial assets in the course of market transformation. However, with few exceptions (as in Slovenia), these policies proved unsuccessful, and a renewed wave of reform in the late 1990s and 2000s pushed toward a reinvigorated externalization strategy where FDI became the dominant industrial policy of restructuring and redevelopment. These policy shifts occurred across the region. In the Czech Republic, where reforms under Prime Minister Klaus seemed for a while to make Czech national capitalism viable, the approach was abandoned in favor of FDI. In Slovakia statist control of the economy under the authoritarian regime of Prime Minister Vladimír Mečiar was quickly undone by a new generation of reformers who helped turn Slovakia into one of the prime destinations of FDI in the 2000s. In Poland, whose economy seemed to manage well without significant FDI in the 1990s, the shift came in the 2000s, as well as in Romania, where the late 1990s saw an abrupt, largely politically motivated turn toward an FDI-based strategy.

Another factor influencing the switch to FDI was change in the market strategies of TNCs. As Chapter 4 shows, OPT proved to be of limited use given that the region was quickly outcompeted in low-cost, low-end production in labor-intensive manufacturing by other developing regions, particularly in industries such as textiles and clothing. This led TNCs to turn elsewhere as costs of production climbed. In some cases, OPT was not sustainable for East European firms either, as it involved downgrading capabilities to engage in more basic production tasks. Ellen Comisso (1998) recounts the case of the Czech electronics firm Tesla Pardubice, once a producer of sophisticated surveillance systems, reduced to assembling toasters and coffee makers for a German brand. In cases like Tesla Pardubice and other advanced sectors such as computers, East European enterprises lacked the technologies and, in the 1990s, also the access to finance to invest in upgrades in ways that would make them competitive as OPT partners or direct marketers in their sectors. Indeed, with the withdrawal of state support, the only way for such advanced sectors to survive under the new constraints and pressures of market competition was to seek strategic partnerships with leading global firms. Joint ventures proved to be of limited benefit given that they demanded foreign partners hand over proprietary technologies in exchange for access to local markets. However, with the reduction of trade barriers that came with economic liberalization, local partners became increasingly unnecessary as TNCs could now enter local markets directly. Hence, for many enterprises dependent on external partners for upgrades, restructuring, and external market access, FDI became the only viable strategy. The need for FDI was compounded by the domestic credit crises of the late 1990s, cutting off one of the few sources of investment in postsocialist economies.

In the early 1990s, partnerships created via FDI could be used to restructure and upgrade domestic enterprises. The VW-Škoda Auto joint venture is a primary example of such foreign-led restructuring. But in the late 1990s and 2000s, industrial FDI increasingly came in the form of greenfield investments, thereby helping expand the domestic industrial base. For policymakers, the shift to FDI crucially aided the process of larger economic recovery as it relieved pressures of unemployment, diversified local industry, and grew the export base. In Hungary, FDI helped construct an automotive industry that had been nonexistent before 1989. The cumulative effect of large and sustained FDI inflows was a structural transformation of the economy that in the process radically reframed the region's policy and developmental challenges.

Concurrently, TNCs themselves were in the process of restructuring and expanding. The consolidation of the European common market after 1992 saw major European firms increasingly turn to offshore production as a cost-reduction strategy, mimicking the restructuring that US corporations (following the lead of Japanese companies) began in the 1980s (Young and Hamill 1992). Major European industrial players like the European Round Table of Industrialists (ERT), an exclusive club of chief executive officers of the largest European TNCs, became vocal advocates for the EU's eastward expansion on those very principles (Holman 2001). They saw in East Europe opportunities for low-cost production in ways that enhanced the global competitiveness of European firms as these firms faced stiffer cost competition from US and East Asian TNCs (Radosevic and Sadowski 2004). In Chapter 4 we see how the entry of TNCs into East Europe paralleled processes of industrial restructuring in Western Europe, and while some TNCs had experience operating in multiple markets, some West European firms used East Europe as a launching pad for their own transnationalization. At the same time, for US and East Asian firms, Central and Eastern Europe was increasingly seen as a low-cost assembly point for goods sold in the EU market. With these parallel changes, the interests of both European and non-European manufacturing TNCs converged on Central and Eastern Europe as a destination for FDI. In other words, in addition to the "pull" factors of Central and Eastern European pro-FDI policies, there were the "push" factors of shifting strategies of TNCs in the course of the 2000s that identified Central and Eastern Europe as a growing hub for global manufacturing operations targeting the greater European market.

Finally, all these processes were accelerated by the accession of Central and Eastern European states to the EU. The dramatic growth in FDI inflows in the early 2000s mirrored the region's progress in EU accession and final admittance in the mid-2000s (Vachudova 2008; Bandelj 2010). The region's governments recognized the boom in FDI inflows, and politicians touted major TNC investments as success stories of European integration and market restructuring. With FDI quickly becoming a major source of domestic investment, governments increasingly competed on benefits and subsidy packages offered to investors, with the key centers of economic policymaking shifting from industrial ministries to foreign investment promotion agencies (Drahokoupil 2009; Appel and Orenstein 2013). More significantly, with growing transnational control over local industry and the harmonization of local regulatory frameworks and governance units with those of the EU, the region shifted from the traditional combination of economic interdependence through trade and domestic policy autonomy toward a "deep" integration that combined an FDI-driven growth model with a neoliberal policy regime that narrowed the scope for developmental alternatives (Bruszt and McDermott 2009; Ban 2016, 152–158; Bruszt and Langbein 2017).

But while policies seem to converge, the *outcomes* of these combined changes were uneven across the region. In cases like post-Soviet Russia and Ukraine, early exclusion from socialist-era transnational production networks and distance from core European markets already left a large gap between domestic industry and TNCs. This gap was preserved by political factors, including privatization policies that favored domestic owners and other legal barriers that limited market access to TNCs. But paths of transnational integration differed even among the Central and Eastern European states that became the prime destination of FDI in the 2000s. In Chapter 4 we see how the globalization of industry in the early 1990s contributed to a growth in exports but led to the reduction in the industry's location in global value chains, as production shifted to more low-skill, labor-intensive work. This feeds into claims that the region has become an increasingly low-skill "assembly platform" for TNCs and has evolved into "dependent market economies" (Nölke and Vliegenthart 2009; Ban 2013). It also highlights the region's growing structural dependence on FDI as a basis of economic growth. Has this been the case across the region? The following sections examine differences in patterns of transnational integration, their effects on industrial specialization, and the emergent role for each economy in networks of transnational production.

Theorizing and Measuring Transnational Integration

The measurement of transnational integration is a continual challenge for scholars of the global economy (Sturgeon et al. 2013). This section relies on a set of simple structural measures to examine patterns of transnational integration across Central and Eastern Europe based on degrees of dependence on external sources for investment, market demand, and technology.

The first measure captures an economy's overall movement across global value chains through a standard measure of ratios of foreign and domestic value added in the country's exports over the period 1990–2012. While expressing differences in value-added processes that go into the making of an economy's exports, the ratio can also be treated as indicating the level of the economy's technological dependence. The assumption is that integration with global production networks involves varied bundles of value-added activities, which thus rely on different skill bases in the host economy (Sturgeon 2001). Transnational integration can have one of two effects. It may upgrade the economy's skill base, leading to higher levels of endogenous technological capacities as host economy workers become involved in more complex and creative tasks in the production (and potential innovation) of goods. Alternatively, transnational integration may reduce the skill base by downgrading the type of skill required in production, by routinizing work and lowering skill and knowledge standards required in production (in a process of de-skilling). This difference signifies movement across the global value chain and the level at which a host economy's domestic production integrates with and contributes to transnational production networks driven by lead firms (Sturgeon 2001; Gereffi, Humphrey, and Sturgeon 2005; Milberg and Winkler 2013). The literature on global value chains acknowledges the possibility for such upgrades in host economy industries given certain opportunities, domestic policies, and international market conditions (Gereffi 2009). The relationship between the capacity to upgrade an industry's position in the value-added chain and the host economy's domestic technological and skill capabilities is highlighted by UNCTAD: "taking advantage of [global value chain] participation (and upgrading opportunities) is dependent on the development of productive capacities, technology and skills" (2013, 20).

The ratio of foreign to domestic value added in exports may tell us about the effects of global value chain integration on domestic industry, but it does not tell us about the extent of an economy's dependence on transnational industries. A macroeconomic measure expressing the degree to which an economy specializes in exports provides another way of getting to this value. Rather than taking the measure of total trade or the proportion of exports in GDP, the degree of export specialization (the dependence of local industry—and thus economic growth—on exports) can be assessed by identifying the primary source of demand for the economy. A general measure such as total trade as a share of GDP combines external and internal demand and as a result obscures the origin of the economy's dominant source of demand. Similarly, examining only exports (gross external demand) as a share of GDP leaves us in the dark about the weight of domestic demand in the economy.

More precisely, a heavily transnationalized economy may specialize in exports in particular sector or market niches, whereas much of the economy's other domestic needs are satisfied by imports. In such a situation, external demand proves crucial for economic growth. This suggests that whether the primary source of demand for an economy is the domestic market or foreign markets has important macroeconomic (and thus policy) implications. Export-oriented economies that also satisfy a great deal of domestic consumption are more likely to weather downturns in global markets by diverting production to meet the needs of domestic consumption (or by temporarily reducing capacity utilization of domestic factors of production). Put differently, in these economies export markets function as extensions of the domestic market, and thus exports supplement domestic demand. This can be contrasted with enclave type production where goods are produced primarily or exclusively for export, and where the domestic market is unable to pick up the slack when external demand falls. These economies are much more vulnerable to external shocks, as were many Central and Eastern European economies after the 2008 global financial crisis (Marer 2010; Fraga and Rocha 2014). In more formal terms, this dimension of the analysis focuses on the problem of demand realization. Economies that exhibit high dependence on external markets for their demand realization can be said to display high levels of export specialization, and thus contain more firms and production networks that depend heavily on demand in external markets. A case in point is Slovakia's automotive industry. On a per capita basis, Slovakia frequently ranks among the top producers of automobiles in the world. In 2015 the output of the automotive industry in Slovakia was over one million automobiles. However, the vast majority of these automobiles are destined for the export market, as it is certainly beyond the means of Slovakia's population of five and a half million to purchase a million new cars every year.

During downturns in global markets, firms in these economies (or, in the case of Slovakia, global automotive subsidiaries and their suppliers) cannot simply divert production toward the domestic market. Insufficient domestic production also means that domestic levels of consumption cannot be sustained without worsening the economy's current account balance, since new imports need to be financed through foreign borrowing (by contrast, export economies with robust domestic demand may also suffer from unemployment during downturns but are less reliant on foreign borrowing to finance domestic consumption). In the measure used here, market dependence is calculated as the difference between net domestic demand (gross domestic consumption minus total imports) and gross external demand (total exports) in any given year. Higher positive values indicate that domestic production satisfies a greater portion of domestic consumption, while negative values indicate not only higher exports but also a greater reliance of the economy on imports to satisfy domestic consumption (hence, greater export specialization).

Transnational economic integration is also captured by the conventional variable of FDI dependence, that of how dependent an economy is on FDI as a source of investment. FDI is a pervasive feature of the global economy, but a deeply transnationalized economy is one where FDI looms as a dominant source of investments. For most analysts, reliance on FDI for investment constitutes the key defining element of the "dependent" nature of Central and Eastern European economies (Nölke and Vliegenthart 2009; Bohle and Greskovits 2012; Ban 2013). However, when examined comparatively, FDI dependence varies significantly across the region. The degree to which an economy has relied on FDI (as opposed to domestic investment) to maintain economic growth over the long run can be defined as another dimension across which transnationalization differs. The measure used here is the share of FDI in total investments. In Chapter 4, the focus is on the total *volume* of FDI and its distribution across the region. By using the share of FDI in investments, the analysis here looks at the *domestic* weight of FDI. The higher the share of FDI in total investments (over the long run), the more is economic transformation dependent on FDI. Juxtaposed against the dimension of export specialization, the variable indicates the degree to which export specialization has been obtained via reliance on TNC-driven FDI or on domestic capital.[1] Alternatively, FDI may be primarily of the market-seeking variety (seeking to access local markets), which would reflect in high levels of FDI dependence but low levels of export specialization.

In combination, technological, market, and investment dependence provide three key dimensions across which modes and intensities of economic transnationalization differ. The quantitative comparison of these indicators is not to assess their marginal effects, but serves the goal of using observed differences to inductively construct typological categories of distinct political economies in the manner of what Robert Boyer (2005) calls the "structural method."[2]

Figure 5.1 shows the distribution of economies based on the two dimensions of transnationalization during 1990–1997 and 1998–2008. A number of observations stand out. During 1990–1997, Slovenia and Slovakia already emerge as highly reliant on exports, but only in Hungary is FDI important for domestic transformation. During 1998–2008, representing the height of the region's FDI-driven transformation, FDI became increasingly important across the region (with Slovenia the only exception). In Bulgaria and Hungary, FDI constituted the dominant source of investment, though in the latter case this is combined with high levels of export specialization. Export dependence also

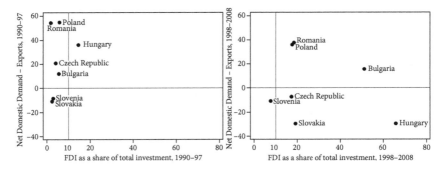

Figure 5.1. Levels of FDI dependence and export specialization during 1990–1997 and 1998–2008 (mean values)

NOTE: The x-axis shows investment dependence based on the share of FDI in total domestic investment. The y-axis measures market dependence through the difference between net domestic demand (gross domestic consumption minus imports) and gross external demand (exports). Negative values signify greater export specialization.
SOURCE: Author's calculations based on World Bank World Development Indicators.

intensified for the Czech Republic. Slovakia and Hungary came to exhibit the highest levels of export dependence, capturing the depth of both economies' export orientation and transnational integration.

Figure 5.2 shows that domestic value added still dominated over foreign value added in the countries' exports. In other words, a significant amount of domestic technology continued to constitute the exports of most economies in the region, highlighting the continuing role in these economies of high-skilled labor in manufacturing, even as exports grew. The two exceptions to this pattern, Slovakia and Hungary, both exhibit high export and high technological dependence. Overall, Poland and Romania score lower on measures of transnationalization, while Hungary scores extremely high on all measures. Slovenia and Bulgaria emerge as polar opposites at another level: Slovenia is highly export-market dependent, but achieved this role largely by reliance on domestic investment and production; by contrast, Bulgaria still relied mainly on domestic markets, consumption, and technology to drive growth, but depended heavily on FDI for investments.

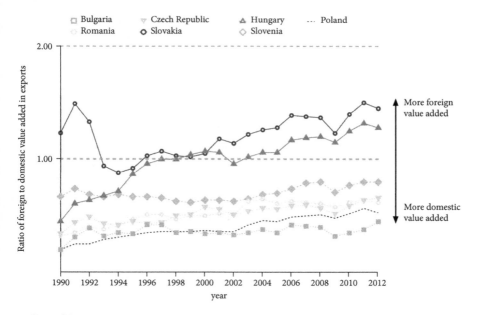

Figure 5.2. Ratio of foreign to domestic value added in exports, 1990–2012
SOURCE: Author's calculations based on data from the UNCTAD-EORA GVC database (Lenzen et al. 2012; Lenzen et al. 2013).

A number of structural shifts can be observed when the 2000s are compared to the early 1990s. One standout feature of the 1990s is the lower dependence on external markets (see Figure 5.1); in other words, exports were less critical to the economy, as most production and consumption took place within the domestic economy. Investment dependence was also lower on average. Technological dependence was much lower; for the most part, domestic value added dominated over foreign value added in exports, even in Hungary. Overall, in the 1990s, these economies were more self-reliant. The heightened globalization period of 1998–2008 introduced a number of important structural changes, such as differentiating the smaller from the larger economies, and the more export-specialized economies from those that relied more heavily on domestically driven growth. While external market dependence grew for all economies, export specialization is more dramatic in the smaller countries like the Czech Republic, Slovakia, and Slovenia than in Poland and Romania.

Summarizing Differences

To summarize patterns in the 2000s, Table 5.1 represents the distribution of countries along the categories of investment (FDI) and market (export) dependence. Across these dimensions, we observe that patterns of transnational integration in the 2000s are quite distinct. In one set of countries, we have the emergence of high levels of export specialization (the Czech Republic, Hungary, Slovakia, Slovenia), while in others we see the continued importance of domestic demand as a driver of growth.[3] These market factors are critical because to policymakers they imply different sources of pressure and different strategies of adjustment. On the crucial dimension of FDI dependence, there is variation between economies where FDI strongly outweighs domestic investment, and in others where domestic investment continues to be significant. Once again, policymakers are presented with different constraints depending on whether domestic or foreign capital dominates investment decisions.

Table 5.1. Distribution of countries across levels of FDI and export dependence in the 2000s

| | FDI dependence | | |
Export dependence	Low	Intermediate	High
High	Slovenia	Czech Republic	Hungary, Slovakia
Low	Russia	Poland, Romania	Bulgaria

In terms of technological dependence, data show that, over the 2000s, domestic value added assumed a smaller and, in some cases, even marginal role in exports when compared to foreign value added. The value-added composition of exports speaks directly to the relative position of the economy in terms of global value chains. In the case of Central and Eastern Europe's transformation, it helps determine the extent to which the region's growing export complexity in the 2000s and 2010s reflects the enhancement of domestic skill and technology, or whether export complexity is largely reflective of the economy's reexporting of high-technology goods as a result of integration into transnational production chains. In the latter cases, domestic production can be said to primarily serve the function of downstream, low-skilled assembly work of inputs that are sourced from elsewhere, even when the final output is high-technology goods. This partly addresses the question of whether TNC-driven economic transnationalization contributes to the upgrade of the domestic technological base, or whether it serves to undermine that base by encouraging the downgrading of domestic skill and technological capabilities, favoring low-skilled *maquiladora*-type development.

Table 5.2 compares countries across ratios of domestic and foreign value added in exports and their share of high-technology exports.[4] Clearly, economies differ widely in the composition of their exports, with Hungary and the Czech Republic leading in high-technology exports. However, differences in value-added levels suggest strong contrasts in the sources of those high-technology exports. On average, more of Hungary's exports are based on high-end foreign inputs. Given the decline in ratios of domestic and foreign value added, Hungary's transnationalization has contributed to its rise as a major

Table 5.2. Distribution of countries across ratios of domestic and foreign value added in exports and portion of high-technology exports in total exports

	Portion of high-technology exports	
Ratio of domestic and foreign value added in exports	Low	High
More domestic	Poland, Slovenia, Bulgaria, Romania	Czech Republic
More foreign	Slovakia	Hungary

SOURCE: World Bank World Development Indicators (data for 2007) and author's calculations from UNCTAD-EORA GVC database.
NOTE: High-technology exports are classified as high when the share of high-technology goods is 10 percent or more of total exports.

high-technology exporter, but the cost has been the relative diminishment of the role of domestic skill in manufacturing. Slovakia has also experienced a similar decline in the value-added composition of its exports, but unlike Hungary, it was not rewarded with a more complex export profile. High-technology exports constituted only 5 percent of Slovakia's exports.

By contrast, the Czech Republic and Slovenia are also highly dependent on exports, but domestic value added plays a larger role in constituting each country's export profile. Czech exports consist of more high-technology exports than Slovenian exports. This is reflective of a longer history of industrial development, but more crucially the capacity of the Czech political economy to preserve the economy's innovative capabilities during the era of transnationalization. Slovenia's export profile consists primarily of intermediate goods, also reflecting a preserved industrial specialization during the course of the longer transformation from socialism. Given similar starting points in the late 1980s, Slovenia could have presumably chosen the Hungarian path of pursuing an FDI-heavy and TNC-driven road of upgrading its export profile, but the cost would have likely been loss of domestic skill and technological capabilities.

Paralleling the importance of FDI in domestic investment is the role of TNCs and their importance as sources of domestic output and employment. TNCs account for close to one-half or more of total turnover in manufacturing across most states, with TNCs controlling one-half and up to two-thirds of turnover in manufacturing in Bulgaria, the Czech Republic, Hungary, Romania, and Slovakia (Table 5.3). By contrast, the role of TNCs in the manufacturing output of Slovenia and Poland is less prominent. Paralleling their prominent role in manufacturing and other sectors, TNCs account for nearly a quarter of total employment in the Czech Republic, Hungary, Romania, and Slovakia. What these structural variations mean substantively is discussed next.

Table 5.3. Distribution of countries based on level of turnover in foreign-controlled enterprises in manufacturing as a percentage of domestic totals

Level	Proportion	Economy
Very high	70% or higher	Slovakia
High	60–69%	Czech Republic, Hungary, Romania
Intermediate	50–59%	Bulgaria
Low	49% or less	Poland, Slovenia

SOURCE: Eurostat (2011 figures).

Transnational Integration and International Market Roles

In combination, the preceding observations indicate the existence of at least *two alternative paths of transnational integration*, leading to *three distinct international market roles* of Central and Eastern European economies in the course of their transformation in the 2000s. Paths differed on the speed and depth of export specialization and reliance on FDI (and the corresponding growth of the TNC sector) in driving that process. In this we see that Hungary and Slovakia pursued a high-FDI path relying heavily on an export-driven strategy. This policy has reflected in TNCs playing a major role in domestic output and employment; indeed, with the figure standing at 78 percent in 2011, Slovakia had the highest rate of control of domestic manufacturing turnover by TNCs in the region and, according to other measures, across the entire OECD. This high-FDI, export-driven path has also been associated with the increased reliance on foreign value added as a basis for those exports.

The path of low-FDI, high-export specialization appears in only one case, Slovenia. A low-FDI path means that greater pressure was placed on domestic firms to adjust to world market pressures, and a greater role was given to domestic investment in absorbing the costs of such adjustment. Between these two extreme paths are intermediate tracks where the expansion of the TNC sector is not combined with a downgrade of domestic skill (the Czech Republic), or where export specialization is partly stunted by the continued importance of the domestic market (Bulgaria, Poland, and Romania).

The weight of FDI in domestic investment and its impact on the domestic economic structure was not the only differentiating factor. Measures of technological dependence indicate that an additional dimension differentiated the globalizing economies of Central and Eastern Europe. This factor is the structural location that domestic industry captured in global value chains and the character of the economy's exports (high- versus medium- and low-technology goods). These features suggest significant differences in roles assumed by postsocialist economies in transnational production and international markets. As previously mentioned, these economies came to occupy one of three roles in the course of the 2000s: assembly platform, intermediate producer, or combined. Rather than true-to-detail empirical descriptions, these roles represent theoretical ideal types whose fit with empirical cases will be assessed subsequently.

An *assembly platform* role suggests that the economy has come to serve primarily as a site for downstream, low-cost, low-skill assembly of foreign inputs, relying primarily on imported capital goods. While such assembly tasks may involve the manufacture of sophisticated goods, the economy's domestic capacities for innovation and technological development are reduced due to the less significant role of endogenous product development. An assembly platform role is also accompanied by the relative de-skilling of the workforce, as even sophisticated product manufacture depends on mass-production technologies that require little creative work on the part of workers. Managerial work similarly depends on the steering of employees on the basis of organizational models and practices imposed from the outside. Hierarchical control by TNCs suggests that firms' key strategic decisions are made in parent organizations located outside of the host economy, whose primary interest lies in using subsidiaries toward cost and efficiency gains. In combination, this inhibits both product and organizational innovation in the subsidiary firm and firm-led investment in skill formation. Critics of FDI have long warned that high dependence on FDI carries such risks. When economies assume the assembly platform role, these risks materialize.

An *intermediate producer* casts the economy in the role of an exporter of sophisticated manufactured goods and where domestic value-added activities play a much larger role in the production process. In these economies, firms tend to exhibit greater domestic managerial control and potentially higher levels of domestic ownership of key export industries. Domestic firms and workers possess higher levels of technological competence and innovative capabilities. Because more domestic firms compete in markets as direct sellers and subcontractors (rather than operating as TNC subsidiaries), they face greater pressures to innovate and compete on cost and quality. As a result, rather than serving mainly as a processing point of foreign-sourced inputs, the economy originates more of its exported products, some of which constitute competitive high-technology exports. With these capacities, the economy's firms possess more "specific resources," including human capital and proprietary technologies, enabling them to retain "sustained competitive advantages" (Barney 1991) over the long run. These allow domestic firms to assume niche market identities and compete directly in world markets. These firm-level capacities differentiate intermediate producer economies from assembly platforms, which are more strongly characterized by firms relying on more widely available technologies, production processes, and the more easily replicable tasks and replaceable labor of mass production. An intermediate producer is not necessarily devoid of TNC subsidiaries in the local economy, but intermediate producers have richer ecologies of local firms against which TNC subsidiaries compete with or rely on as suppliers providing a wide array of inputs and high-end services. This suggests that, when present, TNCs in intermediate producer economies generate greater horizontal spillover effects. TNCs spur local firms to enhance competitiveness via upgrades in technology and increases in productivity. As a result, TNC subsidiaries often perform roles that are complementary to those of local firms, rather than as substitutes for them (the so-called crowding out effect).

Finally, the *combined* role signifies an economy that specializes fully neither as an assembly platform nor as an intermediate producer. These roles instead differ across sectors. The development of an international market role is also an institutionally more muted process given the higher relative importance of the domestic market for producers. Table 5.4 summarizes the characteristics of the two main ideal types described here.

Applying these three ideal types to the empirical cases suggests the distribution presented in Table 5.5. Hungary and Slovakia both exhibit features of the assembly platform role. These are two highly FDI-dependent, export-specialized economies that produce relatively sophisticated products (such as

Table 5.4. Distinctions in firm behavior, innovation, skill, and product market regulation in assembly platforms and intermediate producers

	Assembly platform	Intermediate producer
Dominant market presence of firms	Subsidiaries	Direct market participants
Firm management	Implementation of external organizational models	Greater autonomy of managers to engage in organizational experimentation and innovation
Innovation	Disjuncture between economy's low innovative capabilities and complexity of exports	Better match between complexity of exports and domestic innovation
Skill	Worker de-skilling due to prevalence of replicable mass-production techniques (spatially reproducible tasks with replaceable human capital)	Firms rely on worker skill to overcome competitive pressures (specific firm resources in human capital)
TNC role	Enclave-type operations with sparse links to domestic firms	Complementary operation with dense links to and high-technological and productivity spillovers among domestic firms
Product market regulation	Liberal (deregulated) market policies attract TNC investment	Regulated market raises barriers of entry

Table 5.5. Distribution of cases across international market role types

International market role	Cases
Assembly platform	Hungary, Slovakia
Intermediate producer	Czech Republic, Slovenia
Combined	Poland, Romania, Bulgaria

automobiles and electronics). But their role as reexporting economies makes such sophisticated exports largely the output of assembly work, often carried out by means of mass-production techniques, of foreign-imported components, under the control of TNC subsidiaries. The assembly platform role leads us to expect that innovation levels in these economies are low, economies undergo considerable de-skilling, and there are few TNC spillovers for domestic firms. As political economies, their institutions and policies reflect features of the "competition state" (Cerny 1997), where tax policy, product market regulation, and labor markets are organized on the basis of liberal market rules that are geared toward supporting and incentivizing continued TNC investments.

By contrast, the Czech Republic and Slovenia occupy an intermediate producer role. The Czech Republic figures among the region's most sophisticated exporters and Slovenia among the region's most successful export-oriented economies. The intermediate producer role, however, has been obtained by different routes. In Slovenia, this route followed a path favoring domestic ownership of export industries. The comparative advantages of Slovenian exports were preserved in the course of the 1990s and 2000s, making Slovenia one of the most export-oriented countries in the region. Unlike its neighbors, which export more final consumer goods, Slovenia specializes in the export of intermediate products such as electrical and mechanical components and equipment. Additional facts that make Slovenia a prime case of an intermediate producer include a more marginal role of TNCs in manufacturing, and the resulting pressures export firms face to compete directly in export markets. The Czech case is somewhat different, given that Czech governments after 1997 pursued a more FDI-based growth policy. As a result, the share of TNC control in Czech industry is much greater. However, this has not reduced the competitive and innovative capacities of Czech firms, suggesting that spillover effects of TNCs are greater.

Finally, Poland, Romania, and Bulgaria exhibit the combined role. Across these cases, this role is partly made possible by the importance of the domestic market, which drives many local firms (including small producers and small business) to service the needs of domestic clients. Poland represents the primary case of a combined role given both the size of the domestic market and the fact that sizable FDI inflows did not translate into the economy's domination by TNCs. Particular sectors, however, may variously display features of assembly platform and intermediate producer roles. In the TNC-based automotive industry, the sector's role as an assembly platform is prominent. In the shipbuilding sector, domestic (and largely state) ownership create a very different base for the organization of production, supply chain linkages, international competition, and sectoral development. These radical sectoral differences make combined cases less fully classifiable as belonging to either of the two types. Trends may push combined cases toward assuming one or another role. While paths of future development are not fully determined, Bulgaria, on the one hand, is tending toward the intermediate producer role, given the growing importance of exports in its economy after 2008. Romania, on the other hand, is tending toward the assembly platform role, given the growing weight of TNCs in the economy and losses in the role of domestic value added in exports.[5]

International Market Roles and Features of the Domestic Political Economy

Beyond general macroeconomic and structural features, the assembly platform and intermediate producer roles suggest significant differences in the institutional and policy features of these political economies. A number of assumptions are made about differences in firm performance, innovation-oriented activity, and public policies. How well do the features described in the ideal types capture the *institutional* and *policy* realities found in empirical cases? The following analysis shifts toward the examination of the landscape of firms and public policy within individual political economies to inspect the degree of fit between the ideal types and the empirical features of cases. This section looks at four factors: capacities for innovation, TNC spillovers, domestic skill, and product market regulation. Capacities for innovation and TNC spillovers should be comparatively lower in assembly platforms. With the prevalence of mass-production techniques, skill training and education focused on the preparation of the industrial workforce should favor general over specific skill. And the high dependence of exports, employment, and overall economic growth on TNC investments in assembly platforms should be associated with governments pursuing greater product market deregulation—that is, policies that accommodate the competitive and efficiency-seeking interests of TNCs. How do the cases match up with these expectations?

Two indicators are used to examine capacities for innovation, examining both innovation-oriented public policy and firm-level capacities for innovation. The first measure uses data on public spending on R&D. As Table 5.6 shows, R&D spending in intermediate producers is considerably higher than in assembly platforms or combined cases. While such spending is nonetheless below the OECD average, intermediate producers Slovenia and the Czech Republic top the region in levels of public investment in R&D. In the other group, we observe major differences between Hungary and Slovakia, which as assembly platforms ought to perform the worst on this measure. Indeed, Slovakia spent the least on R&D, but Hungary did better than Poland and Romania. Rather than economically oriented innovation, this may partly reflect the higher quality of the education system and the more advanced state of scientific research in these states. For example, both Hungary and Slovakia do better than the combined cases in measures of scientific performance, such as numbers of scientific articles per million population.[6] While Slovenia and the Czech Republic outperform these two economies in these measures as well, Hungary and Slovakia generate a greater amount of scientific output than Poland and Romania.[7] In addition, the vast majority of government expenditures for R&D in Hungary and Slovakia go toward generic (nonspecialized) public research. By contrast, the question of innovation pertains to the spillovers scientific research has in economic applications. Ideally, public investments in science ought to translate into an economy driven by more endogenous innovation. The assumption for assembly platforms is not that public investments in R&D are necessarily low in comparative terms, but that there is a mismatch between public investments in R&D and innovation at the firm level. Because TNCs perform most of their product and process development in the home economy, their ties to the national innovation system in assembly platforms are more tenuous. In assembly platforms, more than simply low public expenditures on R&D, we should observe a persistent gap between national innovation policies and the innovation rates of firms.

The comparative data on public policy, firm innovation, and market regulation demonstrate significant and consistent differences between assembly platforms and intermediate producers (see Table 5.6). Not only are there important differences in terms of public and private investment in R&D, but in

Table 5.6. Public policy, firm innovation, and market regulation indicators across three groups of states

	Public policy				Firm innovation				Market regulation	
	Government expenditure on R&D (% of GDP) (2012)	Business expenditure on R&D (% of GDP)	Government budget appropriations and outlays for R&D (% of GDP)	Tertiary education expenditure (% of GDP) (2011)	R&D expenditures of foreign affiliates (% of total R&D expenditures of enterprises) (2007)	Trademarks abroad (2012)	Product and process innovators (as a % of all firms) (2010)	Total patents filed under the Patent Cooperation Treaty (per 100,000 pop.) (2014)	Product market regulation (2013)	Employment protection (individual and collective dismissals) (2013)
Intermediate producer										
Czech Republic	1.9	1.2	0.7	1.5	55	0.24	9.3	2.23	1.39	2.92
Slovenia	2.6	2.0	0.5	1.4	29	0.34	10.2	7.59	1.70	2.6
Assembly platform										
Hungary	1.3	0.8	0.3	0	63	0.17	7.5	2.31	1.33	1.59
Slovakia	0.8	0.3	0.4	1.1	38	0.16	6.5	1.21	1.29	1.84
Combined										
Poland	0.9	0.3	0.4	1.3	31	0.09	6.8	0.94	1.65	2.23

INDICATORS AND SOURCES: Public policy: all figures from *OECD Science, Technology and Industry Outlook 2014* (OECD 2014b). Firm innovation: all figures from *OECD* (2014b), with the exception of "Total patents filed under the Patent Cooperation Treaty (per 100,000 population), which is based on author's calculation using data from OECD Patent Database. Market regulation: Product market regulation from OECD Indicators of Product Market Regulation 2013 and employment protection data from OECD Employment Protection Indicators (version 1).

NOTE: Shaded cells indicate consistently higher values within the group. Comparable data for Bulgaria and Romania are unavailable. Product market regulation values reflect economy-wide regulation in the areas of state control, barriers to entrepreneurship, and barriers to trade and investment. Higher values reflect greater overall regulation. Employment protection indices measure legal regulation of employment, including ease of dismissals. Higher values indicate higher levels of employment protection.

innovation measures as well. Intermediate producers are better product and process innovators, reflecting the greater autonomy of firms and the more direct competitive pressures firms face. These are associated with a higher number of innovations measured in terms of international trademarks and patents. Their high levels of innovation reflect not only public policy orientations but also firm interests. As more innovative firms are direct market participants and rely on endogenous resources to compete in domestic and international markets, public investments in R&D are more likely to be complementary to firm-level R&D.

Similarly consistent differences emerge in the area of market regulation. Given the heavily outward-oriented and externally dependent structure of business sectors, the basic economic policy orientation of assembly platforms is FDI competition. This necessitates broad deregulation in order to create institutional environments that favor business flexibility—that is, that give a freer hand to firms and management to carry out market transactions and make cost-cutting decisions while facing fewer regulatory or bureaucratic hindrances. In other words, institutions and policies in assembly platforms more deeply reflect the designs of a neoliberal policy regime. Market regulation indicators again point to the consistently less regulated markets of assembly platforms. Two measures are used here: product market and labor market regulation. The first measure combines regulatory levels in three areas: state control over the economy, legal and bureaucratic barriers to entrepreneurship, and legal and bureaucratic barriers to trade and investment. Hungary and Slovakia score lower average levels of regulation in all three areas. The second measure is degrees of employment protection that the law provides to workers, reflecting the scope of managerial power to hire and dismiss workers and trade union involvement in employment. Again, Hungary and Slovakia display much lower levels of labor market regulation than do the Czech Republic and Slovenia. In these measures, Poland occupies a middle ground, reflecting the cross-cutting pressures of business interests and government policy in the combined role. While product and labor market regulation is higher in Poland than in the assembly platforms, many of the public policy and firm innovation indicators fall on the lower end of the scale. Unfortunately, due to the unavailability of comparable data for Bulgaria and Romania, developing a clearer image of patterns and differences among states in the combined role is more difficult.

Another institutional perspective across distinct political economies can be gained by comparative surveys of business managers who operate in these environments. Instead of reporting objective performance measures and out-comes such as quantifiable expenditures and outputs, these types of surveys reflect the subjective views of business actors on the quality of institutions and business environments. The World Economic Forum's *Global Competitiveness Report* (*GCR*) represents one such worldwide survey that rates countries based on the views of business actors in these areas (Schwab 2015). While the *GCR* ranks countries on a large array of indicators, a focus on areas of interest to the typology constructed here is instructive as a gauge of the degree to which the analytical descriptions of institutions constructed here correspond with views of business actors operating in those environments. One of these areas reflects views on skill and technological capacities, and another on the nature of the business environment in terms of business sophistication—the quantity and quality of local suppliers, cluster development, value chain breadth, interna-tional distribution, production process sophistication, marketing, and other aspects relevant to international business operation in the local economy. The measure of skill examines what the *GCR* calls "technological readiness" and is a measure of "the agility with which an economy adopts existing technologies to enhance the productivity of its industries" (Schwab 2015, 36). Such agility refers not only to the capacity of the economy to develop new technologies but also the ease with which local actors adapt to and apply existing (including for-eign-sourced) technologies in production. In this implicit measure of domestic skill capacities, the intermediate producers perform better than the assembly platforms. Indeed, some of the combined economies such as Bulgaria perform better on this measure than the assembly platforms. In terms of business so-phistication, which indicates the breadth and depth of local supply networks, the *GCR* survey again confirms the superiority of intermediate producers. In-deed, in this area the gap between intermediate producers and assembly plat-forms is much larger. Hungary, especially, falls behind not only the combined group but also Slovakia.

A final area where we should see differences is in FDI spillovers. Recall that the central claim is that intermediate producers differ from assembly platforms not necessarily by the degree of presence of TNCs in the local economy but by the structural location they assume in local production networks. Rather than substituting for domestic firms, TNCs may potentially complement them and, additionally, their presence may create greater horizontal spillover effects in areas such as technology and productivity among local business. Vertical (di-rect) spillovers take place when TNCs transfer technology and organizational practices into the host economy, leading to gains in efficiency and productivity. With vertical spillovers, these gains are confined to TNC sectors and individual subsidiaries under TNC control. By contrast, horizontal (indirect) spillovers occur when the presence of TNCs causes productivity and technology gains among *local firms*. There are a variety of channels by which horizontal spillovers can occur, and only a small set are mentioned here. The first is *direct competition* against TNCs for market share, which could lead domestic firms to improve organizational practices, technologies, and products (Pula 2017a). Second, TNCs may impose higher quality standards on local suppliers, causing them to invest in upgrades and product improvements. Third, the presence of TNC subsidiaries facilitates the circulation of personnel. As professional and skilled workers circulate between TNC subsidiaries and local firms, they transfer knowledge and organizational experience. Economists who have examined FDI spillovers in Central and Eastern Europe using econometric techniques find overwhelming positive evidence for vertical spillovers, but there is no consensus on the positive or negative effects of horizontal spillovers (Iwasaki and Tokunaga 2016). Among major comparative studies, the analysis by Jože Damijan and colleagues (2003) examines the effects of FDI on efficiency gains in capital and labor among domestic firms for the period 1994–1999. They find little evidence of horizontal spillover effects, and instead find evidence of positive spillovers from trade in the Czech Republic, Slovenia, Poland, and Romania. In Slovenia they find that spillovers from trade are more important than those from FDI, reflecting the locally rooted nature of exporting firms. In the Czech Republic they find evidence of horizontal spillovers, but that these spillovers are positive only among firms that already had high levels of endogenous R&D accumulation. In other words, in the Czech Republic, FDI incited the upgrade of technology and productivity among *advanced domestic firms*. Balázs Szent-Iványi and Gábor Vigvári (2012) agree with much research that finds that FDI spillovers are highly dependent on host economy characteristics, including technological absorption capacities and the nature of foreign ownership. For example, firms that have only partial foreign ownership retain more ties with local suppliers, making horizontal spillovers more likely in comparison to fully owned subsidiaries that bring with them their own suppliers. In their development of an index for spillover potential, Szent-Iványi and Vigvári compare the Czech Republic, Hungary, Slovakia, and Poland between 2003 and 2007 to find that potential significantly higher in the Czech Republic. While spillover effects are weakest in Poland, the large gap between the Czech Republic, on the one hand, and Hungary and Slovakia, on the other, demonstrates that, even for FDI-dependent economies, the benefits of FDI are not always widely shared. In other words, there is no question that in assembly platforms FDI has brought important benefits in terms of technology and productivity gains. But, as expected, these gains are more narrowly concentrated in TNC-led sectors and even individual TNC subsidiaries. In intermediate producers, the gains from FDI are more likely to emanate beyond TNC-led sectors and diffuse among local manufacturing firms.

Conclusion

This chapter develops a comparative analysis of the political economy of Central and Eastern European states building inductively from their international market roles developed through the period of heightened globalization in the 2000s. The period was characterized both by a more central role for FDI and TNCs in the local economies and by a deepening export specialization, as well as EU accession, which embedded Central and Eastern European economies firmly within the emerging political economy of the European global region. An increasing convergence on FDI and reliance on leading global firms drove the process of domestic industrial restructuring and production network integration.

However, through a structural comparison of paths and outcomes of transnational integration, this chapter demonstrates that there were significant *divergences* in regional patterns of integration, based on the role of FDI, the degree of export specialization, and the location assumed by domestic industry in global value chains. These differences point to the fact that the experience of globalization in the 2000s generated significant rifts in structural and institutional patterns across the region. Even under the shared conditions of EU-led market integration and deepening transnational linkages of local industry, there is more heterogeneity in the region's political economies than is typically acknowledged in accounts and classifications of Central and Eastern Europe as a set of dependent market economies (King 2007; Nölke and Vliegenthart 2009) or as varying by regional cluster (Bohle and Greskovits 2012). These differences imply not only divergent developmental paths but also the emergence of distinct structural pressures and organizations of producer interests with significant impact on sectoral organization, dominant market orientation of firms, and the performance of political economies in the areas of skill formation and innovation.

This chapter proposes three distinct international market roles assumed by Central and Eastern European states in the process of globalization in the 2000s: assembly platform, intermediate producer, and combined. Assembly platforms globalized quickly with the rapid incorporation of domestic industry in transnational production networks via reliance on TNC-led FDI, which raised the export profile and complexity mix of domestic industry, but at the cost of the hollowing out of domestic skill, including capacities for innovation. Hungary and Slovakia exemplify this role. Their international market role corresponds closely with key aspects of their domestic political economy, including high concentration of control in TNCs, low levels of firm-based R&D and innovation, and relative isolation of domestic firms from the TNC sector. In public policy, these states favored liberal market policies oriented toward the competition for FDI and deregulation in product markets and employment protection that were consonant with a neoliberal view of global market competition and the demand for a transnationally oriented competition state. Assembly platforms fit most closely with standard descriptions of dependent market economies, in the sense that the process of structural and institutional adjustment to global competitive pressures led to relative improvements in market positions and export complexity, but at the price of the loss of domestic skill and innovative capacities and pressures for thoroughgoing liberalization of the economy. Put differently, by drawing their competitive advantage primarily on cost, assembly platforms run a higher risk of hitting the developmental trap of a middle-income economy that faces increasingly stiffer competition from low-wage economies in serving as a base for export-oriented manufacturing, but also lacking the institutions and organized interests that enable the economy to move up the technological frontier and compete against advanced economies in areas of high skill and innovation (Kharas and Kohli 2011; Doner and Schneider 2016).

By contrast, intermediate producers were better able to maintain domestic innovative capacities, even when their economy became reliant on FDI and the expansion of the TNC sector, as in the Czech Republic (with Slovenia representing the most unambiguous case of an intermediate producer). These political economies were better structured to provide capabilities for innovation and skilled labor, judged by public and private investment in R&D, the performance of local economies in measures of innovation, levels of legal protection given to workers, and other aspects of domestic product market regulation. Intermediate producers were the ones to mobilize and use the opportunities of globalization of domestic industry toward broader developmental goals and move up the value chain ladder of the global economy, despite the largely second-tier status of their industry (specializing largely—though not exclusively—in in-termediate components and producer goods). In the third type, the combined roles, neither assembly platform nor an intermediate producer role emerged clearly. Instead, such roles surface variously at the sectoral level. In addition, less prominent TNC sectors and the larger role of the domestic market create wider scope for policymakers and present less coherent organization of inter-ests that drive the restructuring and adjustment of the political economy. Con-sequently, institutional and policy features in combined roles fell less neatly within the patterns of either an assembly platform or an intermediate producer.

Emerging international market roles in the 2000s were not the direct outcome of socialist experiences of globalization (or protoglobalization; see Chapter 4). The legacy of socialist protoglobalization was not determinant of postsocialist developmental patterns; rather, it provided a legacy that could be mobilized toward those goals in the context of the changing international market opportunity structure in the 1990s and 2000s. The advantages that economies like Hungary, Romania, Poland, and Slovenia had due to their lon-ger experiences with transnational production (see Chapter 3) could and were mobilized politically toward varied ends. In Hungary, the process of rapid post-socialist globalization was taken to its farthest possible extent, accommodated politically through robust pro-FDI and pro-TNC policies, resulting eventually in an assembly platform role. In Romania, despite the country's long experi-ence in Western trade, political elites in the early 1990s put greater emphasis on domestic state-led development and made acquisition of local industry by TNCs more cumbersome. In Slovenia, a regime that was similarly less open to TNC entry was combined with the rise of a robust (domestically owned) export sector. And in Poland, the early wholesale approach to market reform and privatization was in the course of the 1990s and 2000s replaced by sectoral policies that gave different political weight to labor, regional governments, and state-led industrial policies that made the entry of industrial FDI more com-plex and uneven. These differences indicate the importance of political factors in directing the process of local industry's deepening transnational integration and postsocialist institutional adjustment. Chapter 6 turns to the analysis of these political factors and their impact on institutional change.

Critical Junctures and the Politics of Institutional Adjustment

6

Explaining Divergence

No legacy lasts forever.
—Ruth Berins Collier and David Collier, *Shaping the Political Arena*[1]

The previous chapter details structural and institutional divergences in the development of Central and Eastern European economies through the 2000s. While legacy factors were causally significant during the early reform period, Chapter 5 suggests that political factors ultimately determined the direction of postsocialist development and international market specialization. International market roles of individual economies built on the cumulative advantages in transnational production that Central and Eastern European economies gained during their socialist experience, but it was the *political* challenge of turning those cumulative advantages into a sustained *comparative institutional advantage* that would bring important gains in the capital, technological, and skill base of the economy. Accomplishing this feat is what concerned the politics of reform in the 1990s and 2000s. It was here that politics became critical and where the interplay between industrial restructuring and reform of other institutions of the political economy came to matter, including financial systems, educational systems, labor markets, and industrial relations.

The explanation in this chapter puts its focus on the critical junctures of the postsocialist period. It suggests that the developmental strategies of postsocialist elites had much to do with the institutional outcomes of economic restructuring and reorientation. My analysis assumes that, while postsocialist economic reforms in East Europe were generally oriented toward building markets, reformers saw markets in developmental terms. I suggest that, in broad terms, two major sets of policy orientations were pursued after 1989. The first were *externalist* (outward) strategies, implemented by reformers who saw developmental gains in terms of rapid transnational integration, relying on the role of external (foreign) actors, particularly TNCs. This strategy favored economic openness in terms of trade and capital account liberalization, privatization reliant on FDI, and rapid export-driven growth. By contrast, reformers employing *internalist* (inward) strategies favored domestically driven development. While also favoring economic openness, they saw domestic firms and investment as the main drivers of restructuring. This partly reflected in privatization policies that gave priority to domestic owners and other fiscal, industrial, and credit policies that supported domestic industry.

Externalist and internalist strategies did not simply reflect contrasting preferences of successive reformers in power, but were constituted in the critical junctures of postsocialist transformation. Rather than purely individual or party-political differences, these orientations were carried out by governments consisting of reformers who sometimes came from opposing parties. As a result, they reflected a particular kind of socioeconomic consensus (or hegemony) on the orientation of reform among elites and society more generally, and sustained until a crisis or external pressures demanded change in approach and direction. There were at least two region-wide critical junctures in the making of such policy orientation in postsocialist polities. Clearly, the political revolutions of 1989–1990 constituted the first such critical juncture, by opening the political space for radical policy reorientation. A second juncture emerged in the late 1990s, when first-wave reforms had run their course and the economies of Central and Eastern Europe faced serious, sometimes dire recessions. The political effects of these latter pressures were also compounded by the process of EU accession, which also intensified in the late 1990s and early 2000s. In many cases, the result of these events was a shift in reform strategy, leading in most cases to the abandonment of internalist strategies. However, following the logic of path dependence, the *institutional residues* of previous strategies remained; they constrained the effects of subsequent strategy orientations.

The following discussion broadly outlines the difference between inward and outward strategies. It then applies the strategies to the empirical cases, comparing the experience of the intermediate producers and assembly platforms, and discussing the conundrums faced by states assuming the combined role.

Outward Versus Inward Strategies of Postsocialist Reform

The literature on postsocialist economic reform is vast, as are the intricacies of reform policies carried out over successive decades. This discussion does no justice to the minutiae of economic reform politics and policies and their differences across individual postsocialist states. Rather, it builds on family resemblances between particular policy sets and their overall orientation to construct two basic but consequential ideal-typical orientations in economic reform policy. It is important to highlight where some of the key differences lied. For example, while some differences emerged between the region's governments in the early 1990s in areas such as import and tariff policy, capital controls, and exchange rate regimes, these did not differ dramatically across states (EBRD 1994, 108–109). One key policy difference lay in the orientation of privatization and FDI policy. Indeed, in the early 1990s, for the most part, privatization favoring domestic owners tended to be accompanied with more restrictive FDI policies and more protective trade, capital account, and exchange rate policies, and is thus most indicative of the reforming governments' internalist orientation.[2]

Postsocialist governments introduced three general waves of economic reform. The first wave included the so-called liberalization and stabilization measures pioneered by the neoliberal "shock therapy" policies of Leszek Balcerowicz in Poland, which aimed at macroeconomic adjustments in areas such as price, currency, and trade liberalization with the goal of inducing market shocks in the economy. Stabilization reforms endeavored to control spiraling inflation through a combination of interest rate and wage control mechanisms. The basic designs of these initial reforms were shared across the region (Bruno 1992; Lavigne 1999). Privatization constituted the second pillar of economic reform, whose objective was the transferring of state-owned industries to private owners in order to restructure the supply side of the economy in accordance with market principles. Finally, parallel and subsequent reforms tackled other market institutions. These institutional reforms ranged from judicial reforms to the creation of independent monetary authorities to the establishment of regulatory agencies and organizations such as stock exchanges necessary for the exercise of property rights and the operation of markets.

Privatization policy formed a crucial element of the reform process. Unlike liberalization and stabilization reforms, approaches to privatization varied significantly across countries. Privatization policy was geared either toward catering to domestic interests (creating a class of domestic owners) or toward selling assets off to foreign owners. These radically different orientations reflected not only ideological preferences of postsocialist political elites or the interests of dominant elite factions but also a developmental orientation reflecting the varied political and social blocs that stood behind them, particularly in key industrial sectors. The making of capitalism and markets in postsocialist contexts was an institutional transformation taking place in the context of heavily industrialized economies. Reformers were aware that market pressures would make certain economic sectors obsolete, but many believed that certain comparative advantages could be protected and harnessed (Landesmann and Ábel 1995). Some industries, especially in the heavy industry sectors, were too costly politically to let disappear, given powerful voter constituencies or managerial elites with ties to ruling parties. As Nove (1995) observes, the industry- and employment-preserving pressures of powerful social and political constituencies and the destructive forces of the world market constituted one of the key contradictions of the postsocialist transition process. Hence, inward and outward policies were not only about the principle according to which assets were distributed to new owners but were also strategies that elites (both political and economic) used to cope with the sudden unleashing of world market pressures after the breakdown of the domestic institutional system that had undergirded past governance of the industrial economy.

The *outward* strategy gave in almost entirely to world market pressures, given confidence that ceding control of domestic industry to external actors was the best means toward the long-term restructuring of the economy. To be sure, in the early 1990s, this was a high-risk undertaking both politically and as a developmental strategy. It relied on the present and ongoing interest of TNCs to make direct investments in the economy. In addition, as previous chapters make clear, not all states were positioned to pursue such a strategy successfully. It worked in Hungary. In Bulgaria, efforts to attract industrial FDI in the early 1990s were much less successful. By contrast, the *inward* strategy relied more heavily on domestic ownership and counted on domestic actors to lead and the state to facilitate the process of economic restructuring as economies adjusted to world market pressures in an approach that Ban (2016) calls "neodevelopmentalist." Privatization policy was skewed toward domestic ownership, and the state introduced a variety of explicit or implicit industrial and credit policies aimed at supporting the restructuring of domestic industry. This strategy carried its own set of risks. That is, instead of leading to economic restructuring, it could encourage rent-seeking behavior by economic elites. Rather than restructure firms, elites would rely on the state to continue with subsidy-seeking actions, with those subsidies now additionally serving the goals of private (and often illicit) gain (Hellman 1998; Grzymala-Busse 2007). An elaboration of the conditions under which inward strategies were more likely to succeed lies beyond the scope of this analysis. But in general terms, the likelihood of success depended on the combination of (1) the existence of or the potential for export growth, particularly with advanced capitalist markets, and (2) the capacity of the state and of political elites to reduce monitoring costs in ways that reduced the likelihood of rent-seeking in the enterprise sector. This implied ruling parties able to forge developmental coalitions with dominant producer groups and a robust and effective state (Grzymala-Busse and Luong 2002; McDermott 2004; Grzymala-Busse 2007; Crowley and Stanojević 2011; Bohle and Greskovits 2012; Easter 2012).

Internalist and externalist strategies were pursued variously across Central and Eastern Europe in the 1990s. Initially, most governments pursued inward-oriented policies, though with the exception of Slovenia, this orientation was largely abandoned by the early 2000s. By contrast, Hungary pursued an outward-oriented strategy from the get-go. It should come as no surprise that, as a result of sustained reform orientations, Slovenia and Hungary represent most fully cases of straightforward transformation into an intermediate producer and an assembly platform, respectively. By contrast, in the other cases (Bulgaria, the Czech Republic, Slovakia, and Romania), the path to an outward-oriented strategy in the 2000s passed through largely unsuccessful attempts at restructuring economies and restarting growth via reliance on domestic actors. In these cases, the transformation is more arduous and their paths laid with more sudden turning points. In Poland, but also partly in Bulgaria and Romania, combined roles are the result of less coherent orientations resulting in experimentations with both inward and outward strategies, but also the less prominent pressures in the enterprise sector of making gains in export markets due to the continuing role of the domestic market. In Slovakia, a radical switch from an internalist to an externalist policy in the early 2000s is constrained and deeply affected by the institutional and political legacies of the previous policy period, leading to a significant but less comprehensive transformation into an assembly platform. The discussion now turns to the analysis of empirical cases and the political dynamics leading in shifts in policy and their consequences.

Outward-Oriented Policies and Political Economies in Hungary and Slovakia

Hungary was a trailblazer in outward-oriented policy. Chapters 3 and 4 highlight Hungary's leadership in import-led growth policies in the 1970s and rapid transnationalization in the 1990s. The path for openness in the post-Communist era was set by the fact that many important institutional reforms were already introduced by the Hungarian Socialist Workers' Party in its last years in power. Reforms in 1988 introduced one of the most liberal foreign investment laws seen in the still existing Soviet bloc. These reforms legalized foreign ownership, allowed full profit repatriation, instituted import duty exemptions, and provided a variety of tax benefits to foreign investors (Jermakowicz and Drazek 1993). In 1990 the still Communist-led parliament adopted Hungary's privatization law, setting up a privatization agency that favored foreign investors (Bartlett 1992). This outward orientation set early on during the Communist regime's last days was maintained and enhanced after the transition to democracy. The post-Communist government of József Antall introduced market reforms that preserved this basic orientation. In 1991, 80 percent of the privatization agency's revenues came from sales to foreign entities (OECD 1993, 73). This trend continued throughout the first privatization wave, during which sales to foreign buyers overwhelmingly dominated over transfers to domestic owners (Hanley, King, and János 2002). With the sale of most industrial assets largely completed, a second privatization wave in 1995 turned to areas such as energy, mining, telecommunications, and banking, which had until then been held as reserved strategic sectors slated to remain under domestic control. This second privatization wave, carried out under the leadership of Gyula Horn of the Hungarian Socialist Party, also led to the ceding of control of major telecommunications, energy, and banking firms to foreign owners, completing Hungary's transition to an almost entirely FDI-dominated economy.

TNCs' entry into Hungary's economy also had much to do with the eventual role assumed by Hungary in its economic transformation. As Comisso (1998) notes, most TNCs in Hungary, particularly in the manufacturing sector, established an "enclave" presence where links with domestic firms were few and interest of TNCs was driven primarily toward cost savings. The weak ties between foreign and domestic firms became an issue of concern to successive Hungarian governments, which have since the 1990s attempted to introduce programs encouraging better integration between TNCs and local suppliers.

These programs ranged from the Socialist government's "Suppliers' Charter" of 1998 to more recent use by the right-wing Fidesz government of "strategic partnerships" with individual TNCs (Hungarian Investment Promotion Agency 2015). These measures have proven of limited effect.

The establishment and consolidation of a TNC-led economy was followed by institutional reforms aimed at accommodating the needs of large employers and encouraging further TNC investment in the growing regional competition for FDI. This regional competition heightened in the late 1990s and early 2000s, when Hungary, once a leading destination for FDI, became increasingly eclipsed by the Czech Republic and Slovakia. Romania and Bulgaria, with their international positions newly bolstered by the promise of EU membership, had during this period fully entered the regional FDI market, and this contributed to the feeling that Hungary had lost its competitive edge. The government's response was to introduce some of the region's most generous incentive packages to foreign investors, some of which had to be rolled back prior to Hungary's EU accession because they violated EU competition rules. Among the other concerns was the rising cost of labor: By the 2000s, Hungary had one of the region's higher paid workforces, particularly compared to Poland, Slovakia, Bulgaria, and Romania. Thanks to a trade union movement in disarray, Hungary's reformers had already introduced one of the region's most liberal employment laws in 1992. A variety of other measures undermined trade unions, including the weakening of tripartite institutions (Ost 2000; Tóth 2001). Even socialist governments in the 2000s were timid in their support tripartite bodies. As a result, Hungary came to have one of the lowest rates of union membership and collective bargaining coverage in the entire EU. Reforms in the educational system introduced in 1993 devolved the control of educational institutions to local governments. Among the consequences of those reforms was the precipitous decline of enrollment in vocational training programs, which had prior to 1989 enrolled most of Hungary's secondary students. The elimination of vocational programs and the shift toward general education at the secondary level was accompanied by an expansion of tertiary education, all the while public funding for tertiary education was being reduced. While Hungary's outward orientation helped preserve the country's industrial base, reforms in the educational system led to persistent shortages of vocationally skilled workers (OECD 2012, 106; 2014a, 37–39). The skill gap became evident in demographic shifts as well. While in the early 1990s, young workers were more likely to be employed than older workers (many of whom lost jobs due to restructuring), the situation entirely reversed after 2008, with high levels of youth unemployment contrasting starkly with high employment levels among older workers. As a result, the labor market became geared toward catering to job seekers with general education profiles; in industry, the burden of creating a skilled workforce fell increasingly on employers. Realizing the detrimental effects of the skill gap, the Fidesz government in 2011 introduced educational reforms that recentralized the educational system by placing curriculum and other areas of primary and secondary education under the control of the national ministry of education. The effects of this change have been mixed. While provoking the ire of local governments and the rage of teachers' unions, they have not significantly turned around the orientation of the Hungarian education system and are far from restoring the popularity of vocational programs to their prior heights (OECD 2015).

Hungary adopted its outward strategies early on in the postsocialist reform period and combined them with deeply liberalizing measures in trade, finance, and employment and industrial relations. Slovakia's path toward the assembly platform role was more circuitous and politically contentious. Indeed, after its split with the Czech Republic, Slovakia followed an internalist orientation, a position bolstered by the fact that as a newly independent nation, the defense of Slovak sovereignty was construed as a primary task for Mečiar's nationalist government. Mečiar canceled the voucher privatization program that had been introduced under the Czechoslovak federal state and replaced it with a program that favored sales to domestic owners. The government used these to construct a patronage-based system of rule. This was accompanied by policies that provided a variety of soft credit and other indirect support to companies favored by the ruling party. Measures such as these contributed to criticism against the government for corruption. In combination with the authoritarian turn against independent media, opposition parties, and ethnic minorities, Mečiar's regime increasingly lost international legitimacy, leading to major rebuttals and increasing diplomatic isolation from the EU and the United States. In 1998 Mečiar and his Movement for a Democratic Slovakia (HZDS) were ousted in parliamentary elections by a united opposition under the leadership of Mikuláš Dzurinda. Dzurinda and his coalition proceeded to dismantle the HZDS patronage network and restarted privatization. This time, priority was given to foreign investors and as a result levels of FDI in Slovakia skyrocketed. The breakup of the Mečiar-era steelmaker and industrial conglomerate VSŽ-Košice, the country's largest employer, and the sale of its steel business to US Steel in 2001 was among the events that marked Slovakia's transition toward an outward strategy. TNC acquisitions in telecommunications, energy, and banking, flagged Slovakia's new role as a major FDI destination. After the contentious elections of 2002, Dzurinda formed a second cabinet, this time with a narrower political base that excluded his former center-left allies. Under the leadership of Finance Minister Ivan Mikloš, Dzurinda's second government implemented a radical and comprehensive program of neoliberal restructuring. In addition to drastic austerity measures, the government's reforms included the introduction of a flat income, corporate, and value-added tax of 19 percent as well as the elimination of dividend taxes, real estate transfer taxes, the gift tax, and the inheritance tax. Pension privatization and health care reforms seeking to induce a financial logic of control in the sector followed, as did privatization measures in higher education. These combined changes quickly gained Slovakia popularity among conservative and neoliberal circles, who described Dzurinda's government as Central and Eastern Europe's neoliberal champion. Indeed, the radical nature of the reforms became a concern even for otherwise market-friendly economists at international financial institutions (Fisher, Gould, and Haighton 2007).

The second Dzurinda government's goals of neoliberal restructuring also targeted the labor market. Describing labor market regulation as a primary cause for Slovakia's persistently high unemployment rate, Dzurinda's reformers pushed for radical liberalization by undermining existing employment and collective bargaining institutions. Unlike in Hungary, where a liberal labor market regime was instituted early on, the internalist strategy pursued under Mečiar cultivated the regime's ties with trade unions and led to the adoption of regulated employment laws and an important role for collective bargaining. The goal of the second Dzurinda government was to roll back these gains, which had been preserved and reaffirmed during his first government (indeed, the support of the Confederation of Trade Unions of the Slovak Republic [KOZ SR], Slovakia's largest trade union confederation, was key in the democratic opposition's victory in 1998). In line with Slovakia's new outward strategy and transformation into an FDI-seeking competition state, Slovak neoliberals believed undermining the influence of trade unions would be welcome by foreign investors. In 2002 reforms stripped employment legislation of much of its protections and dismantled collective bargaining at the national level. In combination with public sector cuts, the reforms depressed wages in an already low-cost economy. Among the most dramatically growing sectors in the 2000s was automobile production, driven exclusively by the rapidly growing presence of major automotive TNCs. The rise of the sector best embodied Slovakia's turn to its new role as a low-cost assembly platform.

The institutional residues of the internal strategy were not that easily done away with, however. While the FDI-led restructuring of the enterprise sector largely succeeded in transforming Slovakia's economic base, issues over employment legislation, industrial relations, and other aspects of social policy lingered. In 2006 Slovak voters threw out Dzurinda's party in favor of a government led by the center-left SMER-SD party under Robert Fico. During his first term, and again in his second after 2012, governments led by Fico have proceeded to reverse some of the more drastic neoliberal reforms, including those in labor legislation, pensions, and other areas. In the area of education, Dzurinda's reforms focused on educational financing more than implementing major changes in curriculum and program structure. As a result, unlike Hungary, Slovakia retained industrially based vocational training programs throughout. Tertiary education expanded at a much slower pace than in Hungary, as well as countries like Poland (Herbst and Wojciuk 2014). Unlike in these latter cases, where vocational training came to be increasingly seen as a dead-end path leading to diminished chances of employment or pursuit of a tertiary degree, in Slovakia (as in the Czech Republic, Slovenia, and Bulgaria), secondary vocational schools, while sometimes lacking in quality and often wanting of more job-relevant training, were still considered by many as a path toward a steady job.

Trade unions, with their ability to influence the social policies of the center-left, as well as the legacy of vocational training, were institutional residues of Slovakia's inward strategies, and their weight continued to be felt after Slovakia's externalist turn in the 2000s. As a result, while exhibiting assembly platform features in patterns of Slovakia's *outward* integration with production networks, its *domestic* institutions of the political economy have continued to be shaped by the legacies of early inward policies during the nationalist era, and also helped energize the political reaction to the radical neoliberal reforms of Dzurinda's second government.

Institutional Legacies and Economic Reform in the Making of Intermediate Producers: The Czech Republic and Slovenia

Like Slovakia, the Czech Republic experienced a similar shift from an inward to outward strategy. As in Slovakia, the outward turn was distorted by the institutional residues of the previous policy posture. In the Czech case, these institutional residues went beyond the domains of social policy and the education system and extended into the enterprise sector. The early consolidation of domestic ownership in the enterprise sector helped preserve endogenous industrial capacities in particular high-technology sectors. In addition, the mode of entry of FDI into what would emerge in the 2000s as the Czech Republic's dominant industrial sector, the automobile industry, also preserved the domestic rootedness of the industry despite changing hands in ownership.

The Czech approach to privatization relied on an innovative process developed by a group of local economists under the leadership of Klaus, who served as finance minister in the post-Communist Czechoslovak federal government, and subsequently occupied the position of prime minister of the Czech Republic after 1993. While renowned for his radical neoliberal positions, Klaus nonetheless favored a privatization policy that was biased toward domestic ownership (Myant 2003). Aiming to avoid the concentration of ownership among a small group, Klaus and his associates developed the original scheme of voucher privatization. Under the program, each Czech citizen would gain vouchers that could be converted toward shares in private investment funds. These investment funds would, in turn, own shares in Czech firms. The goal was to create not only private owners but also a market for ownership that would lead the Czech Republic toward the development of capital markets dominated by small investors (Appel 2004).

The scheme was implemented successfully, and Czech privatization officially concluded in 1995. But the new system was characterized by serious structural problems. Ownership shares came to be concentrated in a small set of investment funds, many of which were controlled by banks. In addition to corrupt dealings in vouchers and shares, shady investors sought to gain control of profitable companies on the cheap or sell shares at inflated prices. The system also encouraged risky investments and loans by banks to their subsidiary industries. In 1998 a major financial crisis erupted that ultimately led to Klaus's downfall. The succeeding government, led by the Czech Social Democrats, drove the turnaround that increasingly steered Czech economic policy toward an outward orientation. The greatest threat to the Czech economy lay in the banking sector. As a result, foreign privatization of banks was among the new government's priorities.

The outward turn also restructured domestic industry. The lack of direct control of privatized companies limited the Czech government's hand in directing a renewed FDI effort into domestic industry (McDermott 2007). But the financial crisis was followed by a wave of bankruptcies of industrial firms that diminished the role of domestic ownership just as FDI inflows were intensifying. Indeed, investors considered the Czech Republic an attractive destination for FDI even in the 1990s. However, following the implementation of voucher privatization, most industrial FDI was directed toward greenfield projects.[3] Because voucher privatization left certain industries under domestic control, the impact of FDI was directed toward expanding the existing industrial base. Hence, FDI complemented, rather than substituted for, the activity of domestic firms, and worked to limit the rise of enclave forms of transnational industry. Another factor that bolstered domestic industry was the mode of entry of TNCs into what would become the Czech Republic's dominant export sector, the automotive industry. The first incarnation of TNC control took place in the form of the VW-Škoda Auto joint venture (see Chapter 4). Because the acquisition largely preserved Škoda Auto's organizational structure, the new firm inherited much of the old company's domestic supply chain, which became firmly integrated into the new transnational enterprise. Volkswagen's decision to preserve the Škoda brand name and its own independent line of models also contributed to the retention of parts of Škoda's internal R&D operations (Pavlínek 2008). By contrast, in Hungary, Slovakia, and Poland, global automobile brands preferred to establish local manufacturing subsidiaries that performed more basic assembly tasks for vehicles sold in European markets. This put them on the lower rungs of the value chain in transnational production networks (Pavlínek, Domański, and Guzik 2009).

The combination of domestic ownership over specific, especially high-end and high value-added manufacturing industries and the entry of FDI in a complementary mode into the Czech economy contributed to the making of the Czech intermediate producer. This made the Czech path of transnational integration different from that of Slovakia. While the Czech case does not represent a pure type of intermediate producer given the depth of TNC presence, it indicates a case where transnational integration via FDI did not lead toward the marginalization of local industry in transnational production networks. The institutions of the Czech political economy were also shaped in ways that complemented the Czech economy's skill-based manufacturing orientation. As in the other cases, political rather than purely economic factors played a role in this. First, unlike Hungary's abandonment of vocational schools, Czech educational reforms kept intact the Czech system of vocational education at the secondary level. The Czech Republic maintains some of the highest levels of student enrollment in vocational programs in the OECD, and the rate of employment of high school graduates is often higher than that for university-educated graduates. Vocational programs are divided into technical upper-secondary schools that lead to a secondary school diploma and apprenticeships that end with apprenticeship certificates. Both technical upper-secondary schools and apprenticeship programs include, in addition to classroom learning, direct practical training provided in workshops and companies. In recent years upward of 90 percent of technical upper-secondary students had some kind of direct work experience as part of their education (Kuczera 2010). While critics voice concerns over the quality of programs and the integration of training with labor market needs, these programs stand better than homologous programs in Hungary and Poland, where vocational programs do not provide direct job training and are much less desirable to students because they present much less meaningful paths to employment.[4]

In the labor market as well, major reforms carried out in 2002 fell short of full liberalization, and subsequent laws have preserved the bulk of protective rules for employees. Indeed, levels of protection in employment legislation in the Czech Republic are among the highest in the OECD. One of the key reasons for this was political: Major labor market reforms were carried out by the Social Democrats, who maintained close ties with the largely unified trade union confederation. While trade union membership has been in decline and is relatively low in comparative European terms, the electoral link with the Social Democrats has enabled trade unions to resist pressures toward radical labor market liberalization.[5] The political economy literature has long recognized the complementary institutional links between a regime of vocationally oriented skill formation and protective employment legislation, given that the combination mitigates risks associated with skill investments (Estevez-Abe, Iversen, and Soskice 2001; Thelen 2004; Busemeyer and Trampusch 2012). The degree of integration in the Czech political economy between employment protection, skill formation, and employer interests may be more imperfect than in traditional coordinated market economies, given the divergent roles and orientations of small and large companies, and domestic and foreign companies, and a weaker role for corporatism and a more central role for the state. However, the combination of a manufacturing-oriented economy with supportive institutions of the political economy, leading to the country's complex export profile, suggests a very different institutional arrangement than that found in assembly platforms.

While the outward turn in the late 1990s deepened the role of TNCs in the Czech economy, such a shift did not occur in Slovenia, which presents more comprehensively the features of an intermediate producer. This includes a higher rate of domestic business ownership, particularly in the manufacturing and export-oriented industries. Slovenia pursued a privatization policy that favored firm insiders, including management and workers. The role of FDI was even more limited than in the Czech Republic, as Slovenian legislation was comparatively less friendly to FDI. Slovenia's postsocialist governments could afford the "go it alone" path partly due to the strength of Slovenia's export industries, which had been developed during the Yugoslav period. Slovenia was among Yugoslavia's high exporting regions (Mencinger 2004). During the 1980s, about two-thirds of Slovenian exports went to EC and EFTA countries. These long-standing ties with Western firms allowed Slovenia to more easily absorb the shocks of economic disruptions in Comecon as well as the loss of ex-Yugoslav markets. The maintenance of a positive trade balance through the transformational period aided the country's macroeconomic stability, and negotiated reforms under the liberal-left coalition of the Liberal Democratic Party moved Slovenia toward the development of strong corporatist institutions (Feldmann 2006; Crowley and Stanojević 2011; Bohle and Greskovits 2012). The limited role for FDI and the preservation of domestic ownership over Slovenia's key export industries, particularly in the intermediate goods sectors, led to an enterprise sector that differed significantly from both assembly platforms as well as the Czech Republic. Unlike the Czech Republic, Slovenia experienced no major recessionary or fiscal crisis in the 1990s or early 2000s. This enabled the maintenance of the liberal-left's hegemony all the while Slovenia moved along the process of EU accession.

In combination with the country's competitive export industries, Slovenia evolved into the region's singular intermediate producer whose transnational integration happened without the significant presence of TNCs. The ability of Slovenian firms to compete directly against major TNCs has been constrained, as witnessed by the household appliance maker Gorenje and other consumer goods producers' limited inroads into European markets. But Slovenian firms have excelled as producers of intermediate goods, including parts and components for automobiles and electronic equipment.[6] Direct market participation by export firms has contributed to the maintenance of investments in innovation and the significantly higher number of patents and trademarks held by Slovenia in regional comparisons. These have been complemented by the Slovenian government's higher comparative levels of investment in R&D, and higher comparative rates of business investment in R&D. After the global financial crisis of 2008 generated a banking crisis, a major problem of debt overhang in the corporate sector and growing fiscal pressures have induced some amount of foreign privatization in the banking sector and other large firms but have not led to the abandonment of the basic institutional tenets and inward orientation of the Slovenian political economy (Stanojević 2012).[7] Slovenia maintains its intermediate producer role despite major political shifts and restructuring in the enterprise sector, including pressures on labor-intensive sectors such as textiles, clothing, and wood processing, and structural changes such as the weakening of trade unions and the erosion of aspects of Slovenia's neocorporatist system of coordinated market capitalism.[8]

Varied Paths Toward Combined Roles: Poland, Romania, and Bulgaria

The final set of states in our examination includes Poland, Romania, and Bulgaria, which developed along the combined role. The combined role limits the economy's specialization as either assembly platform or intermediate producer. In this model, both roles may be combined and may vary across sectors. The institutions of the political economy are also more heterogenous in combined roles, due to the presence of more diverse and plural interests in their making. Part of the diversity stems from the relatively larger role played by the domestic market. By contrast, the limited role of trade and exports in the political economy affects the structure of business interests, which influences the design of and bargaining over institutional reforms. In particular, small business may gain a greater voice in domestic policymaking, and its interests in areas such as education, labor market regulation, and taxation may diverge significantly from those of large employers. This section briefly discusses trajectories in all three cases.

With its large domestic market and plural politics of reform negotiation, Poland represents the exemplary case of a combined role. Several features distinguished the Polish path of reform and recovery. First, unlike the largely top-down politics of post-Communist transition that characterized Hungary, Czechoslovakia, Romania, and Bulgaria, the Polish transformation was largely effected by the Solidarity mass movement. This created a much more popularly electrified and politicized atmosphere of reform policymaking, reflected in the succession of short-lived administrations that governed Poland for most of the 1990s. Economically, after facing a major downturn and inflationary spiral in 1990–1992, the Polish economy experienced a quick recovery, registering some of the highest growth rates in the region. While privatization moved very slowly, a great deal of this recovery was driven by the rapid expansion of the private sector, particularly small business, and the recovery of output in industrial sectors. Poland's large domestic market partly accounted for the capacity of the Polish economy to remain less dependent on outside developments, unlike small states like Slovenia that relied more heavily on exports.

The recovery of Poland's industrial sectors partly contributed to growth in the 1990s. The shock therapy economic reforms of 1990 under Finance Minister Balcerowicz included plans for rapid privatization, but these stalled as political actors voiced a variety of concerns over the proper method, implementation, and potential beneficiaries. The initial privatization program included plans for direct sales. This, as in Hungary, opened the door for foreign privatization, but the pace in Poland was much slower. After 1993, a new law expanded equity privatization through investment funds and mass distributed shares. The shift was now toward domestic owners. This coincided with the election of the Democratic Left Alliance (SLD), which introduced industrial policies aimed at restructuring firms and improving efficiency and profitability (King and Sznajder 2006). While many of these firms ended up privatized, and many were sold to foreign owners, it improved the survival chances of industrial sectors against the destructive pressures of market forces. The policies also created a much more diverse set of ownership structures in the economy, ranging from equity ownership to direct (foreign or domestic) ownership to state ownership. State ownership is still large in particular sectors of the Polish economy, including energy and mining (Pula 2017b).

In combination with the growth of an independent private sector, these developments made the Polish economy much more heterogenous in composition than in Hungary, where foreign owners quickly prevailed, or Slovenia, where firm control fell largely to insiders. As in the Czech Republic, this was combined with significant levels of greenfield FDI. Greenfield manufacturing investments increased particularly in the 2000s, with the expansion of the automotive industry as part of the growing Central and Eastern European industrial cluster. The outcome of these diverse and countervailing processes was to diversify sectoral specialization. For example, while the textile and clothing industry, mainly domestically owned, depended on the domestic market (particularly after the decline of OPT), the automotive sector turned mainly toward an assembly platform structure, with large automotive TNCs using Poland as a base of low-cost assembly for cars intended for both the Polish and European market.[9] By contrast, the preservation of domestic component makers and suppliers in the aerospace industry has made that sector look more like an intermediate producer. Even though the industry is dominated by Western aerospace producers like Pratt & Whitney, GE, Lockheed, and Airbus, given the complexity of manufacturing and the technical expertise required, their mode of entry has been through the takeover of domestic firms, preserving the local base of skill and expertise.[10] A number of domestically owned producers of aerospace components and equipment are also important actors in that sector.

Romania went down a similar path, though unlike Poland, the country faced more persistent macroeconomic instability. While an industrial recovery took place by the mid-1990s, export growth was slow given past emphasis on heavy industry development (see Chapter 3). The clothing and textile industry benefited from OPT (see Chapter 4), but the mining industry was ailing and political pressures prevented government efforts to restructure.

Privatization in Romania was also biased toward domestic owners and particularly enterprise insiders. While a mass privatization program was eventually launched, most firms were privatized through MEBOs. By 1995, nearly 90 percent of enterprises slated for privatization were privatized using this method. This choice partly reflected the political power of managers. Given weak mass antiregime organization in the late 1980s, the Romanian regime transformation took place with many of the old elites remaining in place. Moreover, given the ensuing political weakness of governments (due to weak party structures and organization), managerial elites were in a particularly strong position (Pop 2006). This situation created a highly contentious and polarized environment in national politics in the early 1990s, as opposition parties rallied against what they perceived to be the continuation of Communist power by other means.

The upside of managerial control and state support for the enterprise sector was the preservation of employment (Ban 2016). High employment rates sustained domestic demand despite macroeconomic troubles. For example, many consumer goods industries survived due to this, as did Romania's flagship automobile manufacturer, Dacia. But the inward policies, which went much deeper in Romania than elsewhere, also held Romania back from pursuing a path of world market specialization through production network integration. In 1996 things took a turn politically. President Ion Iliescu lost the presidency and his National Salvation Front lost control of parliament to the opposition, leading to a new government under Victor Ciorbea. Relying on the warm Western support for his government, Ciorbea instituted a series of structural reforms meant to undermine the power of the old managerial elite, especially by withdrawing state resources in support of industry. Ciorbea's reforms led to macroeconomic instability and major industrial dislocation, while introducing policies accommodating FDI, which had played a negligible role in the Romanian economy until then. Ciorbea's reforms resulted in an industrial collapse and a credit crunch, at the same time creating the opportunity for industries with declining value to be privatized, particularly through the sale of remaining state shares. As a result of the economy's contraction, the weight of FDI in Romania became much higher (as a share of total investments), even if actual inflows were lower than in Slovakia. The government's successful adoption of an outward strategy solidified in 1998, when it succeeded in transferring a controlling stake in Dacia to French carmaker Renault. But unlike Volkswagen's acquisition of Škoda Auto, the deal was settled for a significantly smaller sum. Inflation and the devaluation of the leu caused the world market price of Romanian assets to fall to bargain-basement levels, and the cost of labor became among the lowest in Europe.

These conditions, aided by the prospects of EU membership, helped drive another wave of FDI in the 2000s, peaking with $6.4 billion in inflows in 2004 and constituting nearly half of total investments that year. But these measures were not enough to radically transform the orientation of the economy. While exports grew and the Dacia effect spread to turn Romania into another regional hub for automotive FDI, economic growth also helped in the recovery of domestic demand. This aided the survival of firms in light and consumer industries. In addition, Romania lacked some of the high-technology export sectors found in Hungary, the Czech Republic, and Slovenia. In combination, these worked against export specialization and sectoral divergence in patterns of production network integration.

The weakness of high-technology sectors and specialized intermediate producers also had another homogenizing effect on FDI—that is, the tendency toward an assembly platform role. But again, the effects of this role are muted by other factors. While assembly platform investment prevailed in the automotive

industry, the existence of the Dacia brand cushioned the reduction in local development capacity. At the same time, Dacia's expansion throughout the 2000s
left it as a much less sophisticated brand than its competitors, coming to cater
mainly to the domestic market and other low-cost market segments. Low innovative capacities persisted in other transnationalized sectors, particularly
mining. Other FDI was directed at nonmanufacturing sectors such as retail
sales, banking, telecommunications, and other segments of the service sector.
A recent trend has been the growth in FDI in information and communication technologies (ICT), and while some endogenous innovation has emerged,
the bulk of these have focused on back-office operations such as bookkeeping,
document management, and call centers that rely on medium-skilled workers
hired largely on temporary contracts.[11]

Reforms in the institutional domain have also pushed Romania toward assuming a more assembly platform role in industries that have been transnationally integrated. Institutional reform of the political economy followed the
liberal market designs seen in Hungary, though implemented in Romania during a much later stage of the post-Communist transformation process. As in
Slovakia, this has made reforms in areas such as the labor market much more
contentious and polarizing. Also as in Slovakia, early reforms in the labor market and in industrial relations introduced high levels of employment protection and an institutionalized role for trade unions in collective bargaining. The
initial arrangements were set up in 1997, during Ciorbea's government, which
established a standing tripartite forum for government-employer-trade union
policy coordination. The victory of the Social Democratic Party in 2000 led to
the consolidation of relatively strong employment protection, under legislation
adopted in 2003. The political winds shifted, however, in the early 2010s as Romania faced renewed pressures for fiscal consolidation as a result of the 2008
financial crisis. The crisis created an opportunity for neoliberal restructuring in
the regulation of employment relations, with a new and radically liberal labor
code adopted in 2011 under the leadership of Emil Boc's Democratic-Liberal
Party (Ban 2016). While the reforms provoked a popular backlash, they pushed
the Romanian political economy further away from coordination and toward
decentralized liberal market arrangements. In the sphere of education, Romania did not effect a major restructuring of degree programs and preserved the
system of vocational training. However, unlike in the Czech Republic and Slovenia, the quality of vocational programs in Romania is lower and collaboration
with employers in job training much more limited. With the low quality and

status of vocational training, most students are driven toward tertiary-degree programs to ensure chances of employment. This more limited articulation and coordination between education, the labor market, and industrial relations has also prevented Romania's full international role specialization in either direction, which have worked to make low-cost, low-skill assembly platform-type manufacturing FDI the prevailing kind in the country.

As in Romania, continuities between the *ancien regime* and the new democracy in Bulgaria went deeper, leading to highly polarized and factionalized politics during the 1990s. Moreover, Bulgaria's high dependence on Comecon trade made its economic situation much more precarious. The trade disruption after 1990 led to major declines in investment and output, with economic reforms providing little hope for a serious recovery. With factionalized politics and unstable governments, privatization largely favored insiders and, as a result, Bulgarian economic policy took an inward orientation. But the weakening of the state and a low level of popular mobilization for change left managerial elites free to engage in rampant rent-seeking that decapitalized a great deal of Bulgarian industry (Ganev 2007). Rent-seeking interests quickly overcame the Bulgarian economy, and parts of the banking sector fell prey to financial manipulation and abuse, further encouraged by weak oversight and lax regulation. This led to Bulgaria's financial panic of 1996, which resulted in bank runs, massive currency depreciation, and the effective loss of trust by Bulgarians in the central bank. The deep financial problems further eroded the position of major firms in the enterprise sector, leading to a new wave of bankruptcies.

The crisis opened the path for radical measures, implemented under the leadership of Bulgaria's United Democratic Forces (SNS) led by Ivan Kostov, who became prime minister in 1997. The package of reforms gradually moved Bulgaria toward an outward economic strategy, introducing currency stability as a macroeconomic anchor (through the establishment of a currency board), rapprochement with international financial institutions (with Bulgaria's commitment to service its foreign debt), and the turn to FDI as a base for privatization. As in Romania, after 1998, FDI inflows were still small by regional standards, but given massive devaluation and the collapse of domestic investment, the weight of FDI in overall investments in the Bulgarian economy grew drastically.

The rocky road to economic recovery in the 2000s was responsible for Bulgaria's combined path. It was amplified by limited integration with Western production networks and an inward strategy that was dominated by insiders.

An already flagging trust in institutions was made worse by the economy's per-petual instability and widespread rent-seeking, limiting the chances of a suc-cessful neodevelopmental approach, which was halfheartedly attempted by Bulgarian socialists in the early 1990s. By contrast, the turn toward an out-ward strategy directed early investments primarily toward manufacturing. In the period between 1999 and 2003, roughly half of all FDI in Bulgaria was di-rected into the manufacturing sector. Investments in the service sector, includ-ing retail, consumer services, and banking picked up during the later 2000s, as the country approached EU accession.[12] As in the postrecessionary Czech Republic, the outward strategy served to restructure domestic manufacturing and, in the Bulgarian case, speed up integration into transnational production networks. But the sectoral makeup of Bulgarian industry contributed to its less than perfect combined role; unlike the other countries in the region, the sec-tors most dependent on assembly platform uses of peripheral economies, such as automotive and electronics, did not assume major roles as investors in the country. Indeed, Bulgaria's once large electronics sector languished for most of the 1990s and did not become an important target for acquisition until it restructured and reemerged in much diminished form.[13] Instead, the bulk of manufacturing investments were oriented toward Bulgaria's machinery and capital goods producers as well as in energy and mining, based on the country's large coal reserves and other mineral resources.

These developments pushed Bulgaria toward a more intermediate producer role, but the niche occupied by Bulgarian industries (unlike, say, Czech ex-ports) falls in less technologically advanced market areas. Basic commodities still form the bulk of Bulgarian exports, focused particularly on raw and partly processed minerals (especially metals). But the commodity industry is diver-sified, and in addition to minerals includes wood and agricultural products. Until recently, labor-intensive industries such as textiles and clothing were also important in Bulgaria's export profile. The impact of FDI has been mainly in the growing sophistication of Bulgaria's machinery, components, and chemical exports, largely in the bottom end of intermediate industries. Dominated in the 1990s by ball bearings, forklifts, and simple motors and chemical compounds, by the 2010s Bulgarian manufacturing exports included electrical resistors, transformers, integrated circuits, and pharmaceutical products.

Unlike Romania, this sectoral specialization has been paralleled by less rad-ical measures to liberalize the political economy, particularly in labor market regulations and in education. Bulgaria preserved an orientation toward specific skill formation by maintaining its system of vocational education and training. In 1999 the government adopted a Vocational Education and Training Act, with the goal of improving the quality of vocational education programs and making them more responsive to labor market demands and updating the system of professional certification. By the late 2000s, more than half of upper-secondary students were enrolled in vocational programs. While this rate was on the lower end in regional comparisons, it is higher than in Hungary. But, with the region's lowest rates of enrollment in tertiary education (baccalaureate programs) second only to the Czech Republic (where vocational training is the norm for the majority of secondary students), vocational degrees are of greater importance in the Bulgarian labor market. In labor market regulation as well, while liberalization measures have been introduced, they have been gradual. Bulgaria saw none of the shock liberalization measures implemented in Slovakia in 2003 or in Romania in 2011. In this respect as well, Bulgaria's combined role tends toward a political economy that is more supportive of a manufacturing- and skill-oriented intermediate producer, though lacking the strong corporatism of Slovenia.

Conclusion

This chapter discusses the political factors behind the transnational integration of Central and Eastern European economies toward one of three international market roles: assembly platform, intermediate producer, and combined. The chapter shows that these roles were not directly determined by pre-1989 patterns of transnational integration in the enterprise sector. Instead, it was the intervening politics of reform that mobilized legacies toward one or another direction, leading to divergent paths of industrial and institutional development. In looking at the politics of postsocialist reform, the goal of the chapter is not to provide a complete and comprehensive account of key events, actors, policies, and institutions across six states, but to highlight a key difference in policy orientation across critical reform periods. This orientation lay in the choice that post-Communist elites made between inward-oriented and outward-oriented strategies of postsocialist industrial restructuring. The difference between inward- and outward-oriented strategies lay not in the choice between openness and autarchy. Rather, they represented different strategies of development while domestic industries coped against the unleashing of world market pressures. In inward-oriented strategies, the objective was to support and restructure domestic industry in its goal to become competitive in world markets, particularly through exports. In outward-oriented strategies, the business of restructuring and upgrading of domestic industry was thought as better left to external private actors, particularly TNCs.

To be sure, outward-oriented strategies were more tenable when states possessed enterprise sectors that had already developed dense ties with TNCs before the fall of Communist regimes. That is why the outward-oriented strategy was first and most systematically pursued in Hungary, which had led the way in import-led growth policies in the 1970s. But past ties were not themselves the cause of outward-oriented policies; for example, Slovenia had dense ties with TNCs, but instead pursued an inward-oriented strategy that focused on rebuilding and consolidating the domestic export sector, rather than turning it over to subsidiary production. Hence, while the legacy of socialist protoglobalization (Chapter 4) formed a structural condition for the tenability of an outward-oriented strategy, it was ultimately reform politics that led states toward different paths of international specialization.

But policy orientations were not etched in stone. Critical junctures emerging in the mid- to late 1990s—often the result of failures of previous reforms accompanied by renewed recessionary crises—led to policy reorientations that in most cases resulted in the turn toward outward-oriented strategies. Demands for an outward turn were amplified by the beginning of accession into the EU common market. Moreover, the changing geoeconomics of TNC activity led to greater interest by TNCs toward using Central and Eastern Europe as a base of subsidiary operations as part of strategies that saw the region within the context of the larger European market. These changing opportunity structures offered Central and Eastern European political elites the chance to shift toward outward-oriented strategies in the course of the late 1990s and early 2000s.

Shifts from inward- to outward-oriented strategies were not cost free in institutional terms. Institutional structures and power relations built up during one period could not be replaced overnight with entirely new ones. These institutional residues resulted in less than perfect matches between modes of international market specialization and the organization of domestic political economies (as described theoretically in Chapter 5). Hence, Hungarian reforms became well suited to the making of a political economy of an assembly platform. In Slovakia, by contrast, institutional residues in the political economy, including the legacy role of trade unions, created a backlash against radical liberalization efforts in the political economy. Hence, while Slovakian manufacturing moved decisively toward an assembly platform role, the institutions of the political economy became objects of political struggle between parties that combined outward-oriented strategies with radical neoliberal restructuring, and those committed to preserving existing institutions. As a result, the "competition state" formula of combining FDI-seeking policy with radical domestic neoliberal restructuring became a more polarizing process in Slovakia.

Institutional residues of the past also affected the Czech turn toward an outward strategy after the financial crisis of 1997. Here, institutional residues played a role not only in the political realm but also in the enterprise sector. The initial inward-oriented strategy led to the creation of domestically controlled industrial sectors, particularly in engineering and other high-end manufacturing. The mode of entry of FDI, based more heavily on greenfield investments than direct acquisitions of domestic firms, preserved enclaves of domestic production within an overall economy that was becoming more heavily dominated by subsidiary-based production. Finally, because the entry of major TNC projects, such as the VW-Škoda Auto acquisition, took place using the existing organizational infrastructure of the old enterprise, the Czech Republic was able to preserve greater domestic technological capacities and better integrate domestic firms into TNC supplier networks. As Chapter 5 highlights, studies suggest that FDI spillovers in the Czech Republic are comparatively higher than other states in the region, a finding that is consistent with the intermediate producer role and model of political economy.

Just as socialist legacies of TNC production networks presented a structural constraint in the pursuit of an outward-oriented strategy, another structural condition lay in the role of the domestic market. For postsocialist states with large internal (and, hence, less export-dependent) markets, pressures toward production network integration were lower, enabling inward-oriented policies to play out over longer time periods. The combination of these structural conditions led to combined roles in Poland, Romania, and Bulgaria. In addition, sectoral diversity and difference in these economies also led to distinct role specializations that differed across sectors. In the combined roles, sectoral production network integration could take on either assembly platform or intermediate producer roles, depending on the mode of entry of FDI (local acquisition or greenfield) and the technological nature of the sector. The more the nature of TNC subsidiary operations were of a mass-production type, the more likely the sector would assume an assembly platform role. The more heavily they relied on domestic technological capacities (including R&D and innovation), the more likely they assumed intermediate producer roles.

Sectoral differences and political dynamics have also skewed particular combined cases toward one or another role. Poland represents the primary case of a combined role given its sectoral diversity and large domestic market that orients a great deal of business activity toward it. By contrast, political efforts by center-right parties to move Romania toward a liberal market institutional framework and the dominance of low-cost, mass-production sectors in the composition of manufacturing FDI (and more recently extended toward business services), are pushing Romania toward an assembly platform role. In Bulgaria, this path has been impeded both by greater compromises in liberal institutional reform and by the prevalence of more low-end capital goods and labor-intensive industries, which skews it toward a more intermediate producer role.

On a final note, claims of correspondence between a state's international market specialization and its domestic institutions of the political economy should not be construed as suggesting that there exist institutional "complementarities" (Hall and Soskice 2001; Campbell 2010; Crouch 2010) within individual political economies that reflect the logics of the liberal or coordinated market variety of capitalism. To be sure, the comparative political economy literature recognizes that a degree of institutional adjustment almost always follows periods of strong exogenous and endogenous pressures, particularly those stemming from international markets and domestic recessions (Streeck and Thelen 2005). The critical junctures of post-1989 and the late 1990s were such path-switching events. However, given strong emerging divisions between the different sectors of capital (foreign and domestic, small and large, internal market and export-oriented), falling levels of worker organization (given declining unionization rates), and overall institutional weakness, postsocialist polities in the late 1990s and 2000s typically lacked the political coalitions required to build robust "upgrade coalitions" (Doner and Schneider 2016) that deepen coordinating mechanisms between firms, workers, and the state in the pursuit of national developmental goals. At the same time, the region's neoliberal reformers often faced significant mass political pushback against comprehensive market liberalization and the privatization of social welfare, preventing the emergence of fully "disembedded" liberal market systems (Vanhuysse 2006; Bohle and Greskovits 2012). As a result, the institutions of the political economy reflect the conjunctural interests of countervailing social forces and may consequently operate at cross-purposes and be less articulated across institutional domains than implied by the concept of institutional complementarity in the strong sense.[14] Indeed, the dependent market economy perspective on Central and Eastern European capitalisms suggests that dominance by transnational firms makes the emergence of coordinated market mechanisms near impossible in Central and Eastern Europe (Nölke and Vliegenthart 2009). This chapter does not share such a categorical view. The degree to which complementarity and coordination exist within the comparative political economies of Central and Eastern Europe is a question meriting its own separate study; what this chapter merely suggests is that there is a continuum of coordination and complementarity that is higher in the intermediate producers and much lower in the assembly platforms, with combined cases potentially exhibiting greater regional and sectoral variation (cf. Crouch, Schröder, and Voelzkow 2009). Moreover, all these varied configurations result partly from political forces and partly from the path-dependent transformation of institutions as actors responded to domestic economic pressures and international market opportunities.

Conclusion

Between 2013 and 2015, the European Commission sponsored a large research project with the aim of assessing the development of postsocialist Central and Eastern European economies since their admission into the EU. Composed of a large team of researchers from the region, the project issued a series of research papers covering areas from social cohesion and welfare to innovation policies, structural change, and international competitiveness. The final report lauded the tremendous economic growth recorded by the Central and Eastern European economies since entering the EU, noting that their average growth rates have been higher than those of the older EU members (Gorzelak 2015). It highlighted the role of the EU in opening up postsocialist economies, channeling investments, and fostering democratic institutions. It pointed out improved standards of living across the region. But the report also noted the drawbacks of the open, capital-seeking developmental model adopted by Central and Eastern European states. It noted that the research group's findings had converged on the general insight that there existed a "disjuncture between fast productivity growth and a rather poor performance in developing innovative capacities to support longer-term sustainable growth and assure their competitive positions" (4). It noted, for example, that the region "seems to have reduced its patenting activities drastically in absolute and per capita terms after 1990 and now maintains a stable level below the performance of the EU-15. Thus, the disappearance of the former advantage enjoyed by the [region] in low-cost types of production has not been [replaced] by the generation of new sources of competitive advantage" (6). That is because, among other factors, "techno-logical activities of foreign subsidiaries in [Central and Eastern Europe] are often implemented without significant linkages to various actors in the domes-tic innovation system" (5). In response to these problems, the report suggests that the region shift "towards a new and different stage of development, relying less on FDI and more on endogenous investments, taking advantage of techno-logical multipliers and technological spillovers from multinational companies into the local fabric" (9). The report proposes a number of more specific policy changes involving investments in skill formation and R&D, and recommends addressing unbalanced regional development due partly to the uneven geo-graphic concentration of TNC-led industrial activities.

One report in the series traces the problems of Central and Eastern Euro-pean underdevelopment historically as far back as the nineteenth century and expresses fears that the goal of postsocialist reformers—economic catch-up with the core EU—remains a far-fetched dream (Podkaminer 2013). Interest-ingly, this report speculates that, perhaps, Central and Eastern Europe might have been better off today had Communist regimes fallen in the 1960s or 1970s, rather than in the 1990s. Instead of transnationally oriented and dependent economies that underwent radical liberalization, economic policies might have taken a Keynesian form with industrial policy and capital controls enabling an internally driven development. That is, unlike the transnationalized, heav-ily liberalized economies of today (that appear to have reached the structural limits of their models of growth), what we would have witnessed in Central and Eastern Europe is the blossoming of social democracy and spectacular in-dustrial development that would have led the region to look more like the rest of (core) Europe. There would have, in other words, been more convergence in wealth and, possibly, in shared forms of national institutions.

We can never know for certain, of course, what would have happened if Communism had fallen in the 1960s or 1970s, but we can rely on counterfactu-als to engage in some speculation. From what this book shows, the differences between the two decades were significant, and the economic outcomes of the hypothetical demise of Communism would differ significantly depending on which decade our presumed transition would have taken place. The 1970s in particular prove to have been a pivotal decade for socialist East Europe just as they were for the advanced capitalist world. In the (highly) hypothetical sce-nario that Communism had fallen then, the report's hopeful vision of the re-gion's Keynesian and social democratic future would have probably remained unfulfilled. Patterns of technological subordination to Western industry were apparent across the region, and even intensified as economies entered an era of growing technological complexity. Attempts to restructure socialist economies in the 1970s would have already faced serious structural difficulties, as socialist reformers discovered, even with the political obstacle in the form of Communist Party control eliminated. Introducing markets would have been just as costly, and world market pressures would have been just as high, particularly given the rise of East Asian exporters, who were just beginning to make their weight felt in the world economy. While reform strategies may have differed given a presumed higher tolerance for capital controls, trade restrictions, and import-substitution policies, the lack of capital would have likely involved Central and Eastern European economies relying on continued state involvement and external debt financing. And the arrival of the 1980s would have likely subjected Central and Eastern European governments to similar liberalizing pressures experienced in Latin America. Pressures to engage in structural adjustment reforms would have likely been amplified by debt crises that, even under capitalist arrangements, would have affected the economies in the 1980s (presuming that they would have maintained their rates of foreign borrowing, perhaps even exceeding those made by socialist governments, given greater capital investment needs in restructuring efforts and the loss of the socialist system's collectivized and decommodified means of absorbing the social costs of transformation). It is doubtful, then, that by the 2000s the economies of Central and Eastern Europe would have looked much different than they do today. If the point of comparison are present-day European economies, the non-core economies of Portugal and Ireland are probably better examples of where our hypothetical Central and Eastern European economies would have found themselves in the 2000s, instead of, say, Austria and Finland.

But even Portugal and Ireland may represent expectations that are still too far-fetched. Indeed, some states would likely be worse off. Poland, Romania, and Bulgaria relied on either Comecon trade or Western credit, or both, to invest in upgrading and diversifying their industries through the 1960s and 1970s. If Communism fell in, say, 1971, these paths would have likely been cut off. Under market conditions, these hypothetical post-Communist economies of the 1970s would have to rely more heavily on simple commodity exports and agriculture. Borrowing would have been harder and its impact on development, however skewed or inefficient under the centrally planned system, much lower as monies would have likely been channeled less toward capital investments and more toward supporting social spending, as they were in many Latin American states. The economies would have been harder hit by the energy crisis and higher commodity prices after 1973, lacking cheap Soviet supplies to buffer their impact. Unless these economies joined the EEC—unlikely since even the southern European states did not join until the 1980s—they would have lacked a captive export market for manufactured goods, as they did with the USSR, while facing tough barriers to enter Western markets. For the poorer developing economies, then, the economic outcomes would have likely been no better or possibly even worse than under actual history, even if politically they might have been more democratic. Assuming, of course, that our hypothetical transitions of the 1970s would result in democracy and not in authoritarian regimes of a different variety.

The actual history of the region's globalization did depend on key events and policies undertaken by East European socialist governments in the 1970s. We have seen that an interest in technological upgrade led to increasing participation in transnational production networks, though unevenly across the region. While these were limited interactions within chains of production under emerging global TNCs, they laid the basis for the region's transformation in the 1990s. This process of transformation has been dubbed here as socialist protoglobalization, and it created the structural basis for some of the institutional and organizational changes that happened within industry during the postsocialist period. In the transition to globalized production networks, what mattered most were not only the nature of reform policies but the development of organizational capacities for transnational production at the industry level. In the process of economic restructuring, these capacities operated as a form of organizational capital lying in the enterprise sector that could be mobilized and employed by policymakers toward economic restructuring ends.

Distinguishing Sequences

The preceding discussion can be clarified once the distinct historical sequences examined in the previous chapters are summarized. To recall, sequences are "temporally ordered sets of events that [take] place in a given [historical] context" (Falleti and Mahoney 2015, 213). Sequences can be strings of temporally successive events, but in comparative historical analysis, the purpose of examining sequences is to identify causal mechanisms that make particular temporal sequences *causal* ones. The discussion of sequences in what follows refers to causal, and not just temporally successive, sequences.

The book examines three general causal sequences leading to distinct sets of outcomes, each of which set the stage (or, put in more technical terms, provided the causal conditions) for the next. The sequential analysis focuses primarily around the structure of economic institutions, and particularly how exogenous events shaped goals of both economic actors within those institutions and political actors in charge of reforming them. The three sequences relate to three different time periods when economic institutions in Central and Eastern Europe underwent significant to radical transformations. As a result, the three sequences can be divided into an examination of three sets of outcomes: sequence A, leading from reform socialism to the rise of socialist protoglobalization (transnational production under socialism); sequence B, leading from protoglobalization to the rise of industrial FDI; and sequence C, leading from FDI to distinct international market roles. The diagram in Figure C.1 summarizes causal sequences A and B.

Sequence A: From Reform Socialism to Socialist Protoglobalization

The book argues that socialist protoglobalization was pivotal to the rise of Central and Eastern Europe's globally integrated manufacturing economies of the twenty-first century and is concerned with both documenting this pro-

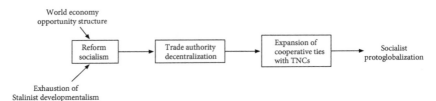

Causal sequence A: From reform socialism to socialist protoglobalization, 1970 to early 1980s

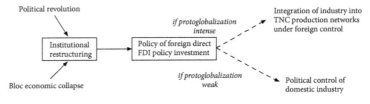

Causal sequence B: From socialist protoglobalization to FDI, late 1980s to mid-1990s

Figure C.1. Diagram representing causal sequences A, leading to socialist protoglobalization, and B, leading to the policy of FDI and its results

cess (Chapter 2) and discussing its implications for the immediate transitional period when the Central and Eastern European economies began the shift to FDI (Chapter 3). The discussion in Chapter 2 also relates protoglobalization to patterns of political reform in Central and Eastern Europe during the 1970s, the era of reform socialism. Hence, causal sequence A is about relating how the political motives of domestic economic reform combined with the changing opportunity structure of the world economy to drive Central and Eastern European socialist economies toward more intense engagements with TNCs and markets of the advanced capitalist nations. The causal narrative thus ties together two independent events, emerging as endogenous and exogenous causes behind the making of socialist protoglobalization. Recall that socialist protoglobalization refers to the process of increasingly growing ties of finance, production, and exchange between industrial enterprises in Central and Eastern Europe and Western TNCs.

Endogenously, socialist states faced steadily falling rates of economic growth due to the exhaustion of postwar Stalinist developmentalism. Chapter 1 examines the historical circumstances leading to the division of Europe's economy into two rival blocs, and the contingent causes behind Central and Eastern Europe's industrial development focused on heavy industries and capital goods. The chapter shows the importance of Soviet-led international economic arrangements for national development in Central and Eastern Europe, but it also shows how East European leaderships were soon confronted by the limits of the socialist developmental model. After Stalin's death in 1953, the region underwent waves of economic reform that attempted to address the shortfalls of the Stalinist system. This included reforming economic institutions in ways that allowed for greater decentralization of economic decision making and introduced market elements. Three important transformations marked this early period of socialist experimentation with reform. First, even when pursued halfheartedly, reforms nonetheless led to the weakening of central authority over the economy, encouraging greater mid-level bureaucratic control. Second, and more specifically, reforms led to the increasing devolution of trade authority from central ministries to FTOs. Among the goals of FTOs became the seeking of new export markets in the West. In some countries, like Hungary, specialized FTOs were set up whose sole task was engaging Western markets. Lastly, at the international level, Khrushchev's unsuccessful domestic reform program in the USSR nonetheless left a legacy of greater openness to world trade within the socialist bloc. The Khrushchev period decisively shifted the economic policy paradigm from the Stalinist contention of the existence of two separate and rival world economies (capitalist and socialist), to one that recognized the unity of the world market, with socialist states as one among its many players (and, moreover, as lying subordinate to the capitalist powers). A major signal in this direction was the adoption within Comecon of world market prices in socialist trade, in addition to Khrushchev's attempts to expand trade relations between the Soviet Union and Western capitalist nations.

A related issue of concern for socialist leaders and policymakers that emerged during this period was the growing technological gap between the socialist economies and the West. The goals of trade openness with the West during the reform socialist period were also understood as expanding opportunities for gaining access to superior technology. These had been long-standing concerns, expressed throughout the 1960s. But the 1970s presented the real opportunity for the pursuit of a policy of industrial upgrade. It is in this context that globalization as we understand it today emerges as another exogenous cause shifting the course of development of socialist economies.

Globalization during this time represents the greater openness of Western economies for trade with socialist countries and, more crucially, the rise of global finance. For socialist states, the last factor was especially critical for the pursuit of the new policy of import-led growth: the importation of Western capital goods and technology as a means of capital reinvestment and industrial upgrade. Throughout the 1950s and 1960s, the problem of importing Western technology had been constrained by the nonconvertibility of East European currencies. The role of global finance, one that evaded direct state authority (and especially restrictive US sanctions against the East European economies), enabled East European planners to overcome this obstacle. Borrowing on international credit markets became the means for socialist planners and enterprises to implement visions of intensive catch-up development. While the sectoral distribution of foreign credit was not always most effectively channeled and reflected the existing bureaucratic interests within the economy, it nonetheless led to a period of renewed investment and technological upgrade in the socialist bloc. The rise of international debt financing was complemented by the relaxation of East-West political tensions, leading in the 1970s to the largest growth in East European exports to Western markets since the end of the war. These structural changes can be referred to as the changing world economic opportunity structure that, in combination with reform socialism, led to deepening ties between socialist enterprises and Western TNCs.

The political easing of tensions, especially within Europe, and the capitalist recessions of the 1970s served as a motivating force for Western TNCs to see East European economies as potential markets and partners in production. Moreover, institutional change at the level of West European trade also drove European ties between East-West increasingly toward firm-level cooperation. That included changes to the EEC treaty in 1973, which had members pledge to allow all existing bilateral trade deals with third countries to expire. Because the treaty excluded cross-border cooperation agreements between firms from this provision, the expansion of direct firm agreements became one of the few areas where EEC members and socialist bloc countries could preserve bilateral connections. For East European policymakers, these connections became the primary means of seeking access to TNC resources, particularly technologies and proprietary knowledge, employed to advance domestic industrial development goals. For TNCs, the recessions of the 1970s demanded that they seek new external markets, and the relatively developed industrial economies of the socialist bloc with untapped consumer bases offered a promising new outlet for growth. These factors fundamentally altered the relationship between socialist enterprise and Western TNCs from one based on the simple exchange of goods to one of more complex organizational relationships that included the transfer of technology and knowledge, including joint ventures and other forms of co-production of goods. This process is what ultimately drove the rise of socialist protoglobalization, given the increasingly growing embeddedness—however limited and marginal—of socialist firms in networks of transnational production. It was through the channels of finance, technology, and production that globalization ultimately led to the structural transformation of East European industry.

Sequence B: From Socialist Protoglobalization to FDI

Using comparative data, Chapter 3 demonstrates that socialist protoglobalization was unevenly distributed across the region. When the political revolutions of 1989 led to the rise of new reformist elites desiring "a market economy without any adjectives" (*Economist* 1990), reorienting trade toward the West became a goal of high importance for ex-socialist economies. The turn to the West was also made more urgent after the demise of Comecon in 1990. Industries and sectors that had been exposed the longest to protoglobalization proved the most capable of weathering the storm. Chapter 3 shows how particular labor-intensive industries rapidly and successfully reoriented towards

Western trade. But this strategy was insufficient for broad industrial recovery, given the large falling capacity in other, more capital- and technologically intensive sectors. Reformers in Central and Eastern Europe embraced FDI as a strategy for economic restructuring. Chapter 3 shows that the diffusion of socialist protoglobalization was one of the primary determinants of the success of FDI strategies. This process, represented by sequence B in Figure C.1, covers the transformational period between the late 1980s and the mid-1990s.

Chapter 3 also shows that the beginnings of postsocialist economic divergence could already be discerned by patterns of integration with TNC networks, as countries like Hungary, which had been at the forefront of socialist protoglobalization, rapidly turned over control of domestic industries to TNCs. In Hungary as elsewhere, the institutional mechanisms that had been constructed during the socialist period to facilitate industrial ties with TNCs became the means by which TNCs entered into the transitioning economies and consolidated control. Hence, joint ventures with local firms, which had been among the chief forms of TNC operation in the 1970s and 1980s, continued to serve as organizational vehicles for TNC entry during the early reform period. With the reinstitution of property rights and privatization, joint ventures increasingly transformed into the direct acquisition of local assets by TNCs. There are strong correlations between countries that had developed the largest number of joint ventures in the 1970s and 1980s and those that received the highest inflows of FDI soon after economic liberalization.

The turn to FDI in the early 1990s, however, was a political choice and was not always the preferred tool of industrial transformation among most countries. Hence, the transnationalization of domestic industry was countered by the exercise of political control over the enterprise sector, either because elites favored domestic capital in privatization (as in the Czech Republic and Slovenia), or because the lack of interest by TNCs led industrial firms to fall under domestic control by default (as in Bulgaria and Slovakia). The behavior of postsocialist reformers, particularly in their choice of an inward or outward economic policy orientation, was an independent causal factor in the process of change. Put simply, an inward policy orientation had reformers bet on domestic industries as capable of leading the economy towards a recovery and withstanding world market competition. An outward policy orientation had them see FDI as the preferred means of securing the survival of domestic industry under the new competitive conditions. While inward and outward policies cover a variety of policy measures, the choice of privatization method was described as best capturing this orientation. When privatization favored foreign owners, it was indicative of a broader outward orientation, including policies like tax exemptions for investors, labor and product market liberalization, and trade and exchange rate policies conducive to capital flows and the operation of foreign subsidiaries. By contrast, when privatization favored domestic owners, elites often resorted to other supportive policies, such as industrial and credit policies aimed at bolstering domestic firms, market protectionism, and providing more extensive product and labor market regulation.

The sequence already points to states most likely to adopt an initial outward orientation; Hungary, which had most extensively transnationalized during the early period of postsocialist reform, also adopted an outward orientation. Socialist protoglobalization could therefore be said to have served as a *structural condition* for Hungary's successful FDI policy. While differences in uneven FDI inflows in the early 1990s could be explained by a variety of institutional, political, and geographic factors, it was socialist-era experience in transnational production that most made ex-socialist manufacturing industries attractive to TNCs. As Chapter 3 explains, past experience with TNCs served not only to mitigate risks and promote relations of trust but also signaled to investors that local sectors could quickly adjust—organizationally and technologically— to the demands of transnational production. As a result, inward policies were more likely in states where transnationalization was weak and an FDI-oriented policy had fewer chances of success. It is important to highlight, however, that the depth of socialist protoglobalization (legacy factor) and postsocialist reform policy orientations (political factor) during the critical juncture of post-1989 economic restructuring are independent and contingently combined. One does not *necessarily* flow from the other; one only made the other *more likely*. Policymakers, after all, operate under structural constraints that limit the chances of success of particular policy options. Hence, in the design of privatization in the early 1990s, it was not as if Bulgarian, Slovakian, and Romanian reformers outright rejected the importance of FDI for postsocialist development, but in some cases more limited past engagement with TNCs hampered their capacity to implement an FDI strategy in a way that seemed to be effective in Hungary and Poland. The Czech case is unusual in that TNC interest after 1989 was strong despite a weaker legacy of transnational production and a reformist government focused on an inward strategy that favored domestic capital. However, as Chapter 3 shows, the propulsion of the Czech Republic to one of the prime destinations of regional FDI in the early 1990s had more to do with the high pricing of a small set of privatized assets rather than the overall mass of FDI inflows.

Sequence C: From FDI to International Economic Specialization

The last sequence is causally more complex because it captures the accumulation of a number of long-term endogenous processes, new political and economic opportunity structures at the international level emerging in the late 1990s, and the agency of political actors during the second reform period, to account for a larger possibility of outcomes. Figure C.2 represents this sequence in parsimonious form. In causal sequence C, the process of transnationalization became overdetermined because of the convergence of multiple causal forces. Transnationalization is no longer a matter of cumulative advantage in the uneven distribution of FDI, but driven by powerful external forces that reshape the region's politics and economies. The question for sequence C is no longer *if* economies transnationalize, but *with what consequence* for domestic institutions and industrial structure. Here we see that past sequences matter in terms of what possibilities existed for political processes to push transnationalization toward distinct outcomes in terms of the role domestic industry came to occupy in global value chains, on the one hand, and the nature of the embeddedness of such industry in the institutions of the domestic political economy, on the other hand. The analysis therefore involves the use of past patterns to explain what may be dubbed *varieties of postsocialist transnationalization*.

Chapter 5 offers a framework that defines a state's international economic role in networks of transnational production in terms of FDI, export, and technological dependency. These structural differences are posited as analogous to institutional variations within political economies, resulting in significant differences across states in areas of economic policy, market regulation, and firm performance. Using these dimensions, the theory identifies three such forms of economic specialization, or emerging international market roles, for Central and Eastern European economies: assembly platform, intermediate producer, and combined. The third causal sequence thus captures the causal path from patterns of initial postsocialist transnationalization to one of these distinct roles that characterizes the Central and Eastern European political economies in the early twenty-first century.

In discussing the impact of forces of European integration in Central and Eastern Europe in the 2000s, Milada Vachudova (2008) uses the formulation "causal behemoth." The term is meant to capture the powerful transformative

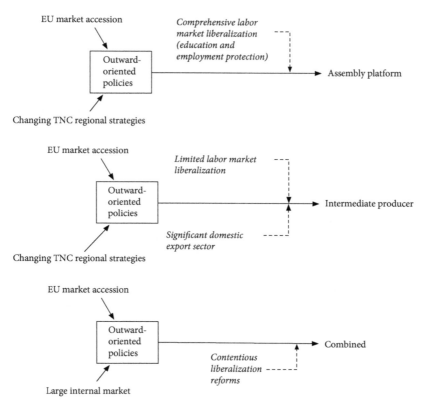

Causal sequence C: From FDI to international economic specialization, mid-1990s and beyond.

Figure C.2. Causal possibilities in sequence C, leading to diversification of international market roles in the context of transnationalized economies

NOTE: The sequences are conservatively represented, excluding specific contingencies within cases.

nature of EU integration in inducing and incentivizing domestic institutional reform in the candidate states of Central and Eastern Europe during the course of their pre-accession reforms. Rather than a singular causal force operating on domestic institutions in an unmediated way, this book conceives of EU integration as a powerful external force presenting a set of constraints as well as a new opportunity structure for domestic political elites (Grzymala-Busse and Innes 2003; Jacoby 2006). The process of integration into the EU common market was accompanied by the concurrent reframing of TNC regional strategies. These strategies saw Central and Eastern Europe as a regional low-cost production hub in the context of the larger European market. TNC regional strategies were no doubt amplified by agglomeration effects, as competitors and other supplemental firms such as suppliers and service providers began following first movers into the region. For example, the 2000s saw a major expansion of the region's automotive sector, largely as a result of agglomeration effects. Recognizing this opportunity, Central and Eastern European political elites began instituting policies that engaged their states in an earnest and intense regional competition for FDI (Bohle and Greskovits 2012). With domestic economic crises in the late 1990s eroding popular support for and patience with inward policies, the 2000s came to represent a period in which FDI-based growth was adopted as the only legitimate economic policy option for industrial redevelopment across the entire region.

As a result, in countries where political elites implemented outward-oriented policies throughout the transformation period (1990–2000s), the result was a continued expansion of the TNC sector. Because the internal market was small, most economic activity, including TNC activity, was export oriented. This resulted in high levels of FDI and export market dependence in the economy. Moreover, TNC operations in the manufacturing sector came to emphasize basic assembly work and focused less on product innovation and R&D. Absolute gains in domestic technology and export complexity came at the cost of relative declines in local skill and innovative capabilities. The skills gap was further widened when governments pulled support away from skill-based training and focused on general education, aiming to match educational reform with liberal labor market models. This was Hungary's path. Slovakia pursued a similar path, but the outward turn came after an initial period of inward-oriented policies.

Across the region in the 2000s, political elites turned to outward-oriented policies, but they faced constraints from the institutional residues of previous policy choices. Prior support for domestic firms had created entrenched domestic managers and trade unions as well as a new segment of domestically owned industry. Initial protective policies were less likely to force the rapid deregulation of labor markets. Trade unions and other actors were more capable of resisting change toward labor market liberalization. Educational reform was less likely to remake educational programs to fit general liberal market models. Instead, policy choices retained emphasis on job-based vocational training geared toward industrial employment. These institutional residues were consequential for the extent to which outward policies could reshape the economy's orientation. This economic reorientation also depended heavily on the structure of the domestic market.

In countries with small domestic markets, such as the Czech Republic, Slovakia, and Slovenia, export-oriented growth became a shared goal of political elites and industrial firms. However, even in countries like the Czech Republic and Slovakia, which made a radical turn toward FDI-driven growth in the 2000s, the outcome very much depended on previous policy choices. The legacy of voucher privatization in the Czech Republic enabled the survival of a core of domestic industrial firms after the shift toward transnationalization. In the Czech economy, TNCs came to complement, rather than substitute for, domestic firms in industrial sectors. As a result, R&D retained a greater role in the economy, and domestic technology and skill continued to play a part in the otherwise heavily transnationalized economy. Moreover, TNCs came to have greater spillover effects in skill and technology among domestic firms, and they became better connected with local firms as suppliers and partners. By contrast, in Slovakia the economic policy strategy after 2002 involved wholesale industrial redevelopment via FDI. This pushed the Slovakian economy toward an assembly platform role, even though other institutions of the political economy did not fully follow paths of liberal adjustment as in Hungary. The educational system retained stronger features of skill-oriented industrial training and the political mobilizing capacities of trade unions were much stronger, leading to a political backlash against the neoliberal reforms of the early 2000s later in the decade.

When internal markets were larger (relative to external ones), outward-oriented policies had less of an impact because most industrial firms could rely on domestic demand. The stultifying effect of large internal markets weakened the impact of TNC-driven transnationalization; hence, FDI and export dependence became concentrated in specific sectors and came to play a less prominent role as the economy's overall basis for growth. The case of Poland best fits this model. In cases where neither assembly platform nor intermediate producer roles fully capture the economy's international specialization, these are defined as combined roles. The importance of internal markets and sectorally based transnationalization also put Romania and Bulgaria in the combined category, though with opposite tendencies. Romanian educational reform in the 2000s, drastic labor market liberalization and abolition of corporatist structures in 2011, and the weakness of domestic high-technology sectors have tended toward the role of an assembly platform, while Bulgaria's increasing export specialization, higher levels of domestic value added in exports, its industry-centered system of skill formation, and more strongly retained elements of corporatism in the political economy make it exhibit features of an intermediate producer.

To sum up, for the purposes of explaining outcomes in the last causal sequence, what came to matter was how the new opportunity structures presented by EU common market entry and TNC regional strategies interacted with the policy choices of postsocialist elites. The impact of these policy choices was constrained both by domestic market structures and by institutional residues remaining from past policy choices. Thus, FDI-based growth policies in the 2000s produced a variety of results in terms of the role that the industrial economy staked out in networks of transnational production. These roles, moreover, had direct consequences on the overall impact of economic globalization on the state's economy. Paradoxically, states that pursued inward-oriented policies were more likely to see gains from globalization in the long run. By contrast, states that were most committed to outward-oriented policies were more likely to see rapid short-term gains at the cost of domestic capacities.

The Politics of Industrial Upgrade and Economic Catch-Up: The Long View

This chapter begins with observations from a recent series of EU-sponsored reports on the state of the Central and Eastern European economies. The two issues raised in those reports speak directly to the broader policy implications of this book's analysis. First, it involves the question of economic catch-up and the potential exhaustion of the region's model of FDI-led development. Second, it involves the policy and governance implications drawn from the analysis of the transnationalization of Central and Eastern European economies. The analysis shows that instead of homogeneity and similarity in transnational economic integration, we see significant diversity. The findings also suggest that a transnationalization strategy, rather than uniform in its consequences, has had different payoffs for different economies, depending on their postsocialist starting point and the sequence of institutional reforms adopted in each country.

If the long-term goal of Central and Eastern European states is the upgrade of domestic industry and catch-up with the advanced capitalist economies, developments since the 1990s have undeniably produced important gains.[1] The transnationalization strategy has not only generated economic growth, but has preserved the industrial character of the Central and Eastern European economies in the context of growing deindustrialization in the rest of Europe. The transnationalization strategy proved to be a clever redeployment of the base of domestic skill and knowledge built over many decades of socialist development in the era of global capitalism. But, the seeds for the success of this project were planted much earlier, with socialist states turning to the capitalist world to acquire means for investment and new capital. That is not to say that what political actors did in the intermediate period did not matter. But the state socialist experience created certain structural possibilities that could be exploited during the period of institutional transformation after 1989.

The growth of economic interdependence and interaction across the different parts of Europe after 1989 was a return to the historical normal; it was the continent's division for most of the second half of the twentieth century that stood out as a historical aberration. In the era of globalization, the terms of that interdependence and interaction changed dramatically, but an integrated European economy stands, at some level, as a restoration of historical patterns of economic flows.

Nevertheless, it is national economies that continue to characterize both the global and the European economic order. At that level, as the introduction to this chapter points out, there is much disappointment and concern over the risks of the path of development that the region has pursued. The idea of the EU common market was premised on convergence—that is, that balancing growth rates and Europe-wide redistribution of public and private investment would begin to level European economies in terms of wealth and development. Surely, the political beating that that idea took in the aftermath of the 2008 global financial crisis and the subsequent euro crisis has also influenced popular sentiment and the thought of political elites in Central and Eastern Europe. Some have in recent years renewed calls, both rhetorically and in actual policy, for a return to national developmentalism. In Hungary, the rise in 2010 of the Fidesz party to power led to renewed calls for state intervention in the economy. In addition to politically attacking and partly nationalizing Hungary's foreign-owned banks, the Fidesz government has also made efforts to support the exports of Hungarian-owned firms as well as raise their profile internationally over the TNCs that dominate Hungary's economy. In Slovakia, Prime Minister Fico of the center-left SMER party reversed many of the neoliberal restructuring measures undertaken by the neoliberal right during the 2000s, to renationalize pension and health care insurance and restoring the rights of trade unions.

In Poland, after gaining control of the government in 2015, the conservative-nationalist Law and Justice (PiS) party announced a new state-led development program known as the Morawiecki Plan (named after the former PiS economy minister and current prime minister, Mateusz Morawiecki) (Poland 2016). The PiS government saw the Polish economy as having entered a "middle-income trap," brought on partly by the weakness of domestic investment. In addition to reducing reliance on foreign investment, the plan envisions a return to targeted industrial policies that will promote "reindustrialization" and high-technology exports of domestic firms. Other countries face similar pressures, though the economic policy turnarounds have not been as dramatic as in Hungary, Slovakia, and Poland, and policy autonomy has been further narrowed by the straightjacket of severe post-2008 fiscal constraints emanating both from EU-mandated austerity policies and from bond market pressures (Myant, Drahokoupil, and Lesay 2013). None of these policy shifts suggest that the Central and Eastern European economies are abandoning FDI-driven growth, but their efforts to question the long-term viability of the developmental model inherited from the 2000s point to the real possibility that another chapter of Central and Eastern Europe's economic history may be coming to an end. That says nothing about the potential for success of the region's presumed neodevelopmentalist turn, or the extent to which such a turn is indeed to be taken seriously.

The analysis in this book breaks from homogenizing depictions of the Central and Eastern European economies by discriminating between different outcomes in transnationalization. The three roles I propose—assembly platform, intermediate producer, and combined—correspond with particular directions of institutional reform after socialism. In the current juncture, these institutional configurations present political elites with varying kinds of developmental challenges, sectoral interests, and sources of popular pressures. It may be no surprise that popular dissatisfaction with FDI-led growth echoes loudest in the countries that have been most dependent on FDI—that is, in the assembly platforms (Hungary and Slovakia). In these cases, most of the policy maneuvering has been aimed at reforming supplemental institutions such as those of financial, fiscal, and social policy without placing excess pressure on TNCs or hampering capital inflows. It may also be of no surprise that part of the industrial policy goals of the Morawiecki Plan, in a combined state like Poland, involves the state extending greater support for intermediate producer sectors such as aerospace and machine building, and emerging sectors like biotechnology, while pushing TNCs in assembly platform sectors like automotive to shift more investment toward locating R&D operations in-country. In the Czech Republic, in addition to favoring high-technology sectors in FDI policy, among the major strategic goals of the government has been to seek export markets for Czech products beyond the EU. In Slovenia, severe fiscal and financial pressures on the state and the enterprise sector after 2008 have demanded deep institutional adjustments but have ultimately not led to the abandonment of the distinct intermediate producer structure of the Slovenian political economy. In Romania, the post-2008 period saw the rise of a set of policies drawing from a "disembedded neoliberalism" (Ban 2016) that undermined the political compromises between the state and trade unions in the 2000s alongside continued dynamic growth in TNC-led sectors that further entrenched their dominance in the Romanian economy. And Bulgaria's improving performance as a globalizing industrial state has been accompanied by ongoing structural problems of high unemployment and widespread informality in employment and underinvestment in infrastructure and education, all of which have been exacerbated by Bulgaria's center-right government's conservative fiscal posture throughout the post-2008 period.

These somewhat cursory observations of economic policy fissures after 2008 point to the potential importance of international market roles in the manner in which Central and Eastern European political economies respond to the most recent crisis as political elites and electorates realize the limits of the FDI-driven growth paradigm, all the while having economic growth structurally dependent on the local economy's global integration through TNC-led networks. Nonetheless, the international market roles identified in this book offer new ways of examining relationships between a broad array of economic policies and their impact on the making—or the undermining—of their respective competitive institutional advantages in the global economy and assess the long-term capacity of these economies to take new directions of sectoral development or enable their existing industries to climb the ladder of global value chains.

A study of the region's comparative institutional advantages ought to begin by examining processes of long-term industrial development while taking into account the profound impact periods of major institutional change have had on how institutions have evolved. In expanding the framework of Central and Eastern Europe's process of economic development as a long-run, episodic process within which both the continuities and discontinuities of socialist development play an important role, and highlighting the fact that postsocialist globalization has generated diverse responses and forms of adjustment within the region, I hope one of the contributions of this book is to open new avenues for research and debate as the region confronts new sets of uncertainties and opportunities.

Acknowledgments

This book would not be possible without the inspiration, assistance, and support of many along the way. The original idea for the project came from my curiosity in the politics of East European debt in the 1970s while I was a visiting scholar at the Institute for Public Knowledge (IPK) at New York University. A conversation on my then sketchy ideas with Craig Calhoun, at the time director of IPK, sparked my interest in studying the historical relationship between socialist economies and the dynamics of capitalism and launched my deep immersion into the intellectual arenas of political economy. The project evolved during my stint as a postdoctoral researcher at the Center for the Study of Social Organization (CSSO) at Princeton University's Department of Sociology, supported by an American Sociological Association / National Science Foundation fellowship. Princeton provided the time and the space to develop the groundwork for the comparative research. Paul DiMaggio, Viviana Zelizer, Miguel Centeno, and the graduate students coalescing around CSSO's workshops provided critical support, inspiration, and guidance. The book took its ultimate shape at my current home institution, the Department of Political Science at Virginia Tech, which supplied the intellectual environment for a work that commits multiple acts of "trespassing," as Albert Hirschman called it, across disciplinary boundaries in the social sciences.

Cornel Ban provided intellectual support and much important feedback as a reviewer, as well as a great deal of logistical help for fieldwork in Romania. Another reviewer, Rudra Sil, helped sharpen the insights and arguments of the book. Along the way, aspects of the book and its arguments were enriched from discussions with Nina Bandelj, Colin Beck, Mark Beissinger, Johanna Bockman, Irina Culic, François Debrix, Magnus Feldmann, Venelin Ganev, Ştefan Guga, Jan Hagemejer, Krzysztof Jasiecki, Lawrence King, James Mark, Deborah Milly, Mitchell Orenstein, David Ost, Petr Pavlinek, Victor Petrov, Florin Poenaru, Martha Poon, Grigore Pop-Eleches, Matija Rojec, Andrew Scerri, Miroslav Stanojević, and Edward Weisband among many others. Paul Avey, Ho-fung Hung, Timothy Luke, Scott Nelson, and J.P. Singh patiently read through drafts of the manuscript that led to innumerable improvements in content, approach, and style. Peter Szewczyk provided valuable research support in Poland, and the Group for Research in Applied Economics in Warsaw gave me an opportunity to present some of the findings to an audience of economists, which I found both intriguing and challenging. A grant from the National Council for East European and Eurasian Research supported fieldwork in Slovenia and Hungary, and generous support was also provided by my home institution for research in the Czech Republic, Romania, and Poland. A special thanks goes to the Vienna Institute for International Economic Studies, which made available to me its entire bank of Comecon economic data. J.P. Singh's faith in my competence and the manuscript's potential opened the door to the book's publication. Margo Beth Fleming, Kate Wahl, Steve Edward Catalano, Olivia Bartz, and the team at Stanford University Press made the process of getting the manuscript to print extremely smooth. Fortuitously, it turned out that this would be among the last books Margo would contract for the press before she moved on to other, grander pursuits in the publishing world. Generous support from the Provost's Office, the College for Liberal Arts and Human Sciences, and the Department of Political Science at Virginia Tech helped make the publication of this book possible.

Interviews with informants across the region helped shape much of the thinking that appears in this book. Rather than serve as "data sources" in the narrow sense, the interviewees instead aided my immersion into these local contexts, particularly as the region was still reeling and unsettled from the effects of the 2008 global financial crisis and its political fallouts. I hope this book contributes at least marginally to the collective process of sense-making I felt was taking place across the region at a time when the dominant narrative of the "transition to the market" had exhausted its explanatory capacity. My conversations with the interviewees on the politics and economies of Central and Eastern Europe raised questions and concerns that at some point became both too interesting and too wide-ranging to address in a single book, and which will likely preoccupy me for many years to come. None of the interviewees and their organizations are responsible for the views expressed in this book, nor should any of the interviewees be considered to share or endorse them.

Though officially enlisted as a political scientist, I was very fortunate to learn the craft of comparative historical research from a set of masterful teachers and mentors at the University of Michigan's Department of Sociology. This includes George Steinmetz, Margaret Somers, Michael Kennedy (now at Brown University), Howard Kimeldorf, Ronald Suny, Julia Adams (now at Yale University), Jeffrey Paige, Mark Mizruchi, and Fatma Müge Göçek. This book took me far from the historical worlds I studied while a graduate student at Michigan. Whatever competence this book demonstrates in turning the intellectual tools of comparative and historical analysis to the transformations of socialism and postsocialism should be attributed to these teachers; the failures, by contrast, are all mine. My intellectual trajectory in thinking about issues of postcommunism began at what now seems many ages ago at Georgetown University's Center for Russian, Eurasian, and East European Studies. Marjorie Mandelstam-Balzer persuaded me that an ethnographic sensibility is something not only anthropologists need, while Charles King at one point gave me the best lesson in fieldwork by letting me do it with him.

On a personal level, my wife, Shpresa, and our children, Rioll, Norik, and Andrra, bore the brunt of my absence during periods of fieldwork and the writing of this book.

In the course of my work on this book, my father was diagnosed with a debilitating illness. He has in some ways inspired this research, given that he spent a great deal of his career in the world of foreign trade both under and after socialism. I have, perhaps without intending to do so initially, partly ended up exploring and historically reconstructing that world. For this, and for the unending love and support he and my mother have given to me, I dedicate this book to my parents.

List of Interviews

Jacek Adamski, Advisor to the Board, Polish Confederation Lewiatan (Warsaw)

Jarolím Antal, Director, Centre for European Studies, University of Economics (Prague)

Jacek Bartkiewicz, Board Member, National Bank of Poland (Warsaw)

Marcin Boroń, Senior Expert, Economic Analysis Division, Economic Development Department, Polish Information and Foreign Investment Agency (Warsaw)

Andras Bozoki, Professor, Department of Political Science, Central European University (Budapest)

Blaž Brodnjak, Board Member, Nova Ljubljanska Banka (Ljubljana)

Radu Burnete, Public Affairs Expert, Foreign Investors Council (Bucharest)

Gonzalo Caprirolo, Researcher, Institute of Macroeconomic Analysis and Development (Ljubljana)

Valentin Cojanu, Faculty member, International Economics and Business, Bucharest Academy of Economic Studies (Bucharest)

Dumitru Costin, President, Blocul Național Sindical (BNS) trade union confederation (Bucharest)

Adrian Dimache, General Manager, Italian Chamber of Commerce in Romania (Bucharest)

Katarzyna Dwórznik, Political and Legal Expert, Chamber of Commerce in Poland (Warsaw)

Pavel Fára, Deputy Director, Confederation of Industry of the Czech Republic (Prague)

Jakub Faryś, President, Polish Automotive Association (Warsaw)

Nenad Filipović, Professor, Bled School of Management (Bled and Ljubljana)

Ştefan Guga, Graduate student and researcher, Central European University (Budapest and Bucharest)

Jan Guz, President, Ogólnopolskie Porozumienie Związków Zawodowych (OPZZ) trade union confederation (Warsaw)

Jan Hagemejer, Economist, GRAPE / National Bank of Poland (Warsaw)

Anca Harasim, Executive Director, American Chamber of Commerce in Romania (Bucharest)

Tony Housh, Chairman, American Chamber of Commerce in Poland (Warsaw)

Florentin Iancu, ICT trade union activist (Bucharest)

Mihai Ivascu, Advisor to the President, Romanian Chamber of Commerce and Industry (Bucharest)

Krzysztof Jasiecki, Professor, Institute of Philosophy and Sociology, Polish Academy of Sciences (Warsaw)

Jakub Kasiński, Director, Research and Analysis Centre, Employers of Poland (Warsaw)

Jacek Kocerka, Deputy Director, Department of Statistics, National Bank of Poland (Warsaw)

Primož Krasovec, Activist, Workers and Punks University (Ljubljana)

Martin Kratochvíl, Information and Marketing Specialist, CzechInvest (Prague)

Kryštof Kruliš, Research Fellow, Association for International Affairs (Prague)

Marko Krzan, Activist, Workers and Punks University (Ljubljana)

Norbert Kusiak, Advisor to the President, Ogólnopolskie Porozumienie Związków Zawodowych (OPZZ) trade union confederation (Warsaw)

Maciej Lachowski, Counsellor to the Minister, Large Investment Support Development, Ministry of Economic Development, Government of the Czech Republic (Prague)

Łukasz Leśniewski, Head of Economic Analysis Division, Economic Development Department, Polish Information and Foreign Investment Agency (Warsaw)

Krzysztof Makowski, Economic Expert, Balance of Payments Direct and Portfolio Investment Section, National Bank of Poland (Warsaw)

Andrzej Malinowski, President, Employers of Poland (Warsaw)

Sebastian Metz, Director, German-Romanian Chamber of Commerce (Bucharest)

Agnieszka Pałka, Department for Key Investments Support, Ministry of Economic Development, Government of Poland (Warsaw)

Petr Pavlínek, Professor, Department of Geography and Geology, University of Nebraska-Omaha and Charles University (Prague)

Florin Poenaru, Scholar and activist (Bucharest)

Petr Pojer, Researcher, Research Institute for Labor and Social Affairs (Prague)

Matija Rojec, Professor, Faculty of Social Sciences, University of Ljubljana (Ljubljana)

Uroš Rožič, State Secretary, Ministry of Economic Development and Technology, Government of Slovenia (Ljubljana)

Vit Samek, Vice President, Czech-Moravian Confederation of Trade Unions (Prague)

Katarzyna Soszka-Ogrodnik, Press Secretary, German-Polish Chamber of Commerce (Warsaw)

Miroslav Stanojević, Professor, Faculty of Social Sciences, University of Ljubljana (Ljubljana)

Victoria Stoiciu, Program Coordinator, Friedrich Ebert Stiftung—Romania (Bucharest)

Robert Szewczyk, International Department, Niezależny Samorządny Związek Zawodowy (NSZZ) Solidarność (Gdańsk)

Andrei Țărnea, Executive Director, Aspen Institute Romania (Bucharest)

Patryk Tuczapski, Foreign Affairs Expert, Employers of Poland (Warsaw)

Marius Tudor, Secretary General, Association of Automobile Producers and Importers (Bucharest)

Soňa Veverková, Researcher, Research Institute for Labor and Social Affairs (Prague)

Mateja Vranicar, State Secretary, Ministry of Finance, Government of Slovenia (Ljubljana)

Zbigniew Zimny, Professor, Vice-Director at Akademia Finansow i Biznesu, and former economist at UNCTAD (Warsaw)

Martin Zuštík, Board Member, Association for Foreign Investment / Technoprojekt (Ostrava)

Notes

Chapter 1

1. Here I associate "transitology" with what Thomas Carothers (2002) terms the "transition paradigm" in the study of democratization and economic reform.

2. The terms "postcommunism" and "postsocialism" are used interchangeably throughout this book to refer to the varied sets of political, economic, and cultural transformations undergone by the ex-socialist states and societies.

3. The terms "state socialism" and "socialism" are used interchangeably throughout this book to mean the political and economic systems of "actually existing socialism" in Europe and Eurasia in the twentieth century, characterized by a Leninist party dictatorship exercising monopolistic control over the state and economy. For a complete definition, see Valerie Bunce's account (1999b, 21–37).

4. As Chase-Dunn put it, "socialist ideology may simply be one of the most powerful legitimations of capitalist accumulation" (1980, 515, n. 11).

5. As Gorin adds, "numerous empirical questions, posed *within* the conceptual framework of world-systems theory, have been raised with regard to the validity of world-systems interpretations of socialist societies. These questions remain unanswered" (1985, 365; emphasis in original). In Wallerstein's later synthetic works on world-systems analysis (e.g., 2004), the socialist experience largely disappears from historical view.

6. As Jowitt puts it, it would be "demagogues, priests, and colonels more than democrats and capitalists who will shape Eastern Europe's general institutional identity" (1992, 300).

Chapter 2

1. Quoted in Wilczynski (1976, 136).

2. For critical assessments of the theories and practices behind Soviet-style central planning that inform this chapter's analysis, consult Alec Nove (1983) and János Kornai (1991).

3. The text of Comecon's founding statement is reprinted in *Comecon: Integration Problems of the Planned Economies* (Kaser 1967, 11–12). Michael Kaser's interpretation of

the origins of Comecon still stands. As he points out, in the division of European economies, "both halves of the continent contributed to the break." On US trade restrictions see Mastanduno (1992).

4. According to CIA estimates reported by Frankyln Holzman (1976, 104).

5. Mongolia became a full member of Comecon in 1962. Full membership was granted to Cuba and Vietnam in the 1970s.

6. The economic model that Yevgeni Preobrazhensky proposed in the 1920s was more an inspiration than an actual blueprint of Soviet central planning. Preobrazhensky believed that agricultural savings could be mobilized for industrialization through the state's monopsony role as dominant buyer of agricultural goods, whereas Stalin accomplished it through forced confiscation. See Robert Allen's analysis (2003, 172–186).

7. Randall Stone's (1996) archival research confirms that the Soviet technocracy continuously expressed concerns over the costs of subsidizing Central and Eastern Europe's economies.

8. Compelling arguments assert that the introduction of central planning in the USSR increased the rate of industrialization, at least in the short run, by increasing the rate of investment and rapidly mobilizing productive resources (Nove 1964). Allen (2003) ran simulations using historical data and showed that Soviet industrialization in the 1930s would not have been as rapid had the USSR and/or Russia followed other developmental paths, attributing growth to the regime's coercive mobilization of resources.

9. By number of projects, these were 116 in Bulgaria, 98 in Romania, 91 in Poland, and 53 in Hungary, while only 19 and 16 in East Germany and Czechoslovakia, respectively.

10. In a longer historical view, Khrushchev's efforts to engage Western companies was a return to the traditional goals of Soviet foreign economic policy. Soviet industrialization throughout the 1920s and 1930s had relied heavily on Western technology and technical expertise. For more on this, consult Timothy Luke (1985), Bruce Parrott (1983), and Antony Sutton (1968, 1971, 1973).

11. Or, as one Czech economist quipped at the irony of having to use capitalist prices for socialist trade: "When the world revolution comes we shall have to preserve at least one capitalist country. Otherwise we shall not know at what prices to trade" (quoted in Nove 1983, 109).

Chapter 3

1. *Time Magazine*, April 26, 1975, quoted in Frank (1977, 120).

2. Reprinted in Smith, Laibman, and Bechtel (1977, 56).

3. "Free" prices were not entirely free. The Material and Price Office still had a role in administering price levels.

4. MFN status was granted to Romania in 1975 and Hungary in 1978.

5. Jozef Wilczynski quotes a socialist economist who says of small Western firms that they are "petty-minded and suspicious [and] more difficult to negotiate with" (1976, 32). By contrast, TNCs are "more experienced in international dealings, and as they operate in several fields their approach to industrial cooperation is more positive" (32).

6. The relationship with capitalist firms was not entirely one-sided, however. As Margarita Maximova (1977, 20–21) points out, Western firms were also interested in Comecon technologies in areas such as metallurgical equipment, turbines and generators, nuclear reactors, electrical power stations, polygraph equipment, and precision mechanics and optics. Wilczynski (1976) makes a similar point.

7. Similar sentiments were expressed in an interview with Tony Housh, chairman of the board of the American Chamber of Commerce in Warsaw, who relayed anecdotes of foreign investors finding factories in the early 1990s sitting on top of relatively new technology that remained unused or underutilized because of the lack of access to Western markets.

8. Figures are from officially published UNECE data given in Lavigne (1991, 324).

9. According to data presented by Iliana Zloch-Christy (1987, 32) and Helgard Wienert and John Slater (1986, 404).

10. Data given in Wienert and Slater (1986, 405–412).

11. The sectors are energy, fuel, metallurgy, engineering and metal working, chemicals, wood and paper, textiles, food, other light industry, and "other."

Chapter 4

1. Quoted in Bourdieu and Wacquant (1992, 91).

2. The term "economic transnationalization" in this chapter refers to the full integration of postsocialist industry in TNC-dominated networks of production and exchange. The process of transnationalization should not be understood as the entry of collective actors into an authority-less field existing outside the purview of state power but rather their incorporation into hierarchical structures of domination that operate both through and across the territorial jurisdictions of nation-states.

3. In a critical realist sense, transnational organizational capital is conceptualized as a causal structure (or mechanism) (Steinmetz 1998; Gorski 2009). The concept thus corresponds to Bourdieu's concept of capital as capabilities (powers) that are generated over time and exercised variably by agents in particular social fields (Bourdieu and Wacquant 1992, 16–19, 90–91).

4. Several case studies of individual postsocialist firms carried out in the 1990s demonstrate how past relationships with Western firms proved central in facilitating their acquisition via FDI (see King 2001, 47–97; Artisien and Rojec 2001, 24; Estrin, Richet, and Brada 2000; Bandelj 2008, 131–143).

5. Classifications of privatization policy and their implementation across postsocialist states follow those of the EBRD (1999).

6. On a methodological note, the reader should bear in mind that the correlations are not offered as demonstrations for the existence or nonexistence of causal relationships. Rather, they are mobilized as evidence in support of the overall process-tracing analysis aiming to narratively reconstruct relationships between past events and observed outcomes.

7. This calculation is based on UNECE (1996) data for Bulgaria, the Czech Republic, Hungary, Poland, Romania, and Slovakia.

8. Interview with Adrian Dimache, Italian-Romanian Chamber of Commerce, Bucharest, June 20, 2015. In the 1990s Dimache was directly involved as an agent contracting OPT work in Romanian factories for Italian clothing and shoe manufacturers.

9. According to Czech national statistics reproduced by Zemplinerova (2001, 135). This pattern also further contradicts the suggestion that complex manufacturing was the main driver of FDI.

10. Interview with Petr Pavlínek, Charles University, Prague, June 29, 2015.

11. The OECD classified agreements into the following four types: agreements involving (Western) plant or equipment in exchange for products, joint production (co-production) of goods, subcontracting, and joint ventures (Wiener and Slater 1986, 339).

12. My informants in the Czech Republic indicated that these kinds of investments, especially in low-skilled, labor-intensive work, were largely resented by both government agencies and policymakers.

13. Slovakia's unusual rise in the ratio of domestic over foreign value added in its exports may be the result of decreased dependence on Czech inputs after the country's independence.

Chapter 5

1. To be sure, this is a simple measure that excludes other intricacies of transnational financial dependence in the enterprise sector, such as cross-border credit and other indirect financial flows that may support domestic private investment.

2. As Boyer (2005, 18) points out, the structural method compares structural features of states and economies across a given set of dimensions and is best suited for identifying and constructing theoretical models of comparative political economies.

3. An alternative measure of export specialization shows similar patterns. In the 2000s the Czech Republic, Hungary, Slovakia, and Slovenia exhibited higher levels of export concentration (less product diversity) than Bulgaria, Romania, and Poland, as measured by the standard Herfindahl-Hirschman Index of export concentration of goods (according to data from UNCTADstat).

4. High-technology exports are defined based on UN Comtrade criteria and include exports with high R&D intensity, such as aerospace, computers, pharmaceuticals, scientific instruments, and electrical machinery.

5. Unlike Poland, Romania also has greater TNC presence in the energy and mining and quarrying sectors as a result of aggressive sectoral privatization in the 2000s.

6. According to Eurostat data.

7. Data for Bulgaria is unavailable.

Chapter 6

1. Collier and Collier (1991, 33).

2. In the period 1990–1994, effective import tariffs ranged between 5 and 22 percent, with the highest rates found in Bulgaria and Romania. In the Czech Republic and Slovakia, low tariffs were offset by quantitative import restrictions covering an extensive range of goods. Only Slovenia adopted a fully liberal trade regime (EBRD 1994, 108–109).

3. Interviews with Martin Kratochvíl, Information and Marketing Specialist, Czech-Invest (Prague), June 25, 2015; Pavel Fára, Deputy Director, Confederation of Industry of the Czech Republic (Prague), July 1, 2015.

4. Interview with Soňa Veverková and Petr Pojer, Research Institute for Labor and Social Affairs (Prague), July 2, 2015.

5. Interview with Vit Samek, Vice President, Czech-Moravian Confederation of Trade Unions (Prague), July 7, 2015.

6. Interview with Matija Rojec, Faculty of Social Sciences, University of Ljubljana (Ljubljana), May 8, 2013.

7. Interview with Uroš Rožič, State Secretary, Ministry of Economic Development and Technology (Ljubljana), May 7, 2013.

8. Interview with Miroslav Stanojević, Faculty of Social Sciences, University of Ljubljana (Ljubljana), June 23, 2016.

9. Interview with Jakub Faryś, President, Polish Automotive Association (Warsaw), June 27, 2016.

10. Interviews with Tony Housh, Chairman, American Chamber of Commerce in Poland (Warsaw), June 27, 2016; Maciej Lachowski and Agnieszka Pałka, Ministry of Economic Development (Warsaw), June 17, 2016; Łukasz Leśniewski and Marcin Boroń, Polish Information and Foreign Investment Agency (Warsaw), June 15, 2016.

11. Interviews with Florentin Iancu, ICT trade union activist (Bucharest), June 20, 2015; Andrei Țărnea, Executive Director, Aspen Institute Romania (Bucharest), June 19, 2015.

12. According to FDI data published by Bulgaria's National Statistical Institute.

13. In the 1980s Bulgaria developed a large electronics industry as part of its Comecon specialization. In the 1990s the sector teetered on the verge of collapse, unable to break into foreign markets or spark acquisition interest among any major electronics TNCs. What remained of the sector was salvaged by an investment from the Hungarian group Videoton, which in 1999 acquired the flagship producer DZU from the Bulgarian state for the petty sum of $54,200.

14. As Colin Crouch points out, *complementarity in the strong sense* means "two or more phenomena [such that] each can be defined in terms of what is lacked by the other(s) in order to produce a defined whole" (2010, 118). The position taken here is more closely aligned with the neorealist view of institutional change in capitalism (Amable and Palombarini 2009) than the firm-centered approach of Peter Hall and David Soskice (2001).

Conclusion

1. This statement, of course, brackets much of the social costs of transformation, which includes factors such as demographic decline due to migration, lower birth rates, and shortened life expectancies, decline in health care and educational coverage, shortages in public investment, and the increased economic vulnerability of marginalized social groups. For a summary, see Iván T. Berend's account (2009, 177–254).

Bibliography

Adam, Jan. 1989. *Economic Reforms in the Soviet Union and Eastern Europe Since the 1960s*. New York: St. Martin's.

Allen, Robert C. 2003. *Farm to Factory: A Reinterpretation of the Soviet Industrial Revolution*. Princeton, NJ: Princeton University Press.

Allen, Roy E. 2009. *Financial Crises and Recession in the Global Economy*. Northampton, MA: Edward Elgar.

Amsden, Alice H. 2001. *The Rise of "The Rest": Challenges to the West from Late-Industrializing Economies*. New York: Oxford University Press.

Anderson, Robert E., Simeon Dejankov, Gerhard Pohl, and Stijn Claessons. 1997. *Privatization and Restructuring in Central and Eastern Europe. Viewpoint: Public Policy for the Private Sector; Note 123*. Washington, DC: World Bank.

Appadurai, Arjun. 1996. *Modernity at Large: Cultural Dimensions of Globalization*. Minneapolis: University of Minnesota Press.

Appel, Hilary. 2000. "The Ideological Determinants of Liberal Economic Reform: The Case of Privatization." *World Politics* 52 (4): 520–549.

———. 2004. *A New Capitalist Order: Privatization and Ideology in Russia and Eastern Europe*. Pittsburgh: University of Pittsburgh Press.

Appel, Hilary, and Mitchell Orenstein. 2013. "Ideas Versus Resources: Explaining the Flat Tax and Pension Privatization Revolutions in Eastern Europe and the Former Soviet Union." *Comparative Political Studies* 46 (2): 123–152.

Arrighi, Giovanni. 1999. "Globalization and Historical Macrosociology." In *Sociology for the Twenty-First Century: Continuities and Cutting Edges*, edited by Janet Abü-Lughod, 117–133. Chicago: University of Chicago Press.

Arrighi, Giovanni, and Jessica Drangel. 1986. "The Stratification of the World-Economy: An Exploration of the Semiperipheral Zone." *Review (Fernand Braudel Center)* 10 (1): 9–74.

Artisien, Patrick, and Matija Rojec. 2001. "Foreign Investment and Privatization in Eastern Europe: An Overview." In *Foreign Investment and Privatization in Central and Eastern Europe*, edited by Patrick Artisien and Matija Rojec, 3–33. New York: Palgrave Macmillan.

Artisien, Patrick, Matija Rojec, and Marjan Svetlicic, eds. 1993. *Foreign Investment in Central and Eastern Europe*. New York: Palgrave Macmillan.

Åslund, Anders. 2007. *How Capitalism Was Built: The Transformation of Central and Eastern Europe, Russia, and Central Asia*. New York: Cambridge University Press.

Ban, Cornel. 2012. "Sovereign Debt, Austerity, and Regime Change: The Case of Nicolae Ceausescu's Romania." *East European Politics and Societies* 26 (4): 743–776.

———. 2013, December 2. "From Cocktail to Dependence: Revisiting the Foundations of Dependent Market Economies." Global Economic Governance Initiative Working Paper 3, Boston University, Boston, MA.

———. 2016. *Ruling Ideas: How Global Neoliberalism Goes Local*. New York: Oxford University Press.

Bandelj, Nina. 2008. *From Communists to Foreign Capitalists: The Social Foundations of Foreign Direct Investment in Postsocialist Europe*. Princeton, NJ: Princeton University Press.

———. 2009. "The Global Economy as Instituted Process: The Case of Central and Eastern Europe." *American Sociological Review* 74 (1): 128–149.

———. 2010. "How EU Integration and Legacies Mattered for Foreign Direct Investment into Central and Eastern Europe." *Europe-Asia Studies* 62 (3): 481–501.

Barney, Jay. 1991. "Firm Resources and Sustained Competitive Advantage." *Journal of Management* 17 (1): 99–120.

Bartlett, David. 1992. "The Political Economy of Privatization: Property Reform and Democracy in Hungary." *East European Politics and Societies* 6 (1): 73–118.

Bauman, Zygmunt. 1998. *Globalization: The Human Consequences*. New York: Columbia University Press.

Beach, Derek, and Rasmus Brun Pedersen. 2013. *Process-Tracing Methods: Foundations and Guidelines*. Ann Arbor: University of Michigan Press.

Beck, Ulrich. 2000. *What Is Globalization?* Translated by Patrick Camiller. Cambridge, MA: Polity Press.

Beissinger, Mark R., and Stephen Kotkin, eds. 2014. *Historical Legacies of Communism in Russia and Eastern Europe*. New York: Cambridge University Press.

Beramendi, Pablo, Silja Häusermann, Herbert Kitschelt, and Hanspeter Kriesi, eds. 2015. *The Politics of Advanced Capitalism*. New York: Cambridge University Press.

Berend, Iván T. 1998. *Decades of Crisis: Central and Eastern Europe Before World War II*. Berkeley: University of California Press.

———. 2009. *From the Soviet Bloc to the European Union: The Economic and Social Transformation of Central and Eastern Europe Since 1973*. New York: Cambridge University Press.

Biberaj, Elez. 1990. *Albania: A Socialist Maverick*. Boulder, CO: Westview Press.

Birch, Kean, and Vlad Mykhnenko. 2009. "Varieties of Neoliberalism? Restructuring in Large Industrially Dependent Regions Across Western and Eastern Europe." *Journal of Economic Geography* 9 (3): 355–380.

Bockman, Johanna. 2011. *Markets in the Name of Socialism: The Left-Wing Origins of Neoliberalism*. Stanford, CA: Stanford University Press.

Bohle, Dorothee. 2006. "Neoliberal Hegemony, Transnational Capital, and the Terms of the EU's Eastward Expansion." *Capital and Class* 30 (1): 57–86.

Bohle, Dorothee, and Béla Greskovits. 2012. *Capitalist Diversity on Europe's Periphery.* Ithaca, NY: Cornell University Press.

Bojkó, Béla. 1977. "Results and Problems of Cooperation with Western Firms in Hungarian Light Industry." In *East-West Cooperation in Business: Inter-firm Studies,* edited by Christopher T. Saunders, 152–165. New York: Springer-Verlag.

Bornstein, Morris. 1985. *The Transfer of Western Technology to the USSR.* Paris: Organization for Economic Cooperation and Development.

Böröcz, József. 1992. "Dual Dependency and Property Vacuum: Social Change on the State Socialist Semiperiphery." *Theory and Society* 21 (1): 77–104.

Bourdieu, Pierre. 1986. "The Forms of Capital." In *Handbook of Theory and Research for the Sociology of Education,* edited by John G. Richardson, 242–258. Westport, CT: Greenwood Press.

———. 1990. *The Logic of Practice.* Stanford, CA: Stanford University Press.

———. 1993. "Some Properties of Fields." In *Sociology in Question,* edited by Pierre Bourdieu, 72–77. London: Sage.

Bourdieu, Pierre, and Loïc Wacquant. 1992. *An Invitation to Reflexive Sociology.* Chicago: University of Chicago Press.

Boycko, Maxim, Andrei Shleifer, and Robert W. Vishny. 1995. *Privatizing Russia.* Cambridge, MA: MIT Press.

Boyer, Robert. 2005. "How and Why Capitalisms Differ." MPIfG Discussion Paper 05/4. Max Planck Institute for the Study of Societies, Cologne.

Brada, Josef C. 1985a. "Soviet Subsidization of Eastern Europe: The Primacy of Economics of Politics?" *Journal of Comparative Economics* 9 (1) : 80–92.

———. 1985b. "Soviet-Western Trade and Technology Transfer: An Economic Overview." In *Trade, Technology, and Soviet-American Relations,* edited by Bruce Parrott, 3–34. Bloomington: Indiana University Press.

———. 1988. "Industrial Policy in Eastern Europe." In *Economic Adjustment and Reform in Eastern Europe and the Soviet Union,* edited by Josef C. Brada, Ed A. Hewett, and Thomas A. Wolf, 109–146. Durham, NC: Duke University Press.

Bruno, Michael. 1992. "Stabilization and Reform in Eastern Europe: A Preliminary Evaluation." *IMF Staff Papers* 39 (4): 741–777.

Brus, Włodzimierz. 1979. "The East European Reforms: What Happened to Them?" *Soviet Studies* 31 (2): 257–267.

Bruszt, László, and Béla Greskovits. 2009. "Transnationalization, Social Integration, and Capitalist Diversity in the East and the South." *Studies in Comparative International Development* 44 (4): 411–434.

Bruszt, László, and Julia Langbein. 2017. "Varieties of Dis-embedded Liberalism. EU Integration Strategies in the Eastern Peripheries of Europe." *Journal of European Public Policy* 24 (2): 297–315.

Bruszt, László, and Gerald A. McDermott. 2009. "Transnational Integration Regimes as Development Programmes." In *The Transnationalization of Economies, States, and*

Civil Societies: New Challenges for Governance in Europe, edited by László Bruszt
   and Ronald Holzhacker, 23–60. New York: Springer.

Brzezinski, Zbigniew. 1967. *The Soviet Bloc: Unity and Conflict*. Cambridge, MA: Harvard University Press.

Bunce, Valerie. 1999a. "The Political Economy of Postsocialism." *Slavic Review* 58 (4):
   756–793.

———. 1999b. *Subversive Institutions: The Design and the Destruction of Socialism and
   the State*. New York: Cambridge University Press.

Busemeyer, Marius R., and Christine Trampusch. 2012. "The Comparative Political
   Economy of Collective Skill Formation." In *The Political Economy of Collective Skill
   Formation*, edited by Marius R. Busemeyer and Christine Trampusch, 3–40. New
   York: Oxford University Press.

Butler, William E., ed. 1978. *A Source Book on Socialist International Organizations*. Alphen aan den Rijn, The Netherlands: Sijthoff and Noordhoff.

Campbell, John L. 2004. *Institutional Change and Globalization*. Princeton, NJ: Princeton University Press.

———. 2010. "Institutional Reproduction and Change." In *The Oxford Handbook of
   Comparative Institutional Analysis*, edited by Glenn Morgan, John L. Campbell,
   Colin Crouch, Ove Kaj Pedersen, and Richard Whitley, 87–116. New York: Oxford
   University Press.

Campbell, John, and Ove K. Pedersen. 1996. "The Evolutionary Nature of Revolutionary Change in Postcommunist Europe." In *Legacies of Change: Transformations of
   Postcommunist European Economies*, edited by John Campbell and Ove K. Pedersen,
   207–246. New York: Aldine De Gruyter.

Cantwell, John A. 1989. *Technological Innovation and Multinational Corporations*. Oxford: Basil Blackwell.

Cardoso, Fernando Henrique, and Enzo Faletto. 1979. *Dependency and Development in
   Latin America*. Translated by Marjory Mattingly Urquidi. Berkeley: University of
   California Press.

Carothers, Thomas. 2002. "The End of the Transition Paradigm." *Journal of Democracy*
   13 (1): 5–21.

Cerny, Philip G. 1997. "Paradoxes of the Competition State: The Dynamics of Political
   Globalization." *Government and Opposition* 32 (2): 249–274.

Chase-Dunn, Christopher K. 1980. "Socialist States in the Capitalist World-Economy."
   Social Problems 29 (5): 505–525.

Chirot, Daniel, ed. 1989. *The Origins of Backwardness in Eastern Europe: Economics and
   Politics from the Middle Ages Until the Early Twentieth Century*. Berkeley: University
   of California Press.

Clark, Cal, and Donna Bahry. 1983. "Dependent Development: A Socialist Variant." *International Studies Quarterly* 27 (3): 271–293.

Collier, David. 2014. "Understanding Process Tracing." *Political Science and Politics* 44
   (4): 823–830.

Collier, Ruth Berins, and David Collier. 1991. *Shaping the Political Arena: Critical Junctures, the Labor Movement, and Regime Dynamics in Latin America*. Princeton, NJ: Princeton University Press.

Comisso, Ellen. 1998. "'Implicit' Development Strategies in Central East Europe and Cross-National Production Networks." Working Paper 129. Prepared for Kreisky Forum and BRIE Policy Conference, Foreign Direct Investment and Trade in Eastern Europe: The Creation of a Unified European Economy, Vienna, June 5–6, 1997.

Crouch, Colin. 2010. "Complementarity." In *The Oxford Handbook of Comparative Institutional Analysis*, edited by Glenn Morgan, John L. Campbell, Colin Crouch, Ove Kaj Pedersen, and Richard Whitley, 117–138. New York: Oxford University Press.

———. 2011. *The Strange Non-Death of Neoliberalism*. Malden, MA: Polity Press.

Crouch, Colin, Martin Schröder, and Helmut Voelzkow. 2009. "Regional and Sectoral Varieties of Capitalism." *Economy and Society* 38 (4): 654–678.

Crowley, Stephen, and Miroslav Stanojević. 2011. "Varieties of Capitalism, Power Resources, and Historical Legacies: Explaining the Slovenian Exception." *Politics and Society* 39 (2): 268–295.

Damijan, Jože, Mark Knell, Boris Majcen, and Matija Rojec. 2003. "The Role of FDI, R&D Accumulation, and Trade in Transferring Technology to Transition Countries: Evidence from Firm Panel Data for Eight Transition Countries." *Economic Systems* 27 (2): 189–204.

Darity, William, Jr., and Bobbie L. Horn. 1988. *The Loan Pushers: The Role of Commercial Banks in the International Debt Crisis*. Cambridge, MA: Ballinger.

Delamaide, Darrell. 1984. *Debt Shock: The Full Story of the World Credit Crisis*. Garden City, NY: Doubleday.

Deudney, Daniel, and G. John Ikenberry. 1991. "Soviet Reform and the End of the Cold War: Explaining Large-Scale Historical Change." *Review of International Studies* 17 (3): 225–250.

Djilas, Milovan. 1963. *Conversations with Stalin*. Translated by Michael B. Petrovich. New York: Harcourt Brace.

Doner, Richard F., and Ben Ross Schneider. 2016. "The Middle-Income Trap: More Politics Than Economics." *World Politics* 68 (4): 608–644.

Dos Santos, Theotonio. 1970. "The Structure of Dependence." *American Economic Review* 60 (2): 231–236.

Drahokoupil, Jan. 2009. *Globalization and the State in Central and Eastern Europe: The Politics of Foreign Direct Investment*. New York: Routledge.

Duménil, Gérard, and Dominique Lévy. 2011. *The Crisis of Neoliberalism*. Cambridge, MA: Harvard University Press.

Dunning, John H. 1988. *Explaining International Production*. London: Unwin Hayman.

Easter, Gerald M. 2012. *Capital, Coercion, and Postcommunist States*. Ithaca, NY: Cornell University Press.

Economist. 1990. "A Conversation with Václav Klaus." *The Economist*, February 10, 77.

Ekiert, Grzegorz. 1991. "Democratization Processes in East Central Europe: A Theoretical Reconsideration." *British Journal of Political Science* 21 (3): 285–313.

———. 2003. "Patterns of Postcommunist Transformation in Central and Eastern Europe." In *Capitalism and Democracy in Central and Eastern Europe: Assessing the Legacy of Communist Rule*, edited by Grzegorz Ekiert and Stephen E. Hanson, 89–119. New York: Cambridge University Press.

———. 2015. "Three Generations of Research on Post Communist Politics—A Sketch." *East European Politics and Societies* 29 (2): 323–337.

Ekiert, Grzegorz, and Stephen E. Hanson, eds. 2003a. *Capitalism and Democracy in Central and Eastern Europe: Assessing the Legacy of Communist Rule*. New York: Cambridge University Press.

———. 2003b. "Time, Space, and Institutional Change in Central and Eastern Europe." In *Capitalism and Democracy in Central and Eastern Europe: Assessing the Legacy of Communist Rule*, edited by Grzegorz Ekiert and Stephen E. Hanson, 15–48. New York: Cambridge University Press.

Estevez-Abe, Margarita, Torben Iversen, and David W. Soskice. 2001. "Social Protection and the Formation of Skills: A Reinterpretation of the Welfare State." In *Varieties of Capitalism: The Institutional Foundations of Comparative Advantage*, edited by Peter A. Hall and David W. Soskice, 145–183. New York: Oxford University Press.

Estrin, Saul, Xavier Richet, and Josef C. Brada, eds. 2000. *Foreign Direct Investment in Central Eastern Europe: Case Studies of Firms in Transition*. Armonk, NY: M.E. Sharpe.

European Bank for Reconstruction and Development (EBRD). 1994. *Transition Report 1994*. London: European Bank for Reconstruction and Development.

———. 1999. *Transition Report 1999: Ten Years of Transition*. London: European Bank for Reconstruction and Development.

European Commission. n.d. *Eurostat Database*. Accessed January 8, 2018. http://ec.europa.eu/eurostat/data/database.

Evans, Peter. 1979. *Dependent Development*. Princeton, NJ: Princeton University Press.

———. 1995. *Embedded Autonomy: States and Industrial Transformation*. Princeton, NJ: Princeton University Press.

Eyal, Gil, Iván Szelényi, and Eleanor R. Townsley. 1998. *Making Capitalism Without Capitalists: Class Formation and Elite Struggles in Post-Communist Central Europe*. New York: Verso.

Fallenbuchl, Zbigniew. 1983. *East-West Technology Transfer: Study of Poland, 1971–1980*. Paris: Organization for Economic Cooperation and Development.

Falleti, Tulia G., and James Mahoney. 2015. "The Comparative Sequential Method." In *Advances in Comparative-Historical Analysis*, edited by James Mahoney and Kathleen Thelen, 211–239. New York: Cambridge University Press.

Feldmann, Magnus. 2006. "Emerging Varieties of Capitalism in Transition Countries: Industrial Relations and Wage Bargaining in Estonia and Slovenia." *Comparative Political Studies* 39 (7): 829–854.

Financial Times. 1992. "Philip Morris Wins Tabak Monopoly." *Financial Times*, May 8, 11.

Fish, M. Steven. 1998. "The Determinants of Reform in the Post-Communist World." *East European Politics and Society* 12 (1): 31–78.

Fisher, Sharon, John Gould, and Tim Haighton. 2007. "Slovakia's Neoliberal Turn." *Europe-Asia Studies* 59 (6): 977–998.

Fowkes, Ben. 2000. *Eastern Europe 1945–1969: From Stalinism to Stagnation*. New York: Longman.

Fraga, Vera, and Manuel Duarte Rocha. 2014. "Vulnerabilities Underlying the Impact of the Global Financial Crisis Across Europe: Emerging Versus Advanced Economies." *Eastern European Economics* 52 (2): 28–48.

Frank, André Gunder. 1966. *The Development of Underdevelopment*. Boston, MA: New England Free Press.

———. 1977. "Long Live Transideological Enterprise! The Socialist Economies in the Capitalist International Division of Labor." *Review (Fernand Braudel Center)* 1 (1): 91–140.

Frieden, Jeffry A. 2006. *Global Capitalism: Its Fall and Rise in the Twentieth Century*. New York: Norton.

Friedman, Milton. 1970. "The Euro-Dollar Market: Some First Principles." Selected Papers 34. University of Chicago Graduate School of Business.

Fröbel, Folker, Jürgen Heinrichs, and Otto Kreye. 1980. *The New International Division of Labour: Structural Unemployment in Industrialised Countries and Industrialisation in Developing Countries*. Translated by Pete Burgess. New York: Cambridge University Press.

Frye, Timothy. 2010. *Building States and Markets After Communism: The Perils of Polarized Democracy*. New York: Cambridge University Press.

Fukuyama, Francis. 1992. *The End of History and the Last Man*. New York: The Free Press.

Gabrisch, Hubert, and Michel Vale. 1993. "Difficulties in Establishing Joint Ventures in Eastern Europe." *Eastern European Economics* 31 (4): 19–50.

Ganev, Venelin I. 2007. *Preying on the State: The Transformation of Bulgaria After 1989*. Ithaca, NY: Cornell University Press.

Genillard, Ariane. 1991. "Czechs Find Life After Comecon: Their Largest Foreign Trading Company, Created to Serve the State, Has Found New Markets." *Financial Times*, June 26, 6.

Gereffi, Gary. 2009. "Development Models and Industrial Upgrading in China and Mexico." *European Sociological Review* 25 (1): 37–51.

Gereffi, Gary, John Humphrey, and Timothy Sturgeon. 2005. "The Governance of Global Value Chains." *Review of International Political Economy* 12 (1): 78–104.

Giddens, Anthony. 1990. *The Consequences of Modernity*. Stanford, CA: Stanford University Press.

Gilpin, Robert. 2001. *Global Political Economy: Understanding the International Economic Order*. Princeton, NJ: Princeton University Press.

———. 2002. *The Challenge of Global Capitalism*. Princeton, NJ: Princeton University Press.

Glyn, Andrew. 2006. *Capitalism Unleashed: Finance, Globalization, and Welfare*. New York: Oxford University Press.

Gorin, Zeev. 1985. "Socialist Societies and World System Theory: A Critical Survey." *Science and Society* 49 (3): 332–366.

Gorski, Philip. 2009. "Social 'Mechanisms' and Comparative-Historical Sociology: A Critical Realist Proposal." In *Frontiers of Sociology*, edited by Peter Hedström and Björn Wittrock, 147–196. Boston, MA: Brill.

Gorzelak, Grzegorz, ed. 2015. "Growth-Innovation-Competitiveness: Fostering Cohesion in Central and Eastern Europe," GRINCOH Project Final Report, Contr. Nr. 290657. Warsaw: Centre for European Regional and Local Studies, University of Warsaw.

Gowan, Peter. 1995. "Neo-Liberal Theory and Practice for Eastern Europe." *New Left Review* 1 (213): 3–60.

Granick, David. 1975. *Enterprise Guidance in Eastern Europe: A Comparison of Four Socialist Economies*. Princeton, NJ: Princeton University Press.

Graziani, Giovanni. 1981. "Dependency Structures in Comecon." *Review of Radical Political Economics* 13 (1): 67–75.

Greskovits, Béla. 2004. "Beyond Transition: The Variety of Post-Socialist Development." In *From Liberal Values to Democratic Transition*, edited by János Kis and Ronald Dworkin, 201–226. Budapest: Central European University Press.

———. 2014. "Legacies of Industrialization and Paths of Transnational Integration After Socialism." In *Historical Legacies of Communism in Russia and Eastern Europe*, edited by Mark R. Beissinger and Stephen Kotkin, 68–89. New York: Cambridge University Press.

Griffin, Larry. 1992. "Temporality, Events, and Explanation in Historical Sociology." *Sociological Methods and Research* 20 (4): 403–427.

Grzymala-Busse, Anna. 2007. *Rebuilding Leviathan: Party Competition and State Exploitation in Post-Communist Democracies*. New York: Cambridge University Press.

———. 2011. "Time Will Tell? Temporality and the Analysis of Causal Mechanisms and Processes." *Comparative Political Studies* 44 (9): 1267–1297.

Grzymala-Busse, Anna, and Abby Innes. 2003. "Great Expectations: The EU and Domestic Political Competition in East Central Europe." *East European Politics and Society* 17 (1): 64–73.

Grzymala-Busse, Anna, and Pauline Jones Luong. 2002. "Reconceptualizing the State: Lessons from Post-Communism." *Politics and Society* 30 (4): 529–554.

Hake, Eric. 2000. "The Rise and Fall of Investment Companies in Slovakia." *Journal of Economic Issues* 34 (3): 635–654.

Hall, Peter A., and David W. Soskice, eds. 2001. *Varieties of Capitalism: The Institutional Foundations of Comparative Advantage*. New York: Oxford University Press.

Hanley, Eric. 2000. "Cadre Capitalism in Hungary and Poland: Property Accumulation Among Communist-Era Elites." *East European Politics and Societies* 14 (1): 143–178.

Hanley, Eric, Lawrence P. King, and István Tóth János. 2002. "The State, International Agencies, and Property Transformation in Postcommunist Hungary." *American Journal of Sociology* 108 (1): 129–167.

Hanson, Philip. 1981. *Trade and Technology in Soviet-Western Relations*. New York: Columbia University Press.

———. 1982. "The End of Import-Led Growth? Some Observations on Soviet, Polish, and Hungarian Experience in the 1970s." *Journal of Comparative Economics* 6 (2): 130–147.

———. 2003. *The Rise and Fall of the Soviet Economy*. New York: Routledge.

Hardt, Rolf. 1977. "Looking Back at Ten Years' Cooperation of a West German Firm with Polish Machine Tool Builders." In *East-West Cooperation in Business: Inter-firm Studies*, edited by Christopher T. Saunders, 166–171. New York: Springer-Verlag.

Harvey, David. 2001. "Capitalism: The Factory of Fragmentation." In *Spaces of Capital: Towards a Critical Geography*, edited by David Harvey, 121–127. New York: Routledge.

———. 2005. *A Brief History of Neoliberalism*. Oxford: Oxford University Press.

Held, David, and Anthony McGrew, eds. 2007. *Globalization Theory: Approaches and Controversies*. Malden, MA: Polity Press.

Helleiner, Eric. 1996. *States and the Reemergence of Global Finance: From Bretton Woods to the 1990s*. Ithaca, NY: Cornell University Press.

Hellman, Joel S. 1998. "Winners Take All: The Politics of Partial Reform." *World Politics* 50 (2): 203–234.

Herbst, Mikołaj, and Anna Wojciuk. 2014 "Common Origin, Different Paths. Transformation of Education Systems in the Czech Republic, Slovakia, Hungary, and Poland." GRINCOH Working Papers Series No. 4.07. European Commission, Brussels.

Herrigel, Gary, and Jonathan Zeitlin. 2010. "Inter-firm Relations in Global Manufacturing: Disintegrated Production and Its Globalization." In *The Oxford Handbook of Comparative Institutional Analysis*, edited by Glenn Morgan, John L. Campbell, Colin Crouch, Ove Kaj Pedersen, and Richard Whitley, 527–561. New York: Oxford University Press.

Hoff, Karla, and Joseph E. Stiglitz. 2004. "After the Big Bang? Obstacles to the Emergence of the Rule of Law in Post-Communist Societies." *American Economic Review* 94 (3): 753–763.

Holesovsky, Vaclav. 1977. "Czechoslovak Economies in the Seventies." In *East European Economies Post-Helsinki: A Compendium of Papers Submitted to the Joint Economic Committee, Congress of the United States*, 698–719. Washington, DC: US Government Printing Office.

Hollingsworth, J. Rogers, and Robert Boyer, eds. 1997. *Contemporary Capitalism: The Embeddedness of Institutions*. New York: Cambridge University Press.

Holman, Otto. 2001. "The Enlargement of the European Union Towards Central and Eastern Europe: The Role of Supranational and Transnational Actors." In *Social Forces in the Making of New Europe: The Restructuring of European Social Relations in the Global Political Economy*, edited by Andreas Bieler and Adam David Morton, 161–184. New York: Palgrave.

Holton, Robert J. 2005. *Making Globalization*. Basingstoke, UK: Palgrave.

Holzman, Franklyn D. 1976. *International Trade Under Communism: Politics and Economics*. New York: Basic Books.

———. 1986. "The Significance of Soviet Subsidies to Eastern Europe." *Comparative Economic Studies* 28 (1): 54–64.

———. 1987. *The Economics of Soviet Bloc Trade and Finance.* Boulder, CO: Westview Press.

Hungarian Investment Promotion Agency. 2015. *Hungarian Government Signs Strategic Agreement with Grundfos.* Budapest: Hungarian Investment Promotion Agency.

Huntington, Samuel P. 1993. *The Third Wave: Democratization in the Late Twentieth Century.* Norman: University of Oklahoma Press.

Huszti, Denes. 1969. "Intercooperation—One-Year Balance." *Figyelő,* August 20.

Imlay, Talbot C. 2009. "Exploring What Might Have Been: Parallel History, International History, and Post-War Socialist Internationalism." *International History Review* 31 (3): 521–557.

Iwasaki, Ichiro, and Masahiro Tokunaga. 2016. "Technology Transfer and Spillovers from FDI in Transition Economies: A Meta-Analysis." *Journal of Comparative Economics* 44 (4): 1086–1114.

Jacoby, Wade. 2006. "Inspiration, Coalition, and Substitution: External Influences on Postcommunist Transformations." *World Politics* 58 (4): 623–651.

Janos, Andrew. 1993. "Continuity and Change in Eastern Europe: Strategies of Post-Communist Politics." *East European Politics and Societies* 8 (1): 1–31.

Jermakowicz, Wladyslaw, and Cecelia Drazek. 1993. "Joint Venture Laws in Eastern Europe: A Comparative Assessment." In *Foreign Investment in Central and Eastern Europe,* edited by Patrick Artisien, Matija Rojec, and Marjan Svetličič, 149–170. New York: Palgrave Macmillan.

Jowitt, Kenneth. 1992. *New World Disorder: The Leninist Extinction.* Berkeley: University of California Press.

Judy, Richard W., and Robert W. Clough. 1989. "Soviet Computers in the 1980s: A Review of the Hardware." *Advances in Computers* 29:251–330.

Karl, Terry Lynn, and Philippe C. Schmitter. 1991. "Modes of Transition in Latin America, Southern and Eastern Europe." *International Social Science Journal* 43:269–284.

Kaser, Michael. 1967. *Comecon: Integration Problems of the Planned Economies.* New York: Oxford University Press.

Katzenstein, Peter J. 1985. *Small States in World Markets: Industrial Policy in Europe.* Ithaca, NY: Cornell University Press.

Kennedy, Michael D. 2002. *Cultural Formations of Postcommunism.* Minneapolis: University of Minnesota Press.

Kentor, Jeffrey. 2005. "The Growth of Transnational Corporate Networks, 1962–1998." *Journal of World-Systems Research* 11 (2): 263–86.

Kharas, Homi, and Harinder Kohli. 2011. "What Is the Middle Income Trap, Why Do Countries Fall into It, and How Can It Be Avoided?" *Global Journal of Emerging Market Economies* 3 (3): 281–289.

Kindleberger, Charles P. 1978. *Manias, Panics, and Crashes: A History of Financial Crises.* New York: Basic Books.

King, Lawrence P. 2001. *The Basic Features of Postcommunist Capitalism in Eastern Europe: Firms in Hungary, the Czech Republic, and Slovakia.* Westport, CT: Praeger.

———. 2007. "Central European Capitalism in Comparative Perspective." In *Beyond Varieties of Capitalism: Conflict, Contradictions, and Complementarities in the European Economy,* edited by Bob Hancké, Martin Rhodes, and Mark Thatcher, 307–327. Oxford: Oxford University Press.

King, Lawrence P., and Iván Szelényi. 2005. "Postcommunist Economic Systems." In *Handbook of Economic Sociology,* edited by Neil Smelser and Richard Swedberg, 205–229. Princeton, NJ: Princeton University Press.

King, Lawrence P., and Aleksandra Sznajder. 2006. "The State-Led Transition to Liberal Capitalism: Neoliberal, Organizational, World-Systems, and Social Structural Explanations of Poland's Economic Success." *American Journal of Sociology* 112 (3): 751–801.

Kitschelt, Herbert. 2003. "Accounting for Postcommunist Regime Diversity: What Counts as a Good Cause?" In *Capitalism and Democracy in Central and Eastern Europe: Assessing the Legacy of Communist Rule,* edited by Grzegorz Ekiert and Stephen E. Hanson, 49–88. New York: Cambridge University Press.

Kitschelt, Herbert, Peter Lange, Gary Marks, and John Stephens, eds. 1999. *Continuity and Change in Contemporary Capitalism.* New York: Cambridge University Press.

Klaus, Václav. 1997. *Renaissance: The Rebirth of Liberty in the Heart of Europe.* Washington, DC: Cato Institute.

Kock, Karin. 1969. *International Trade Policy and the GATT, 1947–1967.* Stockholm: Almqvist and Wiksell.

Kohli, Atul. 2004. *State-Directed Development: Political Power and Industrialization in the Global Periphery.* Cambridge: Cambridge University Press.

Kornai, János. 1990. *The Road to a Free Economy.* New York: Norton.

———. 1991. *The Socialist System: The Political Economy of Communism.* Princeton, NJ: Princeton University Press.

Kostevc, Črt, Tjaša Redek, and Matija Rojec. 2011. "Scope and Effectiveness of Foreign Direct Investment Policies in Transition Economies." In *Multinational Corporations and Local Firms in Emerging Economies,* edited by Eric Rugraff and Michael W. Hansen, 155–180. Amsterdam: Amsterdam University Press.

Kotkin, Stephen, and Mark R. Beissinger. 2014. "The Historical Legacies of Communism: An Empirical Agenda." In *Historical Legacies of Communism in Russia and Eastern Europe,* edited by Mark R. Beissinger and Stephen Kotkin, 1–27. New York: Cambridge University Press.

Kotz, David M., and Terence McDonough. 2010. "Global Neoliberalism and the Contemporary Social Structure of Accumulation." In *Contemporary Capitalism and Its Crises: Social Structure of Accumulation Theory for the 21st Century,* edited by Terrence McDonough, Michael Reich, and David M. Kotz, 93–120. New York: Cambridge University Press.

Köves, A. 1979. "Hungarian and Soviet Foreign Trade with Developed Capitalist Countries: Common and Different Problems." *Acta Oeconomica* 23 (3/4): 323–338.

Krippner, Greta R. 2011. *Capitalizing on Crisis: The Political Origins of the Rise of Finance*. Cambridge, MA: Harvard University Press.

Kubik, Jan. 2003. "Cultural Legacies of State Socialism: History Making and Cultural-Political Entrepreneurship in Postcommunist Poland and Russia." In *Capitalism and Democracy in Central and Eastern Europe: Assessing the Legacy of Communist Rule*, edited by Grzegorz Ekiert and Stephen E. Hanson, 317–351. New York: Cambridge University Press.

Kuczera, Małgorzata. 2010. *Learning for Jobs: OECD Reviews of Vocational Education and Training: Czech Republic*. Paris: Organization for Economic Cooperation and Development.

Lampe, John R., and Marvin Jackson. 1982. *Balkan Economic History, 1550–1950: From Imperial Borderlands to Developing Nations*. Bloomington: Indiana University Press.

Landesmann, Michael A., and István Ábel. 1995. "Industrial Policy in the Transition." In *Industrial Restructuring and Trade Reorientation in Eastern Europe*, edited by Michael A. Landesmann and István P. Székely, 313–336. New York: Cambridge University Press.

Lankes, Hans-Peter, and A. J. Venables. 1996. "Foreign Direct Investment in Economic Transition: The Changing Pattern of Investment." *Economics of Transition* 4 (2): 331–347.

Lavigne, Marie. 1991. *International Political Economy and Socialism*. Translated by David Lambert. New York: Cambridge University Press.

———. 1999. *The Economics of Transition: From Socialist Economy to Market Economy*. 2nd ed. New York: Palgrave Macmillan.

Lazarova, Mariya. 1975. "Industrial Cooperation Between Bulgarian Economic Organizations and Firms in Developed Capitalist Countries." *Vunshna Turgoviya*, 2–7.

Lenzen, Manfred, Keiichiro Kanemoto, Daniel Moran, and Arne Geschke. 2012. "Mapping the Structure of the World Economy." *Environmental Science and Technology* 46 (15): 8374–8381.

———. 2013. "Building EORA: A Global Multi-Region Input-Output Database at High Country and Sector Resolution." *Economic Systems Research* 25 (1): 20–49.

Linz, Juan J., and Alfred Stepan. 1996. *Problems of Democratic Transition and Consolidation: Southern Europe, South America, and Post-Communist Europe*. Baltimore: Johns Hopkins Press.

Luke, Timothy W. 1985. "Technology and Soviet Foreign Trade: On the Political Economy of an Underdeveloped Superpower." *International Studies Quarterly* 29 (3): 327–353.

Maddison Project. 2013. *New Maddison Project Database*. 2013 version. The Netherlands: Groningen Growth and Development Centre, University of Groningen. http://www.ggdc.net/maddison/maddison-project/home.htm

Mahoney, James. 2000. "Path Dependence in Historical Sociology." *Theory and Society* 29 (4): 507–548.

———. 2012. "The Logic of Process Tracing Tests in the Social Sciences." *Sociological Methods and Research* 41 (4): 570–597.

Mahoney, James, Erin Kimball, and Kendra L. Koivu. 2009. "The Logic of Historical Explanation in the Social Sciences." *Comparative Political Studies* 42 (1): 114–146.

Marer, Paul. 1973. *Soviet and East European Foreign Trade, 1946–1969: Statistical Compendium and Guide.* Bloomington: Indiana University Press.

———. 1986. *East-West Technology Transfer: Study of Hungary, 1968–1984.* Paris: Organization for Economic Cooperation and Development.

———. 2010. "The Global Economic Crisis: Impacts on Eastern Europe." *Acta Oeconomica* 60 (1): 3–33.

Mark, James. 2010. *The Unfinished Revolution: Making Sense of the Communist Past in Central-Eastern Europe.* New Haven, CT: Yale University Press.

Marrese, Michael, and Jan Vanous. 1983. *Soviet Subsidization of Trade with Eastern Europe: A Soviet Perspective.* Berkeley: Institute of International Studies, University of California.

Mastanduno, Michael. 1992. *Economic Containment: CoCom and the Politics of East-West Trade.* Ithaca, NY: Cornell University Press.

Maximova, Margarita. 1977. "Industrial Cooperation Between Socialist and Capitalist Countries: Forms, Trends, and Problems." In *East-West Cooperation in Business: Inter-firm Studies*, edited by Christopher T. Saunders, 15–27. New York: Springer-Verlag.

Mayntz, Renate. 2004. "Mechanisms in the Analysis of Social Macro-Phenomena." *Philosophy of the Social Sciences* 34 (2): 237–259.

McDermott, Gerald A. 2004. "Institutional Change and Firm Creation in East-Central Europe: An Embedded Politics Approach." *Comparative Political Studies* 37 (2): 188–217.

———. 2007. "Politics and the Evolution of Inter-firm Networks: A Post-Communist Lesson." *Organization Studies* 28 (6): 885–908.

McMichael, Phillip. 1996. "Globalization: Myths and Realities." *Rural Sociology* 61 (1): 25–55.

McMillan, Carl H. 1977. "Forms and Dimensions of East-West Inter-firm Cooperation." In *East-West Cooperation in Business: Inter-firm Studies*, edited by Christopher T. Saunders, 28–60. New York: Springer-Verlag.

McMillan, Carl H., and D. P. St. Charles. 1973. *Joint Ventures in Eastern Europe: A Three-Country Comparison.* Montreal, Canada: C. D. Howe Research Institute.

Mëhilli, Elidor. 2017. *From Stalin to Mao: Albania and the Socialist World.* Ithaca, NY: Cornell University Press.

Mencinger, Jože. 2004. "Transition to a National and a Market Economy: A Gradualist Approach." In *Slovenia: From Yugoslavia to the European Union*, edited by Mojmir Mrak, Matija Rojec, and Silva-Jáuregui, 67–82. Washington, DC: World Bank.

Mendershausen, Horst. 1959. "Terms of Trade Between the Soviet Union and Smaller Communist Countries." *Review of Economics and Statistics* 41 (2): 106–118.

———. 1960. "The Terms of Soviet Satellite Trade." *Review of Economics and Statistics* 41 (2): 152–163.

Merton, Robert. 1988. "The Matthew Effect in Science, II: Cumulative Advantage and the Symbolism of Intellectual Property." *Isis* 79 (4): 606–623.

Milberg, William, and Deborah Winkler. 2013. *Outsourcing Economics: Global Value Chains in Capitalist Development*. New York: Cambridge University Press.

Mosley, Layna. 2003. *Global Capital and National Governments*. New York: Cambridge University Press.

Murrell, Peter. 1990. *The Nature of Socialist Economies: Lessons from Eastern European Foreign Trade*. Princeton, NJ: Princeton University Press.

Myant, Martin. 2003. *The Rise and Fall of Czech Capitalism*. Northampton, MA: Edward Elgar.

Myant, Martin, and Jan Drahokoupil. 2011. *Transition Economies: Political Economy in Russia, Eastern Europe, and Central Asia*. Hoboken, NJ: John Wiley.

Myant, Martin, Jan Drahokoupil, and Ivan Lesay. 2013. "The Political Economy of Crisis Management in East–Central European Countries." *Europe-Asia Studies* 65 (3): 383–410.

National Statistical Institute of Bulgaria. n.d. *Foreign Direct Investments*. Accessed January 8, 2018. http://www.nsi.bg/en/content/6186/foreign-direct-investments.

Nölke, Andreas, and Arjan Vliegenthart. 2009. "Enlarging the Varieties of Capitalism: The Emergence of Dependent Market Economies in East Central Europe." *World Politics* 61 (4): 670–702.

Nove, Alec. 1964. *Was Stalin Really Necessary?* London: Allen and Unwin.

———. 1966. *The Soviet Economy*. New York: Frederick A. Praeger.

———. 1983. *The Economics of Feasible Socialism*. Boston: Allen and Unwin.

———. 1992. *An Economic History of the USSR, 1917–1991*. New York: Penguin.

———. 1995. "Economics of Transition: Some Gaps and Illusions." In *Markets, States, and Democracy: The Political Economy of Post-Communist Transformation*, edited by Beverly Crawford, 227–245. Boulder, CO: Westview Press.

Nykyrn, Jaroslav. 1977. "Inter-firm Cooperation in the Czechoslovak Machine Building Industry." In *East-West Cooperation in Business: Inter-firm Studies*, edited by Christopher T. Saunders, 172–178. New York: Springer-Verlag.

O'Donnell, Guillermo, and Philippe C. Schmitter. 1986. *Transitions from Authoritarian Rule: Tentative Conclusions About Uncertain Democracies*. Baltimore: Johns Hopkins University Press.

Orenstein, Mitchell. 2001. *Out of the Red: Building Capitalism and Democracy in Post-communist Europe*. Ann Arbor: University of Michigan Press.

———. 2008. *Privatizing Pensions: The Transnational Campaign for Social Security Reform*. Princeton, NJ: Princeton University Press.

Organization for Economic Cooperation and Development (OECD). 1993. *OECD Economic Surveys 1993: Hungary*. Paris: Organization for Economic Cooperation and Development.

———. 2012. *OECD Economic Surveys 2012: Hungary*. Paris: Organization for Economic Cooperation and Development.

———. 2014a. *OECD Economic Surveys 2014: Hungary*. Paris: Organization for Economic Cooperation and Development.

———. 2014b. *OECD Science, Technology and Industry Outlook 2014*. Paris: Organization for Economic Cooperation and Development.

———. 2015. *Educational Policy Outlook: Hungary*. Paris: Organization for Economic Cooperation and Development.

———. n.d. *Indicators of Product Market Regulation*. Accessed January 8, 2018. http://www.oecd.org/eco/growth/indicatorsofproductmarketregulationhomepage.htm.

———. n.d. *OECD Indicators of Employment Protection*. Accessed January 8, 2018. http://www.oecd.org/els/emp/oecdindicatorsofemploymentprotection.htm.

———. n.d. *OECD Patent Database*. Accessed January 8, 2018. http://www.oecd.org/sti/inno/oecdpatentdatabases.htm.

Ost, David. 2000. "Illusory Corporatism in Eastern Europe: Neoliberal Tripartism and Postcommunist Class Identities." *Politics and Society* 28 (4): 503–530.

Paige, Jeffrey. 1999. "Conjuncture, Comparison, and Conditional Theory in Macrosocial Inquiry." *American Journal of Sociology* 105 (3): 781–800.

Parrott, Bruce. 1983. *Politics and Technology in the Soviet Union*. Cambridge, MA: MIT Press.

Pavitt, Keith. 1987. "International Patterns of Technological Accumulation." In *Strategies in Global Competition*, edited by Neil Hood and Jan-Erik Vahlne, 126–157. New York: John Wiley.

Pavlínek, Petr. 1998. "Foreign Direct Investment in the Czech Republic." *Professional Geographer* 50 (1): 71–85.

———. 2008. *A Successful Transformation? Restructuring of the Czech Automobile Industry*. Heidelberg: Physica-Verlag.

Pavlínek, Petr, Bolesław Domański, and Robert Guzik. 2009. "Industrial Upgrading Through Foreign Direct Investment in Central European Automotive Manufacturing." *European Urban and Regional Studies* 16 (1): 43–63.

Peck, Jamie, and Adam Tickell. 2002. "Neoliberalizing Space." *Antipode* 34 (3): 380–404.

Perlmutter, Howard V. 1969. "Emerging East-West Ventures: The Transideological Enterprise." *Columbia Journal of World Business* 4 (5): 39–50.

Pierson, Paul. 2004. *Politics in Time: History, Institutions, and Social Analysis*. Princeton, NJ: Princeton University Press.

Pisar, Samuel. 1970. *Coexistence and Commerce: Guidelines for Transactions Between East and West*. New York: McGraw-Hill.

Podkaminer, Leon. 2013. "Development Patterns of Central and Eastern European Countries (in the Course of Transition and Following EU accession)." GRINCOH Working Papers Series, Research Reports 388. Vienna Institute for International Economic Studies, Vienna.

Poland. 2016. *Responsible Development Plan*. Warsaw: Ministry of Economic Development, Government of Poland.

Pop, Liliana. 2006. *Democratizing Capitalism? The Political Economy of Post-Communist Transformations in Romania, 1989–2001*. New York: Manchester University Press.

Pop-Eleches, Grigore, and Joshua A. Tucker. 2017. *Communism's Shadow: Historical Legacies and Contemporary Political Attitudes*. Princeton, NJ: Princeton University Press.

Poznanski, Kazimierz. 1995. "Political Economy of Privatization in Eastern Europe." In *Markets, States, and Democracy: The Political Economy of Post-Communist Transformation*, edited by Beverly Crawford, 204–226. Boulder, CO: Westview Press.

———. 1996. *Poland's Protracted Transition: Institutional Change and Economic Growth, 1970–1994*. New York: Cambridge University Press.

Przeworski, Adam. 1991. *Democracy and the Market: Political and Economic Reforms in Eastern Europe and Latin America*. Cambridge: Cambridge University Press.

Pula, Besnik. 2017a. "What Makes Firms Competitive? States, Markets, and Organisational Embeddedness in Competitive Firm Restructuring in Postsocialist Economies." *New Political Economy* (Prepublication online):1–17.

———. 2017b. "Whither State Ownership? The Persistence of State-Owned Industry in Postsocialist Central and Eastern Europe." *Journal of East-West Business* 23 (4): 309–336.

Putnam, Robert D. 1993. *Making Democracy Work: Civic Traditions in Modern Italy*. Princeton, NJ: Princeton University Press.

Radio Free Europe/Radio Liberty (RFE/RL). 1979, March 23. "Romania Situation Report." New York: Radio Free Europe/Radio Liberty.

———. 1981, February 13. "Czechoslovakia Situation Report." New York: Radio Free Europe/Radio Liberty.

———. 1984, March 14. Romania Situation Report." New York: Radio Free Europe/Radio Liberty.

———. 1985, April 4. "Czechoslovakia Situation Report." New York: Radio Free Europe/Radio Liberty.

Radosevic, Slavo, and Bert M. Sadowski, eds. 2004. *International Industrial Networks and Industrial Restructuring in Central and Eastern Europe*. Boston, MA: Kluwer Academic.

Robertson, Ronald. 1992. *Globalization: Social Theory and Global Culture*. London: Sage.

Robinson, William I. 2004. *A Theory of Global Capitalism: Production, Class, and State in a Transnational World*. Baltimore: Johns Hopkins University Press.

———. 2011. "Globalization and the Sociology of Immanuel Wallerstein: A Critical Appraisal." *International Sociology* 26 (6): 723–745.

———. 2014. *Global Capitalism and the Crisis of Humanity*. New York: Cambridge University Press.

Rodrik, Dani. 1992. "Making Sense of the Soviet Trade Shock in Eastern Europe: A Framework and Some Estimates." NBER Working Paper No. 4112. National Bureau of Economic Research, Cambridge, MA.

———. 2011. *The Globalization Paradox: Democracy and the Future of the World Economy*. New York: Norton.

Rosenbaum, Andrew. 1990. "Bulgaria: The Best and the Worst; $10.2 Billion in Debt, But It Has a Chip and Computer Industry." *Electronics*, November 13.

Rueschemeyer, Dietrich, and John Stephens. 1997. "Comparing Historical Sequences—A Powerful Tool for Causal Analysis." *Comparative Social Research* 17:55–72.

Sachs, Jeffrey D. 1993. *Poland's Jump to the Market Economy*. Cambridge, MA: MIT Press.

Sachs, Jeffrey D., and Wing Thye Woo. 1994. "Experiences in the Transition to a Market Economy." *Journal of Comparative Economics* 18 (3): 271–275.

Sanchez-Sibony, Oscar. 2014. *Red Globalization: The Political Economy of the Soviet Cold War from Stalin to Khrushchev*. New York: Cambridge University Press.

Sassen, Saskia. 1998. *Globalization and Its Discontents*. New York: New Press.

Schenk, Catherine R. 1998. "The Origins of the Eurodollar Market in London: 1955–1963." *Explorations in Economic History* 35 (2): 221–238.

Schmidt, Max. 1978. "East-West Economic Relations Against the Background of New Trends in the World Economy." In *Economic Relations Between East and West: Proceedings of a Conference Held by the International Economic Association at Dresden, GDR*, edited by Nita G. Watts, 7–23. New York: St. Martin's.

Schwab, Klaus. 2015. *The Global Competitiveness Report, 2015–2016*. Cologny, Switzerland: World Economic Forum.

Sewell, William H., Jr. 1996. "Three Temporalities: Toward an Eventful Sociology." In *The Historic Turn in the Human Sciences*, edited by Terrence McDonald, 245–280. Ann Arbor: University of Michigan Press.

Shanker, V. Gauri. 1979. "Taming the Giants: Transnational Corporations in International Arena." PhD diss., School of International Studies, Jawaharlal Nehru University, New Delhi.

Shields, Stuart. 2004. "Global Restructuring and the Polish State: Transition, Transformation, or Transnationalization?" *Review of International Political Economy* 11 (1): 132–154.

Sil, Rudra. 2006. "The Evolving Significance of Leninism in Comparative Historical Analysis: Theorizing the General and the Particular." In *World Order After Leninism*, edited by Vladimir Tismaneanu, Marc Morjé Howard, Rudra Sil, and Kenneth Jowitt, 225–248. Seattle: University of Washington Press.

Simmons, Beth. 1999. "The Internationalization of Capital." In *Continuity and Change in Contemporary Capitalism*, edited by Herbert Kitschelt, Peter Lange, Gary Marks, and John Stephens, 36–69. New York: Cambridge University Press.

Sklair, Leslie. 2001. *The Transnational Capitalist Class*. Hoboken, NJ: Wiley-Blackwell.

Skocpol, Theda. 1977. "Wallerstein's World Capitalist System: A Theoretical and Historical Critique." *American Journal of Sociology* 82 (5): 1075–1090.

Smith, Alan H. 1983. *The Planned Economies of Eastern Europe*. London: Croom Helm.

Smith, Jessica, David Laibman, and Marilyn Bechtel. 1977. *Building a New Society: The 25th Congress of the Communist Party of the Soviet Union*. New York: NWR Publications.

Soederberg, Susanne, Georg Menz, and Philip G. Cerny, eds. 2005. *Internalizing Globalization: The Rise of Neoliberalism and the Decline of National Varieties of Capitalism*. New York: Palgrave Macmillan.

Spechler, Dina Rome, and Martin C. Spechler. 2009. "A Reassessment of the Burden of Eastern Europe on the USSR." *Europe-Asia Studies* 61 (9): 1645–1657.

Spigler, Iancu. 1973. *Economic Reform in Rumanian Industry*. New York: Oxford University Press.

Spulber, Nicolas. 1957. *The Economics of Communist Eastern Europe*. New York: Wiley.

Stalin, Joseph. 1952. *Economic Problems of Socialism in the USSR*. Moscow: Foreign Languages Press.

Staniszkis, Jadwiga. 1989. "Patterns of Change in Eastern Europe." *East European Politics and Societies* 4 (1): 77–97.

———. 1990. "'Political Capitalism' in Poland." *East European Politics and Societies* 5 (1): 127–141.

Stanojević, Miroslav. 2012. "The Rise and Decline of Slovenian Corporatism: Local and European Factors." *Europe-Asia Studies* 64 (5): 857–877.

Steinmetz, George. 1998. "Critical Realism and Historical Sociology." *Comparative Studies in Society and History* 40 (1): 170–187.

Stiglitz, Joseph E. 2002. *Globalization and Its Discontents*. New York: Norton.

Stinchcombe, Arthur L. 1968. *Constructing Social Theories*. New York: Harcourt, Brace and World.

Stokes, Gale. 1989. "The Social Origins of East European Politics." In *The Origins of Backwardness in Eastern Europe: Economics and Politics from the Middle Ages Until the Early Twentieth Century*, edited by Daniel Chirot, 210–251. Berkeley: University of California Press.

Stone, Randall W. 1996. *Satellites and Commissars: Strategy and Conflict in the Politics of Soviet-Bloc Trade*. Princeton, NJ: Princeton University Press.

Strange, Susan. 1986. *Casino Capitalism*. Manchester, UK: Manchester University Press.

Streeck, Wolfgang. 2009. *Re-Forming Capitalism: Institutional Change in the German Political Economy*. New York: Oxford University Press.

———. 2014. *Buying Time: The Delayed Crisis of Democratic Capitalism*. London: Verso.

Streeck, Wolfgang, and Kathleen Thelen. 2005. "Introduction: Institutional Change in Advanced Political Economies." In *Beyond Continuity: Institutional Change in Advanced Political Economies*, edited by Wolfgang Streeck and Kathleen Thelen, 1–39. Oxford: Oxford University Press.

Sturgeon, Timothy. 2001. "How Do We Define Value Chains and Production Networks?" *IDS Bulletin* 32 (3): 9–18.

Sturgeon, Timothy, Linden Greg, Peter Bøegh Nielsen, Gary Gereffi, and Clair Brown. 2013. "Direct Measurement of Global Value Chains: Collecting Product- and Firm-Level Statistics on Value Added and Business Function Outsourcing and Offshoring." In *Trade in Value Added: Developing New Measures of Cross-Border Trade*, edited by Aaditya Mattoo, Zhi Wang, and Shang-Jin Wei. 289–320. Washington, DC: International Bank for Reconstruction and Development.

Sutton, Antony C. 1968. *Western Technology and Soviet Economic Development, 1917 to 1930*. Vol. 1. Stanford, CA: Hoover Institution Press.

———. 1971. *Western Technology and Soviet Economic Development, 1930 to 1945*. Vol. 2. Stanford, CA: Hoover Institution Press.

———. 1973. *Western Technology and Soviet Economic Development, 1945 to 1965.* Vol. 3. Stanford, CA: Hoover Institution Press.

Swank, Duane. 2002. *Global Capital, Political Institutions, and Policy Change in Developed Welfare States.* New York: Cambridge University Press.

Szent-Iványi, Balázs, and Gábor Vigvári. 2012. "Spillovers from Foreign Direct Investment in Central and Eastern Europe: An Index for Measuring a Country's Potential to Benefit from Technology Spillovers." *Society and Economy* 34 (1): 51–72.

Thelen, Kathleen. 2004. *How Institutions Evolve: The Political Economy of Skills in Comparative-Historical Perspective.* New York: Cambridge University Press.

Tilly, Charles. 1984. *Big Structures, Long Processes, Huge Comparisons.* New York: Russell Sage.

———. 2001. "Mechanisms in Political Processes." *Annual Review of Political Science* 4:21–41.

Tismaneanu, Vladimir, Marc Morjé Howard, Rudra Sil, and Kenneth Jowitt. 2006. *World Order After Leninism.* 1st ed. Seattle: Herbert J. Ellison Center for Russian, East European, and Central Asian Studies in association with University of Washington.

Tóth, Andras. 2001. "The Failure of Social-Democratic Unionism in Hungary." In *Workers After Workers' States: Labor and Politics in Postcommunist Eastern Europe,* edited by Stephen Crowley and David Ost, 37–58. New York: Rowman and Littlefield.

Trend, Harry. 1976, November 29. "OPEC Oil Price Changes and Comecon Oil Prices." *Research and Analysis Department Background Report 244.* New York: Radio Free Europe/Radio Liberty.

Tyson, Laura D'Andrea, and Peter B. Kenen. 1980. "The International Transmission of Disturbances: A Framework for Comparative Analysis." In *The Impact of International Economic Disturbances on the Soviet Union and Eastern Europe: Transmission and Response,* edited by Egon Neuberger and Laura D'Andrea Tyson, 33–62. New York: Pergamon.

United Nations Conference on Trade and Development (UNCTAD). 2007. *World Investment Report: Transnational Corporations, Extractive Industries and Development.* New York: United Nations Conference on Trade and Development.

———. 2013. *Global Value Chains and Development: Investment and Value Added Trade in the Global Economy.* New York: United Nations Conference on Trade and Development.

———. 2015. *World Investment Report: Reforming International Investment Governance.* New York: United Nations Conference on Trade and Development.

———. n.d. *UNCTADstat Database.* Accessed January 8, 2018. http://unctadstat.unctad .org.

United Nations Economic Commission for Europe (UNECE). 1996. *Economic Survey of Europe in 1995–1996.* Geneva: United Nations Economic Commission for Europe.

———. n.d. *UNECE Statistical Database.* Accessed January 8, 2018. http://www.unece .org/data.

United Nations Statistics Division. n.d. *United Nations International Trade Statistics (UN Comtrade).* Accessed January 8, 2018. https://comtrade.un.org.

US Congress, Office of Technology Assessment. 1979. *Technology and East-West Trade.* Washington, DC: US Government Printing Office.

Vachudova, Milada. 2005. *Europe Undivided: Democracy, Leverage, and Integration After Communism.* New York: Oxford University Press.

———. 2008. "The European Union: The Causal Behemoth of Transnational Influence on Postcommunist Politics." In *Transnational Actors in Central and East European Transitions,* edited by Mitchell Orenstein, Stephen Bloom, and Nicole Lindstrom, 19–37. Pittsburgh: University of Pittsburgh Press.

Vanhuysse, Pieter. 2006. *Divide and Pacify: Strategic Social Policies and Political Protests in Post-Communist Democracies.* Budapest: Central European University Press.

Vernon, Raymond. 1971. *Sovereignty at Bay: The Multinational Spread of U.S. Enterprises.* New York: Basic Books.

Vickers, Miranda. 1999. *The Albanians: A Modern History.* London: I. B. Tauris.

Viner, Jacob. 1950. *The Customs Union Issue.* New York: Carnegie Endowment for International Peace.

Wallerstein, Immanuel. 1974. "The Rise and Future Demise of the World Capitalist System: Concepts for Comparative Analysis." *Comparative Studies in Society and History* 16 (4): 387–415.

———. 1979. "Dependence in an Interdependent World: The Limited Possibilities of Transformation Within the Capitalist World-Economy." In *The Capitalist World Economy,* edited by Immanuel Wallerstein, 66–94. Cambridge: Cambridge University Press.

———. 1995. *Historical Capitalism and Capitalist Civilizations.* London: Verso.

———. 2004. *World-Systems Analysis: An Introduction.* Durham, NC: Duke University Press.

Wedel, Janine R. 1998. *Collision and Collusion: The Strange Case of Aid to Eastern Europe, 1989–1998.* New York: St. Martin's.

Weinstein, Michael M., ed. 2005. *Globalization: What's New.* New York: Columbia University Press.

Weiss, Linda. 1998. *The Myth of the Powerless State.* Ithaca, NY: Cornell University Press.

Wiedenmann, Paul. 1981. "Economic Reform in Bulgaria: Coping with 'The kj Problem.'" *Eastern European Economics* 20 (1): 90–108.

Wiener, Helgard, and John Slater. 1986. *East-West Technology Transfer: The Trade and Economic Aspects.* Paris: Organization for Economic Cooperation and Development.

Wilczynski, Jozef. 1975. "Cybernetics, Automation and the Transition to Communism." In *Comparative Socialist Systems: Essays on Politics and Economics,* edited by Carmelo Mesa-Lago and Carl Beck, 397–420. Pittsburgh, PA: University of Pittsburgh Center for International Studies.

———. 1976. *The Multinationals and East-West Relations: Towards Transideological Collaboration.* London: Macmillan.

Wiles, P.J.D. 1969. *Communist International Economics.* New York: Praeger.

Wittenberg, Jason. 2015. "Conceptualizing Historical Legacies." *East European Politics and Societies* 29 (2): 366–378.

Wolf, Thomas A. 1988. *Foreign Trade in the Centrally Planned Economy*. New York: Harwood Academic.

Wolff, Larry. 1994. *Inventing Eastern Europe: The Map of Civilization in the Mind of the Enlightenment*. Palo Alto, CA: Stanford University Press.

World Bank. n.d. *World Bank Development Indicators*. Accessed January 8, 2018. https://data.worldbank.org/data-catalog/world-development-indicators.

Yeung, Henry Wai-chung. 2016. *Strategic Coupling: East Asian Industrial Transformation in the New Global Economy*. Ithaca, NY: Cornell University Press.

Young, David. 1993. "Foreign Direct Investment in Hungary." In *Foreign Investment in Central and Eastern Europe*, edited by Patrick Artisien, Matija Rojec, and Marjan Svetličič, 109–122. New York: Palgrave Macmillan.

Young, Stephen, and James Hamill, eds. 1992. *Europe and the Multinationals: Issues and Responses for the 1990s*. Brookfield, VT: Edward Elgar.

Zemplinerova, Alena. 2001. "Foreign Investment and Privatization in the Czech Republic." In *Foreign Investment and Privatization in Central and Eastern Europe*, edited by Patrick Artisien and Matija Rojec, 131–155. New York: Palgrave Macmillan.

Zloch-Christy, Iliana. 1987. *Debt Problems of Eastern Europe*. New York: Cambridge University Press.

Zoeter, Joan Parpart. 1977. "Eastern Europe: The Growing Hard Currency Debt." In *East European Economies Post-Helsinki*, edited by Joint Economic Committee, US Congress, 1350–1368. Washington, DC: US Government Printing Office.

Zubok, Vladislav 2007. *A Failed Empire: The Soviet Union in the Cold War from Stalin to Gorbachev*. Chapel Hill: University of North Carolina Press.

Zwass, Adam. 1989. *The Council for Mutual Economic Assistance: The Thorny Path from Political to Economic Integration*. Armonk, NY: M.E. Sharpe.

Index

Emerging Frontiers in the Global Economy